Septimus Winner

Two Lives in Music

Michael Remson

The Scarecrow Press, Inc.
Lanham, Maryland, and Oxford
2002

Library
University of Texas
at San Antonio

SCARECROW PRESS, INC.

Published in the United States of America
by Scarecrow Press, Inc.
A Member of the Rowman & Littlefield Publishing Group
4720 Boston Way, Lanham, Maryland 20706
www.scarecrowpress.com

PO Box 317
Oxford
OX2 9RU, UK

British Library Cataloguing in Publication Information Available

Library of Congress Cataloging-in-Publication Data

Remson, Michael, 1962–
  Septimus Winner : two lives in music / Michael Remson.
    p. cm.
Includes bibliographical references (p.   ) and index.
  ISBN 0-8108-4540-7 (hardback : alk. paper)
  1. Winner, Septimus, 1827-1902. 2. Composers—United
States—Biography. I. Title.
  ML410.W72 R4 2002
  780'.92—dc21   2002010834

♾™ The paper used in this publication meets the minimum requirements of
American National Standard for Information Sciences—Permanence of
Paper for Printed Library Materials, ANSI/NISO Z39.48-1992.
Manufactured in the United States of America.

To my parents

Contents

Photospread, Figures and Musical Examples

Cover

Septimus Winner, as photographed in either 1847 or 1850 (Charles Eugene Claghorn, *The Mocking Bird: The Life and Diary of Its Author, Sep. Winner*. Philadelphia: Magee Press, 1937, ii.).

Alice Hawthorne, as depicted on the sheet music cover for "Our Good Old Friends" (Philadelphia: Winner and Shuster, 1855. Lithograph created by Sarony and Company, New York.).

Photospread

vii

Photospread (continued)

Photospread (continued)

Figures

Musical Examples

Musical Examples (continued)

Acknowledgments

I would, of course, be remiss if I did not thank those who have provided such valuable assistance along the way. Writing a book is a solitary effort but it is made so much better through the interaction with and assistance of so many people who helped fill in the pieces, suggested new possibilities and shaped my thinking for the last three years.

Certainly, a great deal of thanks is extended to Dr. Cynthia Freeland, Dr. Barbara Rose Lange and Dr. Howard Pollack, all of the University of Houston, for their scholarly insights and Herculean patience as I sifted the remnants of a life from a variety of sources. Their support, guidance and direction as I prepared my initial thesis were central to my decision to undertake this project.

Deep and heartfelt appreciation is due to both Charles Eugene Claghorn (Septimus' great-grandson) and also to Melissa Claghorn (Charles' granddaughter) for providing valuable information and materials that had heretofore not been included or cited in any of the biographical materials. In addition, their collections of original documents and photographs were invaluable in filling in many of the missing links. As it was his 1937 volume that was the only published source of information initially, I was honored to have Mr. Claghorn's support and my regular correspondence with him became a source of inspiration throughout the project.

I am also indebted to Rebecca Massa and especially to Melissa Ray, Jessica McCleary and Andrew Yoder at Scarecrow Press for taking this project on and for all their help throughout the preparation and publication process.

Thanks also to Lynn Farrington, Maggie Cruesi and the very friendly staff at the Keffer Collection at the University of Pennsylvania Special Collections Library for their assistance in helping me assemble a complete catalogue of Winner's works and for key information on the Musical Fund Society. I must also thank the many people in Philadelphia whom I encountered in my travels. For those of you who haven't had the good fortune to travel there, it is one of America's friendliest and most welcoming cities.

I must also extend appreciation to Laura Beardsley, Dr. Dan Rolph and the wonderful staff at the Historical Society of Pennsylvania in

Philadelphia for providing a wealth of resources not only on Winner himself but on the life and times of one of America's most hospitable cities. In addition, their collection of Septimus Winner's diaries, notebooks and letters (initially donated by Charles Eugene Claghorn) was invaluable in developing a complete picture of Winner's life. Unless noted otherwise, all such materials are held in their well-preserved collection.

Many thanks as well to the New York Public Library special collections division, the Duke University online archive of American Popular Music, the Lester S. Levy online collection of American sheet music and the able researchers and associates at the Library of Congress in Washington, D.C. Each helped me piece together the hundreds of songs, arrangements, books and poems that Winner published over the course of his lifetime. When you begin a project of this sort, you begin to realize how vastly important these resources are in preserving America's cultural history and how much they deserve our support.

For their assistance in securing valuable research materials, I am particularly indebted to Jane Daley Witten from the University of North Carolina Wilson Library for securing a copy of Howard Myers' 1950 master's thesis on Winner and his music.

For their assistance and patience as I tried to chase down the very elusive Hawthorne-edited *Musical Journal*, I owe thanks to Rhoda Channing and Leslie McCall from Wake Forest University's Z. Reynolds Smith Library and Alison Bundy at Brown University's Hay Harris Library for securing a copy of one treasured issue.

I'm particularly indebted to Jim Farrington and especially to David Peter Coppen at the Eastman School of Music for their assistance in ultimately locating and allowing me access to what I imagine is one of the only extant sets of the complete *Journal* in this country.

I'm also most thankful to the staff and administration at the College Music Society. The opportunity to present on Winner at their 44th Annual Conference in Santa Fe was extraordinarily helpful in finalizing the framework for this volume. While there, I was also grateful to Dr. Judith Coe, of the University of Colorado at Denver, for her support and feedback at the conference. The women and gender studies world in musicology is a moderately small one and I appreciate Dr. Coe's kind words of support as I worked on the project.

Much gratitude is also extended to the numerous people and organizations who granted their permission to use materials in this volume. They include Charles Eugene Claghorn, Melissa Claghorn, the New York Public Library, Dover Publications, W.W. Norton and G. Schirmer.

Thanks as well to Suny Monk and everyone at the Virginia Center for the Creative Arts for providing a quiet space to contemplate and work as I began the arduous editing process.

A very special thank you to my friends Phil Chao and Eva Cap-pelletti-Chao for a futon in Arlington and for taking in a wayward musicologist on his regular travels to Washington. Welcome to the world, Colton.

I'm also deeply indebted to Judy Malone-Stein and the arts organization Dragon's Gate for providing me with something of a "writer-in-residence" program. Much of this volume was written over the course of many months in what became known as "Michael's room" at Judy's home office in Houston.

I must also thank Diane Downey for her friendship during this project and the many others on which she has supported me during our twenty-year friendship. A more supportive friend one would be hard-pressed to find.

Of course, one is always grateful for the loving support of family and it is rare to have an opportunity to acknowledge them so publicly. Encouraging words are never so welcome as when they come from one's family and for that I must express my love and gratitude to my mother Maureen, my stepfather Dan, my brothers Adam Remson and Daniel Charnas, my sister-in-law Joanne Arledge and my cousin Brad Spencer for patient listening, great repartee and, most importantly, their ongoing moral support not only with regards to this particular project but throughout my various "lives" as composer, librettist, teacher and now, musicologist.

It seems strange to have completed a volume of this sort and yet feel so at a loss for words to say about my late father, Alfred David Remson. When he originally introduced me to Winner, he sent me on a wonderful odyssey through the past. He would have been proud to have contributed to my work in such a meaningful way (as he often did throughout my career). No matter what the distance or the event in my life, he would always be there to cheer me on—without fail and with the full support that only a father can show to a son who ultimately fell closer to the tree than he probably ever realized. It's easy to say that if it weren't for him, I wouldn't be here . . . what's harder to fathom is that if it weren't for him, I wouldn't be who I am.

Introduction

Septimus Winner: Two Lives in Music chronicles the life and achievements of a man with an extraordinarily unusual career in music. Most modern-day readers may have never heard of Septimus Winner or of Alice Hawthorne. But the music *they* created—songs created during the infancy of American popular song—now reside as part of the pantheon of what we might now term "America's folk songs." Most Americans probably remember songs such as "Ten Little Indians" or "Der Deutscher's Dog" ("O Where, O Where Has My Little Dog Gone . . .") from their childhood, just as they may know "Jimmy Crack Corn" or "Oh! Susannah," but few know the men and women who wrote these songs or their significance to generations of nineteenth-century Americans.

In the middle of the nineteenth century, American culture embraced their popular songs just as modern Americans embrace television. Each in their own way was the basis of a cultural common ground—binding us together rather than dividing us from one another. This cultural sharing may have never been more important to Americans than it was as the country braced for civil war and then struggled through the difficulties of Reconstruction. Americans struggled to maintain a nascent sense of cultural identity as a new nation broke apart and then came back together. One of the ways they tried to do this was through popular songs.

Beyond the songs, there were the men and women who wrote them and the lives they led. As musicologists and historians continue to document the history of American music, we have done much due diligence on songwriters and composers from the first half of the twentieth century such as George M. Cohan, Harold Arlen, George Gershwin and Irving Berlin. However, work remains to be done on those who came before them. It was composers such as Septimus Winner, Alice Hawthorne, John Philip Sousa, Stephen Foster, George Root, Will Shakespeare Hays and countless others who developed the foundations of what we now call "American popular song"—without that work we could have never had the golden era of Tin Pan Alley. These first truly "American" composers struggled to merge a European tradition with both the influx of new ideas from an increasingly influential African

American population and the styles and traditions of the countless immigrants who ventured to America in the nineteenth century. Before vaudeville, jazz and ragtime, nineteenth-century composers defined the parameters for the future. Who were these men and women and how did they live?

Septimus Winner (1827–1902) is one of these forefathers of American popular song. In and of itself, his musical contributions are significant: well over three hundred popular songs, over two thousand arrangements of both his own and others' music, and an astounding array of pedagogical books for a broad variety of instruments that were increasingly found in the domestic milieu. There was scarcely a student of music in the late nineteenth century who didn't use a *Winner Methods* book or one of its many pedagogical cousins.

Beyond Winner's significant musical accomplishments, there is the "story behind the story." On some levels, Winner may have impeded his own fame. Certainly, he made it difficult for anyone researching his life to understand the scope of his accomplishments. For well over three decades, Winner published the majority of his original compositions under a variety of pseudonyms. While pseudonyms in and of themselves were a fairly common practice among artists of all types, Winner took the practice to a level that had not previously been seen nor has it been replicated since. His most popular works (and among his most enduring) were published under a female pseudonym, Alice Hawthorne. While Winner was certainly not the first male artist to publish under a woman's name, his case is distinct in that he created an entire persona for Alice Hawthorne and consistently used this pseudonym for well over thirty years. "The Hawthorne ballads", as they were generally known in the middle and late nineteenth century, were among the most popular and successful songs of their day. Why would Winner make such a choice? Especially at a time when women were either struggling for public acceptance against the social conventions of the time or were disguising their own identities with male pseudonyms? It was these questions that led me to begin to explore this anomaly in music history.

As that exploration began, I began to realize that there was another story to be told. This story concerns the complex relationship between one man and the woman he created. Septimus Winner didn't simply create Alice Hawthorne and use that creation for his own purposes. By exploring publication records, I began to realize that Winner may have often been jealous of his creation while at the same time limiting her output to specific genres while he pursued his own success in others. The more successful Alice became, the more Septimus way have tried to hold her back. It was this aspect of the story that became the basis for this book.

My own involvement with Winner began several years ago. As a doctoral student in music, I began to study feminism in music and in particular the female composers who, until the 1980s, were mentioned only in passing. Names like Hildegarde of Bingen, Fanny Mendelssohn Hensel and Clara Wieck Schumann had gained increasing amounts of recognition for their contributions to the musical canon. On the other hand, women in American music history, either in the classical or popular genres, were still waiting to gain that same recognition—Amy Beach being the only possible exception—or were still concealed by assumed identities that helped them conform to the social codes of the time.

As I explored the issues further, I became more and more interested in the history of women in American music. Max Wilk's fascinating but all too brief history of the women composers of ragtime music became a starting point that ultimately led to Judith Tick's excellent work on women composers in pre-1870 America. My father, an avid music lover and a collector of Broadway musicals, also found himself interested in my new course of study. Known for his regular attendance at local flea markets and auctions near his home in Pipersville, Pennsylvania, he came across a bound collection of popular songs by a composer named Alice Hawthorne. This book, now a treasured part of my library, was clearly special to its owners. They had taken a selection of sheet music, almost all by Hawthorne, and had it lovingly hand-bound to preserve the now yellowing and crumbling pages.

Intrigued by this discovery, my father and I began to look for evidence of Alice Hawthorne among our resources on American popular song. I can still remember his phone call to me as he related the story of a man we had never heard of, Septimus Winner, and his almost lifelong career as the pseudonymous Hawthorne. We had a puzzle on our hands and few avenues to begin solving it. Intrigued from a feminist standpoint, I assumed the mantle of research on Winner/Hawthorne and made it the focus of a musicology degree at the University of Houston.

Researching Winner's life proved to be no easy task for two related reasons. First, there is a paucity of material available on his life and many of the specific details of how Winner led his life may never be fully known. While the Winner family and their descendants seem to be what Howard Myers called "collectors," a most fortunate happenstance, there are numerous gaps in the sequence of Winner's life, especially where Alice Hawthorne and her musical activities are concerned. Because Winner was not a performer in the same way that a Cohan or Gershwin was, we have few details of the musical matters of Winner's life and at least some of what appears in this book is conjecture based on the best available facts.

The second reason that Winner's life is something of a mystery is due to the fact that Winner himself was not beyond what, at minimum, might be called fanciful exaggeration and, at maximum, could be labeled outright fabrication concerning the details of his own life. Even the few seemingly reliable sources on Winner's life contradict each other with varying versions of the same story. Rather than simply make up my own mind on what may or may not have been the truth behind these stories, I have presented them all. They are discussed not just from the perspective of which story may be closest to the truth but also from the standpoint of how these stories were part of creating the "myth behind the (wo)man."

This study is the result of hours spent delving into a life that few had bothered to notice until now. Winner is largely mentioned in footnotes and bibliographic entries in most collections of nineteenth-century song or musical reference works. To say the least, the unusual circumstances of his life are almost never explored (in fact, they are mentioned with an almost nonchalant detachment). Sensing something amiss in my own understanding of American music history, I undertook this book to explore my own fascination with one man and the woman he created.

Chapter One (1827-1852)
Early Years

Musical Philadelphia

As one of the important historical, political and economic centers of the United States in its formative years, Philadelphia could not help but emerge as one of the early cultural centers of an infant America. In the years following the Revolutionary War and up through and following the Civil War, the city was an important center of American cultural development through its numerous musical performances. It was also influential through the theatre, the burgeoning music publishing industry and the growth of piano manufacturing—arguably the single most important factor in the rise of American musical culture. It was this world that formed a context within which Septimus Winner, a musically gifted and tirelessly prolific composer and businessman, could grow and be nurtured.

Prior to Winner's birth, one of the earliest effects on popular music in America in general and in Philadelphia in particular occurred with the ban on "theatrical performances and other vain diversions" passed by the Continental Congress in Philadelphia in 1778 following many years of what might best be referred to as reluctant tolerance.[1] The newly minted United States of America was very much a product of its Puritan origins and, despite the ban, music was frequently performed in many of the cities of the northeast.

Ultimately lifted in 1789, the ban noted that the "frequenting [of] play houses and theatrical entertainments has a fatal tendency to divert the minds of the people from a due attention to the means necessary for the defense of their country and preservation of their liberties."[2] The ban urged states to "pass laws to prevent theatrical and musical diversions as are productive of idleness."[3]

With the lifting of the ban, many cities reemerged as active centers of music publishing and performance of which Philadelphia was no exception.[4] Less popular among Americans were the more "classical"

1

or perceived "aristocratic" songs of their English and European ances-
tors. Instead, at least some of the popular songs of the day originated in
the pleasure gardens and theatres of London, where the taste for Italian
opera had passed and the vogue for a popular music, begun as early as
John Gay's *Beggar's Opera* (1728), had taken a firm hold.[5]

By the opening decades of the nineteenth century some of America's most popular songs included "Auld Lang Syne," the perennial
Christmas favorite "Silent Night," Sir Henry Bishop's "Home, Sweet
Home" and the highly influential ballads of Sir Thomas Moore. Comic
songs and so-called Negro songs were also represented and included
such favorites as "Last Week I Took a Wife" and "Do I Do I Don't Do
Nothing." The style of songs such as these would have a profound influence not just on Winner but on the scores of songwriters active in
nineteenth-century America.

Another outcome of the lifting of the ban on popular music was
that each major American metropolis was flooded with ambitious musicians from Europe, largely from England. As Hamm notes these musicians may have been among the most diverse craftsmen ever to immi-
grate to America.[6] Because there was little professional musical or
theatrical infrastructure in place upon which to build, especially in the
smaller cities, musicians of all types were called upon to compose, arrange, perform, conduct, and potentially, sing and publish. Those who
couldn't had two alternatives: to diversify as much as possible or return
home. As a result, many of the musicians who arrived in the United
States were proficient not only on one instrument, but on many. In addition, many of them forged careers in theatre management, publishing,
and as impresarios, conductors, composers and arrangers. This diversity
of skills required is particularly important as far as Winner's career is
concerned—it established a tradition that became the model for both
his business and his musical activities.

One example of such a career model for Winner was the father and
son team of Joseph (1730-1819) and Benjamin (1768-1831) Carr. Their
publishing concern, Carr & Company, stands as a testament to how a
postwar, culturally and geographically isolated America yearning for
diversions kept musicians active and financially solvent. Between 1793
and 1800, Carr & Company established publishing houses not only in
Philadelphia but also in Baltimore and New York. In addition, Benjamin, a prolific composer, both selected and arranged works for publication in the *Musical Journal*, a music magazine based in Philadelphia
that Carr began publishing in 1800.[7] Carr was also active in concert
management and promotion, both in Philadelphia and in New York,
and was organist at both St. Joseph's Church and the Catholic Church
of St. Augustine in Philadelphia. Carr also composed one of the many
works that bear the moniker "the first American opera," *The Archers*
(1796).[8] Before his death, he was instrumental in the founding of the
Musical Fund Society. The society was one of the most influential mu-

sical groups to form in Philadelphia and an important part of Winner's life. Carr's leadership in the Musical Fund Society was crucial to the establishment of regular musical events in the city. A monument that stood well into the twentieth century in St. Peter's churchyard was a testament to Carr's musical abilities and leadership.[9] The inscription on the monument reads as follows:

> Charitable, without Ostentation,
> Faithful and true in his friendships,
> With the intelligence of a man,
> He united the simplicity of a child.
> In testimony of the high esteem in which he was held,
> this monument is erected by his friends and associates
> of the Musical Fund Society of Philadelphia.[10]

The Musical Fund Society was by no means the only musical organization founded in Philadelphia. The Amateurs of Music (1809), the Anacreontic Society (1833) and the Apollo Society (1830) all contributed to an active cultural life in the city. In addition, the Handelian Society, the Haydn Society, the Philadelphia Glee Associates, the Philadelphia Sacred Music Association, the St. Cecilia Society, the Philharmonic Society and the Männerchor of Philadelphia were all active during the first half of the nineteenth century.

As Philadelphia continued to grow in the first half of the nineteenth century, two other important developments occurred which would solidify Philadelphia's cultural importance. The first was the growing acceptance and performance of opera. While operatic performances had become a mainstay in southern cities like New Orleans, Puritan ethics made operatic performances in the northeast less frequent until the early decades of the nineteenth century. Performances at the Chestnut Street Theatre, and later at the Walnut Street Theatre, led to the formation and construction of the Philadelphia Academy of Music (1857), a rival to the Musical Fund Society notwithstanding their performances of different repertory (the society had largely discontinued operatic performances by the 1840s). Performances by both groups of Weber's *Der Freischütz* (1825), Rossini's *Otello* (1833), Bellini's *Norma* (1840) and later Verdi's *Luisa Miller* (1852) and *Il Trovatore*, the inaugural work at the Academy of Music building in 1857, firmly established opera in Philadelphia. These works were joined by popular ballad operas of the time including Arne's *Love in a Village*, Arnold's *Castle of Andalusia*, and more "serious" American works such as *Leonora* by William Fry, often called the American Berlioz.[11]

The growth of opera went hand in hand with the growth of popular music and the minstrel shows in Philadelphia.[12] Following the explosive debut of the Virginia Minstrels in 1843,[13] many cities built theatres

The Musical Fund Society[14]

The Musical Fund Society began as a series of informal get-togethers by a group of Philadelphia musicians from 1816-1820. As the group grew from its initial membership, they ultimately organized in 1820 as a means to create a professional performing group, involve young musicians, and "institute a society for the relief and support of decayed musicians and their families." A group of eighty-five charter members, including Benjamin Carr and composer Raynor Taylor, began a series of concerts in 1821 that featured European and American works in a variety of musical styles.[15] One admirable aspect of their charter was that the society allowed both men and women to be members in equal standing.

With the construction of the Musical Fund Hall in 1824 on the 800 Block of Locust Street, the society established itself as a leading musical influence in Philadelphia. American and European performers visited Philadelphia to perform with the society including a performance by nineteenth-century diva Maria Malibran in 1826 and 1831.[16] The society also presented the first American performance of *The Magic Flute* in 1841. Ole Bull performed at the hall in 1843 and Leopold Meignen, the society's second conductor, led performances of Beethoven's first three symphonies in 1845-1847. The performance of the first symphony in 1845 was so successful the directors reported that "the ability with which these complicated, yet expressive, harmonies were produced and their approval by one of the largest audiences ever gathered in the hall, is gratifying evidence of advancing musical skill and taste in the community." Later performances by Jenny Lind and Louis Moreau Gottschalk only further cemented the society's status in antebellum Philadelphia.

In addition to these concerts, the society functioned in a variety of capacities including financial support for sick or infirm members, funeral expenses for deceased members and a pension fund for surviving widows. This tradition continued well into the twentieth century even after the society stopped accepting new members in 1938. Hannah Winner, Septimus' wife, received such support following his death.

The society also supported itself through rental income. The first convention of the national Republican Party was held there in 1856. An impressive series of speakers used the facility for public events including Horace Mann, William Makepeace Thackeray, Ralph Waldo Emerson and Horace Greeley. While the facility was ultimately rivaled with the building of Philadelphia's Academy of Music in 1857, it remained an important home for musical performances, conservatories, minstrel

(Continued on next page)

The Musical Fund Society—Continued

shows and vaudeville, political meetings, commencements, boxing matches and religious groups.

While the society continues to exist today, the building itself was sold in 1924. Today, the building has been converted into residential condominiums. However, the society itself remains active, sponsoring composition prizes, providing support for members, holding performances and providing grants and scholarships for students and organizations.

---

and featured regular performances. Philadelphia mainstay Sam Sanford built the city's first minstrel theatre in 1853. A member of Sanford's group, John L. Carncross, created the Carncross and Dixey Minstrels (later just the Carncross Minstrels) that performed continuously for twenty-seven years between 1869 and 1896. An original member of Carncross' group, Frank Dumont, turned the Eleventh Street Opera House into a minstrel venue. The theatre still holds the record for continuous production of minstrel shows in America.

The other important development in Philadelphia's musical growth during the nineteenth century was the establishment of the city as an important center of piano construction.[17] As early as 1742, manufacturers such as Gustavus Hesselius had already established factories and stores in Philadelphia. Later eighteenth-century piano makers included James Julian, Charles Albrecht, Charles Taws and their respective families, who continued making instruments into the 1830s and 1840s.[18] The invention of the upright piano not only contributed to its increased presence in the home but also furthered Philadelphia's reputation as a center of manufacturing. Piano makers such as George E. Blake (a founding member of the Musical Fund Society) and the aforementioned Thomas Loud (later of the Loud Brothers) continued this tradition. These companies were strong rivals to some of the best-known American manufacturers such as Knabe in Baltimore, Chickering in Boston, and preceded such companies as Steinway in the United States by at least a generation.

The importance of the explosive growth of piano manufacturing cannot be underestimated. By the Civil War, piano manufacturers were producing more than 20,000 pianos per year for an American population that was barely more than thirty-one million.[19] By 1870, one out of every 1,540 Americans owned a piano. By 1890, that number was almost one of every 800.[20] Having firmly established itself as a political power and with many aspects of its infrastructure in place, America turned more and more to creating a cultural identity and legacy separate from its European origins. The growth of an increasingly affluent middle class further fueled the desire for leisure-oriented activities and it was women who became the primary purveyors of music in the home, often as a means to prepare young girls for courtship and marriage.

It is within this context in which we can better understand the life, creations and accomplishments of Septimus Winner.

Family Background[21]

The Winner family is largely of English descent. Five generations before our subject was born (see Figure 1.1), John Winner (Septimus' great-great-great-grandfather) came to the United States as a privateer captain of the sailing vessel *Wasp*. Born in Thaxted, County Essex, England, some fifty miles north-northeast of London, John Winner settled in southern New Jersey, opposite the Delaware River from Philadelphia, in approximately 1700 and stayed there until his death circa 1725.

James Winner's son (and Septimus' great-great-grandfather) James was named for John's brother. Born circa 1700, he ultimately moved north of Philadelphia, to Bucks County, Pennsylvania, in the 1740s. Family records indicate that he was a farmer, owning roughly fifty acres of land in Falls Township, some twenty-five miles to the north. Records also indicate that he served as a private in the Newton Pennsylvania Infantry in 1756 as part of the growing movement towards American independence.

John Winner's son Joseph was born in approximately 1735. He settled in Bristol, Pennsylvania, some twenty miles northeast of Philadelphia on the Delaware River, in the 1750s where he raised his family. This family included at least one son, also named Joseph (Septimus' grandfather), who was born in Bristol in 1776.

This Joseph married Elizabeth Evans, the daughter of Captain Nathan Evans, of Welsh descent, who, according to family lore, served with distinction in the Revolutionary War. Settling in the city of Philadelphia, Joseph and Elizabeth had at least three sons out of a total of seven children: William, Septimus (our subject's namesake), and Joseph (our subject's father).

William E. Winner is the best-known of the children of Joseph Winner and Elizabeth Evans. Little information can be found about Septimus Winner (our subject's namesake). Business records from the time list him as a combmaker with a shop or home-and-shop combination fairly close to his brothers.[22] Septimus the composer often recounts visiting his uncles in his diaries but there is precious little information regarding the details of their lives.

Joseph Winner (our subject's father) met and married Mary Ann Hawthorne in either 1825 or 1826. Mary Ann was a New York City native. When she came to Philadelphia and how she and Joseph came

A Family Tree

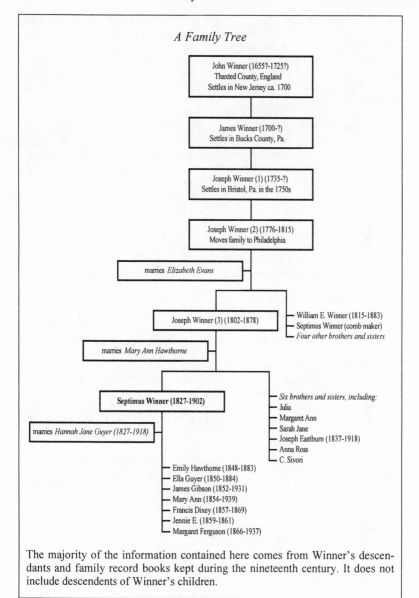

John Winner (1655?-1725?)
Thaxted County, England
Settles in New Jersey ca. 1700

James Winner (1700-?)
Settles in Bucks County, Pa.

Joseph Winner (1) (1735-?)
Settles in Bristol, Pa. in the 1750s

Joseph Winner (2) (1776-1815)
Moves family to Philadelphia

marries *Elizabeth Evans*

Joseph Winner (3) (1802-1878)

— William E. Winner (1815-1883)
— Septimus Winner (comb maker)
— *Four other brothers and sisters*

marries *Mary Ann Hawthorne*

Septimus Winner (1827-1902)

— *Six brothers and sisters, including:*
— Julia
— Margaret Ann
— Sarah Jane
— Joseph Eastburn (1837-1918)
— Anna Ross
— C. Sivori

marries *Hannah Jane Guyer (1827-1918)*

— Emily Hawthorne (1848-1883)
— Ella Guyer (1850-1884)
— James Gibson (1852-1931)
— Mary Ann (1854-1939)
— Francis Dixey (1857-1869)
— Jennie E. (1859-1861)
— Margaret Ferguson (1866-1937)

The majority of the information contained here comes from Winner's descendants and family record books kept during the nineteenth century. It does not include descendents of Winner's children.

Figure 1.1

to be acquainted and ultimately married remains a mystery. Mary Ann was a distant relative of the author Nathaniel Hawthorne, a fact that will prove significant in Septimus' career. After their marriage, they settled in Philadelphia, near his brothers, where Joseph worked to support his wife and growing family. On May 11, 1827, they welcomed the arrival of the first of what would ultimately be seven children. They named him Septimus after his uncle—another indication of how close the family was and would remain.

What has been passed down about Joseph Winner gives every impression of an itinerant not in the habit of keeping jobs for very long. Some sketches list him as a cooper (barrel maker) or a furniture maker but he also made violins. While his musical instruments were not of a very high quality,[23] this vocation would have an important impact on his oldest son and seems to have been the genesis of Septimus' career.

Joseph was also in the habit of taking to drink a little too frequently. Several attempts to reform him met with failure. This ongoing problem was of particular concern to his oldest son. On more than one occasion, Septimus' diaries[24] indicate that not only did he provide moral support to his mother, but as much financial support as he could muster to aid his mother and his younger brothers and sisters.

January 24, 1850
Father is doing very badly and no one knows the intense worriment to my mind it occasions. I acknowledge before God that I have done all in my power to reform him, and I find the more I do for him the less he does for himself. There must be a change sooner or later, for the better or the worse, but as long as I am able to bestow the least help and comfort in mother and her children, God assist me to lend my aid.

Shortly thereafter, on February 5, Winner took his father to see the temperance play *The Drunkard* at Barnum's Museum.[25] Apparently, the play had the desired effect. On March 10, Winner's diaries mention stopping by to visit his parents only to find out that they had gone to attend a temperance meeting. Clearly heartened by the news, Septimus must have felt that, at long last, his father was finally reforming. Shortly thereafter, Winner made the following entry in his diary.

March 13, 1850
Father has reformed and is indeed not only another man, but a true father, everything has gone for the best of late and I hope it may continue so for a period. I am doing all I can to keep him in good spirit, God assist me!

Apparently, however, this success was short lived.

April 22, 1850
Father has commenced his old habit.

Nor did it appear to get any better.

May 4, 1850
Went to see mother, all well but father, he is provoking.

William E. Winner (1815-1883)

William E. Winner was a portraitist and landscape painter of some repute in Philadelphia for the majority of the nineteenth century. Like his nephew, he was involved with groups that formed for the benefit of artists. He served as a member of the Board of Control for the Artist Fund Society beginning in 1843. Family accounts indicate that he exhibited frequently, especially at the Pennsylvania Academy of Fine Arts, where records indicate exhibits as late as 1881.

Family records and Winner's diaries indicate that Septimus was very close with his uncle and that, in many ways, William may have been something of a father figure. However, little else can be found out about William except that he was acquainted with Edgar Allan Poe and may have been a peripheral part of his circle when Poe lived in Philadelphia. It would appear that, at the very least, William's friendship with Poe would be directly responsible for Septimus' first artistic publication. William painted a portrait of the great writer that was rediscovered in 1935. This portrait is now in a private collection.

Septimus' diaries recount several occasions where he visited his uncle, often going as much as two or three times per week. At minimum there were two portraits of Septimus. The first, which is shown on page 119, depicts a young Septimus with his father, probably painted during Septimus' teenage years. The second, now apparently lost, was painted in 1850 and is recorded in Septimus' diaries in May of that year.

Despite various attempts at reform, Joseph would remain a lifelong alcoholic. By August 1850, Septimus was clearly at wit's end.

August 22, 1850
A fine clear day and pleasant day, busy part of the morning, went up home to help mother move, father absent somewhere. Brought mother and the little children home determined to support them myself with the assistance of the Almighty . . .

Joseph Winner (1802-1878)

Comparing the portrait painted by William E. Winner (which dates from the early 1840s) and the April 1863 photo, both of which are shown in the photospread (pages 119-132), it is clear that the years of alcohol abuse had taken their effect on a man who by all accounts was a "handsome, kind and affable man" and "well liked by all who knew him." One of the more interesting stories concerning Joseph Winner, Septimus' father, concerns his service in the Civil War. In and of itself, his service is unusual in that Joseph would have been roughly sixty years old at the time of his enlistment. It is also unusual in that it was a fairly simple matter to have oneself excused from service by paying a substitute to serve in one's place. It is more likely that he would have been pressured to serve by his wife and children given his history of drinking. It is also possible that his numerous arrests at the hands of his wife and children ended up in some kind of forced conscription.

Regardless of the actual reasons behind his service, Joseph Winner was on active duty during the Civil War—serving as a private. On one particular evening when Joseph was more than a little intoxicated, he received orders from his commanding officer to whitewash his entire room while he was away from base. Joseph took the officer at his exact words and proceeded not only to whitewash the room but also the officer's bed, furniture, stove and boots. Family lore doesn't tell the aftermath of this event but it is an indication of the extent of Joseph's "affair with the bottle" and its impact on his children. Most likely, he would have been discharged not only for this antic but also for his consistent drunkenness.

Surprisingly, Joseph's lifelong trouble with alcohol did not result in a shorter life. He most likely lived beyond anyone's expectations—dying in 1878 at the age of seventy-six.[26]

August 23, 1850
A very disagreeable morning, at work until 11 o'clock, went up home and helped mother to finish moving. Father stopped in the afternoon intoxicated, did not come back all night.

August 25, 1850
Father came home at supper-time worse than ever.

The situation apparently became so bad that Septimus had his father arrested and pressed charges against him. This would have most likely been done to protect his mother and siblings.

August 26, 1850
Rose early and went to the South Garden hall with Mother to
make the charge against Father, a trying time indeed to see
him treated thus but something rigid had to be done.

And it would seem to have been an ongoing event, at least for the fore-
seeable future.

January 22, 1851
Father went on a spree, came home at night and made a great
noise for the gratification of all, had him arrested.

January 18, 1852
Had to have father arrested notwithstanding on account of his
drunken and awful behavior.

May 15, 1852
Life possessed no charm this day, business dull, and all things
out of sorts, and to complete the misery, Father got drunk.
Damn the rum! And may I never be tempted with the drug so
help me God!

Despite his constant problems with the bottle, Joseph and Mary
Ann Winner went on to have seven children in total: after Septimus
came Julia, Margaret Ann, Sarah Jane, Joseph Eastburn, Anna Ross and
C. Sivori.[27] The family relationships were close. Septimus was a frequent visitor at the home of his sisters and was, at one point or another,
involved in helping his two brothers make their way in the music business.

Early Years

Septimus Winner was born in the part of Philadelphia known as the
North Liberties.[28] Very little is known about his years as a boy. One
might surmise, given his father's drinking habits, that Septimus' early
years were as difficult for his mother and siblings as they were in his
adulthood but there is no evidence to support it one way or the other.
    What we know about Winner's youth comes largely from stories
he told either to family members or as part of the many newspaper interviews he gave late in life. (Winner's voluminous diaries largely
avoid such anecdotes.) A thorough investigation of many of these articles and stories reveals several different versions of the same events,
thereby making it difficult to separate fact from fiction. The stories
will, therefore, be presented as they were recounted and will also attempt to determine where, if anywhere, the truth lies. Known as an affable and fun-loving man, it's not surprising that Winner might have

embellished his stories for humor's sake. He may have also embellished them to provide interesting fodder for newspaper reporters.

Winner's earliest years were spent in Philadelphia. While we have
physical evidence of the date and place of his birth, there is no evidence
to confirm whether or not he attended school in his early years. While
some earlier directories of Philadelphia residents show no listing for
Joseph, he appears as a chair maker in the 1839 edition, living in the
North Liberties area. As times were most likely hard for the Winner
family in the 1820s and 1830s, it is possible that Septimus was
schooled at home and, as the oldest boy, may have assisted his father as
he struggled to earn a living while he moved from one vocation to the
next.

Joseph made the decision, in either late 1839 or 1840, to relocate
his family to the Wyoming Valley, near Wilkes-Barre, Pa. At the time,
this would have been no small task. At least five of Joseph and Mary
Ann's children would have been born by then, Septimus being no more
than thirteen, and the trip to Wilkes-Barre, some 110 to 120 miles to the
north-northeast, would likely have been arduous. Family records give
no indication as to why Joseph chose to move his family so far away
nor is there any evidence of family in that area. Regardless of the reasons, for thirteen-year-old Septimus, the experiences of that trip would
be recounted for a lifetime.

Winner's fondest memories from the period seem to be most
closely associated with his mother. In one anecdote, Winner recalled
how his mother would dress the hair of her two boys, Septimus and
Joseph, in preparation for Sunday school (from this we can be sure that
Mary Ann was concerned that her children received some form of
Christian education). Normally she would use a can of "bear grease" to
rub on the boys' heads, but on one particular Sunday she reached for
the wrong can and proceeded to rub axle grease on Joseph's hair. In
another story, Winner recalled how his mother always mixed two eggs
together before scrambling them for each family member. In that way if
one egg were bad, then it would be "too bad."[29] Winner's fond memories of his mother would manifest themselves in many ways in later
life.[30]

If Winner's recollections are to be believed, he also attended
school while the family lived in the Wyoming Valley. Winner frequently recounted how his classmates, largely of German descent, had
unusual names. In his row at school, Winner reported two such classmates, Molidore Spiegel and Theopholus Bopholus.[31]

Winner frequently recounted stories of his love for the countryside
and how it affected him in youth. Many of these stories were connected
to his "employment" at the time, having been sent by his parents to
work at the home and farm of one Reverend Thomas P. Hunt, who
lived nearby. Winner's recollections of this time have been recorded in
at least three different ways:

In that delightful section, and amid those glorious scenes of Nature of which poets seem never to tire of singing, was first fostered and brought out whatever of poetry and music there was in him. At the same time, a little of the rebellious spirit, too, made its appearance; for, disgusted with the duties of cow-boy and the many menial services required of him, as-sisted by some older boys, he one day smuggled out his be-longings and ran away from the slow parsonage, succeeding, after many difficulties, in safely reaching home (1897).[32]

This next version, written by a grandson, embellishes this first ver-sion in even more florid and romantic prose but fails to mention his employment at the time:

When still a boy, circumstances brought him to the Wyoming Valley near Wilkes-Barre and it was while living there that young Winner undoubtedly obtained that love for Nature which became one of the ruling passions of his life. He has spoken of his early days among the farms, of midnight rides across the hills, of hunting parties penetrating far into the Po-conos, and across the Indian trails which at that time traversed the mountains. The moonlight shining over the hills, the deep, dark shadows in the valleys; the verdant green of summer, and the white coat of snow in the winter, each touched a respon-sive chord in his gentle, vibrant nature (1903).[33]

This last version, written by his great-grandson, spares us the florid prose in favor of a more straightforward approach:

He enjoyed the country life, with its brooks, trees and animals, displaying a great interest in nature as evidenced in his poetry writing during later years. But at this time the boy was un-happy at the work and menial tasks he had to perform, so one day he secretly carried away his belongings and ran home (1937).[34]

The romanticism of the first two examples should be excused only insofar as they were part of interviews Winner gave or embellishments thereof. It is likely that the third example is the closest to the actual truth concerning Winner's departure from Reverend Hunt's, assuming there was any secretive nature to it at all. Given that the last version was passed down among family members, it seems the most plausible especially when seen in light of the first two. A conspiracy of young boys carried out against a local preacher in an attempt to free only one of them seems unlikely at best. It is more likely to be the late-in-life embellishment of either Winner himself or of a biographer eager to portray his subject in a romantic light.

What these stories tell us, and more importantly their relevance to Winner's career as a songwriter, is that he did attend school. Most importantly, he developed a fondness and respect for nature in all its forms—a prominent feature of his poetry—both in and of itself and for songs that were published later in life.

Again for reasons that remain unclear, Joseph Winner moved his family back to Philadelphia a few years later (the exact date is unknown but it must have been by 1843). Whether Joseph Winner had exhausted all of his business possibilities or simply had worn out his welcome as a result of his difficulties with alcohol remains unknown. As before, the journey home must have been no easier than the one they made to get there.

Upon their return, Septimus attended or was admitted to the First Central High School of Philadelphia.[35] From a modern perspective Winner's attendance at high school may not seem auspicious, but a high school education was far from the norm for teenagers in the nineteenth century. As late as 1870, there were only one hundred and sixty public high schools in the United States.[36] In the 1840s, the number must have been significantly less. While this fact doesn't necessarily demonstrate any newfound affluence on the part of the Winner family, it does indicate that, at the very least, Mary Ann must have felt that her boys (it is unknown whether the girls attended school) would have more potential for advancement should they complete their education—college would have almost certainly been out of the question.

The years of Septimus' attendance at First Central High School are a matter of some debate. Family accounts describe only two years' attendance at the school and a graduation date of 1847. However, one of Winner's school notebooks survives, from a science class taught by a Dr. McMurtrie.[37] This notebook, dated 1843, would place Winner in a Philadelphia school at age sixteen. Two years' attendance would then have Winner graduating in June 1845 at age eighteen, a far more likely scenario. The notebook features notes on physics, chemistry, biology and the elements. However, the notebook also appears to have been something of a scratch pad in later years: it features a variety of poetry that may or may not have been the musings of a teenager. Other notes make reference not only to his wife but also to Alice Hawthorne, as well as containing an 1894 newspaper clipping. As a result, it is difficult to date any of the remaining entries in the notebooks, especially as they pertain to dating any of the poetry.

Winner's diary for the year 1845 shows him already teaching his first students. It is unlikely that Winner would have begun to engage in the business of teaching while still attending high school, thereby giving more credibility to the 1845 graduation date.

Nothing is known as to whether or not Winner received any musical training as part of his high school education. While it is known that at least some form of rudimentary musical training was part of the public school curriculum during Reconstruction, this may or may not have been the case in antebellum Philadelphia. As one of Philadelphia's few high schools, First Central High School may have included music in the curriculum, but Winner made no mention of it in later life and family anecdotes provide no additional information.

Winner did, however, recount stories as to his early musical training. Because Joseph Winner was at least a part-time violin maker, it is reasonable to assume that he provided his oldest son with at least some rudimentary instruction on the instrument. Later in life, Winner told the following stories about his musical education. As it was with his years in Wyoming Valley, there are several differing accounts:

> About this time, he awakened to the knowledge that he had "music in his soul," and this wonderful discovery was brought about by his coming into possession of an old violin, left him by a deceased relation. He sawed at it and worked at it, worried a friend who could play a little to give him some instruction, and by close application and constant practice was, in a year's time enabled to assist a singing-master without "putting out" the whole school. Encouraged by this success, he then took a single quarter's lessons on the violin, and in harmony and thorough-base, from a regular teacher, Professor Leopold Meignen, then a well-known musician and orchestra leader. This was all the regular instruction Mr. Winner ever received; yet we find him, when but a youth of twenty years, a successful music teacher, and also a respected member of the Musical Fund Orchestra (1879).[38]

This first account is almost certainly apocryphal. While the self-insight as to his musical talents may have first been realized at age eighteen, it is highly unlikely that he received a violin from a deceased relative as his father seems to have been the only member of the family with musical inclinations. The avoidance of Winner's father in this particular account is significant in that it demonstrates at least the possibility of some anger or resentment towards him. While Winner's diligent practice must be true on some levels as his later employment as a violinist would indicate, any employment accompanying a singing master (whether it was remunerated or not) is not supported in any other biographical sketches. Beyond that, either Winner's recollection of his studies with Meignen are incorrect, the interviewer misunderstood his subject, or Winner out-and-out lied. His studies with Meignen date from 1853, several years after his twentieth birthday, and did not include instruction on the violin. Given Winner's tendency to exaggerate the details of his life in later interviews, it isn't surprising to find such a confused account. Another description of Winner's musical training follows:

> Mr. Winner's talent is not hereditary, according to his own deduction, but he credits his early training, which he received while his father was manager of Old Temperance Hall, Third and Green Streets, one of the most successful theatres in the city nearly sixty years ago. Young Winner attended the public school during the daytime and at night did clerical duty for his father at the theatre . . . Young Winner learned to compose songs and proved so successful that Sanford (e.g., Sam Sanford) and others frequently asked his assistance in some catchy piece. The result of this was that the young composer cultivated a talent for music of a grander scale and he was next located as violinist in the old Arch Street Theatre (1899, 1901).[39]

This version of Winner's musical training gives at least a perfunctory nod to his father but limits that acknowledgment to a situation rather than to any direct musical support. Given Joseph Winner's on-and-off problems with alcohol, the fact that he may have been employed at the Old Temperance Hall is not surprising. However, the timing of this employment is subject to some debate. Claghorn notes that this employment occurred when his father was "reformed" and referred to him not as a manager but as a custodian.[40] The story implies that Joseph's employment lasted for some time. The sobriety that would have been required simply isn't borne out in any of Septimus' diaries from this time period.

If, in fact, his father did hold such a position, what is likely is that the teenage Septimus *had* to help his father at the theatre as his drinking probably did not permit him to undertake his duties with any completeness on his own. No records have been uncovered that indicate Joseph Winner held this position or that Septimus was engaged in helping him. Additionally, these later newspaper interviews represent the only mention of Winner's being asked to assist performers of the day in composing and/or arranging music at such an early age. While it is entirely possible that Winner was a staff violinist with the orchestra of the Arch Street Theatre, this is not confirmed either by his diaries or in family accounts.

Claghorn's concise telling of the early aspects of Winner's musical education seems more plausible given the lack of any documenting evidence to the contrary:

> He became proficient with the violin while very young, and at the early age of twenty he was in business for himself as a mu-

sic instructor, and making a living at it. His classes included instruction on the guitar, banjo, violin, and other instruments.[41]

Courtship and Marriage

It is very likely that Winner's abilities as a teacher were responsible for his meeting his future wife, Hannah Jane Guyer. Winner's diaries of 1845 (to the extent they can be validated) speak of a student named Guyer taking lessons beginning on October 2. A subsequent diary entry reads: "Evening at H's," suggesting more than a passing level of familiarity.

Little is known about Hannah Jane Guyer, the woman who would become Mrs. Septimus Winner. Family records indicate that she was born on February 12, 1827, and lived a long life, dying on October 12, 1918. It is quite likely that Hannah was in some way related to Winner's student Guyer, possibly an older sister or brother. The coincidence is, on some levels, too much to dismiss.

Of German descent, family accounts report that Hannah was the daughter of Benjamin Guyer, described as a "watchman" which we might assume means a maker of watches and clocks.[42] Benjamin apparently had quite a large family, as a family record in possession of the Winner family indicates that Hannah Jane had at least nine brothers and sisters born between 1810 and 1840.[43]

The courtship of Septimus and Hannah Jane appears, from dated correspondence, to have started by June of 1845. One early note to her, excerpted below, shows his romantic and poetic tendencies:

1.
Accept this while its brightest hint
Imparts unblemished purity
And ere it fades, may it imprint
Upon thy heart one thought of me.

2.
I sought it for its loveliness
And for its chaste sublimity;
I give it, that it may express
A thought bestow'd on thee, by me.

Some letters are of an innocuous nature such as the following undated note scribbled on a sheet of notepaper that had already been used to sketch a poem:

Dear Hannah, I thought it was of no use to cast aside the sheet because of the above lines which is the commencement of a song I once intended for the Weekly Paper. So I have made use of it. It is my intention to proceed to the Musical Theatre tomorrow night to hear the Hutchinson Family. It is likewise my desire that you shall "go along with me". Julia [his sister] went . . . and was there at 10 minutes past 6 . . . and just made out to get a good seat so please to be ready early. I will call before 6 o'clock . . . Yours earnestly, Septimus

As the excerpt from the following courtship letter indicates, Septimus' relationship with Hannah Jane may have been fraught with misunderstandings and difficulties. This was a harbinger of their future together.

April 15, 1846
If ever the true and deepest passion of the heart, responsive to its sharer was evinced, 'tis here. I know not, Hannah, how many hours of unhappiness I may have caused to blight thy days, and mar the calmness of thy peaceful mind. I'll own that I have often acted contrary to my nature, tho I know that I must sadden thee, still I would manifest such evidences of resentment as my spirit could not hide, and tho I were so foolish – finding such returned made me but the worse, and caused me to believe I was not by thee beloved, my Hannah, I would not chide thee for such as it is the nature of every being to retaliate – a feeling not easily to be stifled. That I love thee, and love thee most sincerely, you well know, and coldness on your part is but a torment to my soul. Nevertheless, how often do I bear with such? You may answer that it soon dies. It does, Hannah, but do wounds heal without a scar? There's the point. Could but the impression wrought by its chilling breath pass away as breath then might I rest in happiness. But no! It will cling, it will sicken, and will last.

These misunderstandings were not short-lived.

May 6, 1846
Dearest Hannah, You must know the feelings I now bear. If not, conceive the burden of a heavy heart - enough! You understand me well; you forbid me calling again if I visited . . . [another name, unintelligible] . . . last night. I have done so and well you know the occasion. Now if your heart is so quickly changed, if love can so easily be lost and I be treated with indifference for so frivolous an act, I am greatly deceived in you, but . . .

The fairest flower will quickly fade

And wither while we grasp.
The dearest friend that love hath made
Grows colder while we clasp,
With fervent heart and ardent soul
The hand that gave delight
One friendship lost its sweet control
A passion wore no blight.

I cannot convince myself that such is your real desire nevertheless I will not visit you again till I am fully convinced. If
one can be deceived through actions, it is not easy to be deceived by plain simple language. You have told me plainly
and I understand. Hannah, you know I do not deceive you but
if you leave me, I never can forget. I can write no more. Yours
still faithful, Septimus Winner.

Despite these misunderstandings and difficulties, Septimus and
Hannah were ultimately married by the Reverend Stork at the Presbyterian Church on November 25, 1847. This may have been something of
a double celebration in that Hannah's sister, Caroline, married only
four days earlier.
Given Winner's diary entries after their marriage, it would seem
that the marriage was fraught with the same kinds of difficulties as their
courtship:

February 24, 1848
All scholars present, went out in the afternoon to see Henry
Clay. Hannah got mad cause why!!!

April 21, 1848
Very fine day, went out in the morning, met so many Dutch-
men, quite astonished, ask'd, discovered it was Good Friday,
came home and told Hannah. Got mad because she hadn't had
holiday.

Nor does it seem that any difficulties were resolved in these early
years as this very long entry from May 1849 would indicate.

"The Character of a Woman"

Saturday. Wife complaining incessantly because of having "too much to do," pleads with husband for help, he sym-
pathizes, travels to an intelligence office, pays his quarter and
makes for home. Night. Girl calls, the time fixed to call again,
girl returns. Husband appears much gratified to be accommo-
dated so early, wife looks peeved and wants to know why he,

the Hubby, made himself so sociable with the stranger, thinks
he must have "taken a liking" to her, and doesn't know but
what she did to him. Husband feels vex'd but doesn't think it
worth while to say much, in-as-much as he doesn't care. Both
go to bed in a "huff."

Sunday. Husband remembers all, wife seems unconscious
that anything has taken place, rather inclined to be pleasant.

Monday. Husband pretty quiet all day, busy at work, that
is earning a living until nine o'clock at night. Took a notion to
play checkers and backgammon with his brother-in-law for
amusement, shut up store ten minutes past ten, felt hungry
somewhat, invited brother-in-law to take a plate of oysters at a
neighbors, came home prepared for bed, met the wife, with a
troubled face and arms folded, all because she thought husband had been gambling for refreshments, went to bed in a
sullen mood, never uttered a word, felt as people say "mad" at
which husband smiled.

Tuesday. Wife had forgotten all, the memory of the past
as poets no such thing with her, both retire.

Wednesday. Wife inclined to grumble part of the day but
can't find a subject. Husband steps out at the door to take a
fresh air for a few moments, and enjoying smoke. Wife
nearby, two shad women pass and smile, look back and smile
again. Wife happens to observe same and retires for a con-
venient period, determined to "blow out." Husband smokes
away unconscious of anything that has taken place, drops his
stump and walks in whistling. Wife: "Well, if you're going to
act that way, why do it?"

As their marriage continued, it would appear that things did not
improve despite their feelings for one another:

September 4, 1850
Han had her "dander up" all the evening so I had no pleasure
at home and begin to feel as if I don't expect it anymore and
don't care a straw either. She blames her ugly temper on the
children and the ever-lasting bother with them.

Even later in their marriage, Septimus seemed to be forever apolo-
gizing for his actions or thoughts. On more than one occasion, Hannah
traveled with one or more of their children to visit friends or relatives in
other parts of Pennsylvania and New Jersey. These journeys represent

the only correspondence we have from Septimus to Hannah later in their marriage (Hannah's letters to Septimus appear not to have survived and if Hannah did keep a diary, it has yet to be uncovered). These letters make regular references to Hannah's health and nerves, suggesting that she may have had something of a delicate nature, something which Septimus appears to have been mindful of in the following excerpt, from a letter when Hannah had gone on a visit to Williamsport, Pennsylvania:

> *August 25, 1862*
> Now Han, I want you to try and enjoy yourself as much as possible while you are away and stay just as long as you conveniently can, without discommodating [sic] Mrs. Trainer. Although I would be glad to have you home tomorrow, yet I am willing for you to stay until you are perfectly rested and satisfied . . . I expect to go to the Monster meeting (democratic) to-night for we are going to have a big turnout. If you think it's wrong, I'll go to church to-morrow to atone for the sin.

Septimus also makes regular references, as seen above, to atoning for his sins, an indication that Hannah may have used religion as a means to keep her husband "in line." In a later letter to her, he wrote:

> *July 13, 1873*
> It is nine o'clock, Gibson [their son] is home. He took Hattie a box of candies, a book, a packet full of ground nuts and a half a dozen pretzels, in fact all he could carry, he was up before the sun this morning—I guess he's "gone on her," but he's an awful flirtist when he gets with Laurie, takes after his father I seem to hear you say? Well, "vot uv it," if he lives he'll lose his taste for it, and if he doesn't he won't know what it is. It's naughty but it's nice, and I'd rather be a rake than a sanctimonious sucker . . . I'm afraid I digress—but I'm sorry for my sins and that is enough to acknowledge.[44]

After an interview with Florence Claghorn, the daughter of Winner's daughter Mary Ann and a close friend of the composer in his final years, Howard Myers drew the following conclusions:

> There is no indication that his home was ever in serious danger of breaking up, in spite of the many minor disturbances that occurred during the first fifteen years or so of his marriage. It is possible that his wife was truly in love with him, and his letters to her all indicate a lasting deep affection, at least, on his part. Miss Claghorn remembers her grandmother

as a "saint on earth" who endured her husband's unsaintliness
with fortitude. This leads me to believe that Hannah Jane
dramatized herself as a martyr.[45]

Myers' conclusion may very well have been true, but we only have
Winner's side of the correspondence from which to judge. Especially in
later life, Winner could hardly have been called unsaintly. Several references to his avoidance of alcohol and the relative calm of his domestic life have led this author to conclude that Winner was guilty of no
greater sin that indulging his grandchildren and smoking the occasional
cigar. Without Hannah's own correspondence, it seems as if history is
fated to judge her not only as a martyr, but also as something of a frag-
ile hysteric.

A Musician Sets Out

Upon graduating from high school, Septimus immediately set out to
establish himself in Philadelphia's musical and artistic circles. By his
own account, having had at least some skill as a violinist, one might
assume that Winner would have started out as a performer. However,
records would indicate that performing was only part of his activities.
As early as 1845, business directories of the time list Winner as teaching students and maintaining some form of music stand (although this
may have just been a studio address).[46] This would have put Septimus
in business at the age of eighteen. Myers claims that he had a partnership with his younger brother, Joseph Eastburn Winner.[47] However in
1845, Joseph Eastburn Winner would have only been seven or eight
years old, so this ascription is speculative. What is more likely is that
his father assisted him in some way to get established in the Philadelphia music business, having at least some experience and potentially
contacts as a result of his work as an violin maker. Septimus may have
also needed to supplement his income as a performer as a means to
provide support for his mother.
      As early as September 1845, Winner was beginning to assemble a
roster of students. By January 1846, records indicate that he had at least
ten. There are many possibilities as to what it was Winner taught these
students. We can be reasonably sure that many of these students were
instructed on the violin, but it is also likely that he taught private lessons on guitar and banjo.[48]
      Interestingly, Winner's first published artistic effort was not as a
musician but as a poet. Several biographical sources cite Winner's involvement with Edgar Allan Poe and *Graham's Magazine*. Poe had
been acquainted with William Winner, Septimus' uncle, and had in fact
sat for a portrait at one time. This connection through his uncle may
have provided Septimus' first real opportunity to be recognized as a
poet.

Late in life, Winner said that he had been an occasional contributor to *Graham's Magazine* while Poe was its editor. This was, as so many facts related by Winner are, something of an artful exaggeration. In a late interview, Winner commented about his relationship with Poe:

> I knew him fairly well but although [*sic*] chiefly from the fact that I was not much of a drinker, I was not eligible to member-ship in his set.[49]

Graham's American Magazine[50]

Originally titled the *Casket*, *Graham's American Magazine* began in 1826 as another entry in the burgeoning American magazine market. However, under the leadership of several important writers, the maga-zine quickly began to distinguish itself for its essays, voluminous amounts of poetry and startling color illustrations of domestic scenes and popular fashion.

When George Graham purchased the magazine in 1839, he pub-lished stories of love, American adventure and the Orient, written by important literary figures including Edgar Allan Poe, Russell Lowell, Lydia H. Sigourney, George Pope Morris and Thomas Buchanan Read. They would be followed by an even more impressive roster of literary luminaries including Henry Wadsworth Longfellow, William Cullen Bryant, Mrs. Emma C. Embury, Mrs. Seba Smith and James Fenimore Cooper.

Starting around 1850, *Graham's* began having difficulty compet-ing in an increasingly competitive market that included the highly popular *Harper's Magazine*. With the loss of many of their leading writers, *Graham's* ceased publication in 1858 but, in its day, had estab-lished itself as an important model for literary magazines of the future.

Poe himself was coeditor of the magazine from January 1841 through May 1842 (predating Winner's publication by over four years). However, Poe's influence on Winner may have also been more far-reaching. Myers notes that Poe's poetry may have had a strong impact on Winner, especially Poe's *Ulalume*.[51]

This author's research indicates that Winner was published in the magazine only once, in July 1846, and that by the time of that publica-tion, Poe, although still involved, was no longer the editor. Nineteen-year-old Septimus must have been very encouraged by this acknowl-edgment. Given the timing of this publication, it is more than reason-able to assume that this work, titled "Song," was, at least in part, in-spired by his courtship with Hannah.

The scenes of many days may fade,
Their forms may pass away,
But should the vows of Friendship made
By thee sing to decay,
I ask when lonely hours present
The past once dear to thee,
Thou wouldst but give thy spirit vent
To rest one thought on me.

While ling'ring through this weary life,
If thou shouldst feel undone,
Remember, in the worldly strife,
To love thee there is one;
And if afar from home to rove
Should be thy drear decree,
Think on the friends whom thou didst love,
And then remember me.

Returning to Winner's musical activities, Winner's own diaries do not indicate an official place of business prior to 1845 nor does it seem Winner chose to rent or buy a home for himself until his marriage at the end of 1847. By the beginning of 1848, Winner had opened a teaching studio and some kind of music enterprise at No. 7 Arcade East. Given the lack of entries in his 1847 diary, we might reasonably assume that this was his first place of business without his father. It was also the first in what would become a long series of business addresses. Although the chronology is unclear vis-à-vis his performing career, this first foray into opening his own store may have resulted from a distaste for the rigors of regular performing but may also have been an indication of his relative success as a private teacher as well as the ongoing need to provide support for his family.

The Young Businessman

While Winner's teaching skills were clearly in demand, his skills as a performer were also being called upon. As early as January 8, 1848, Winner writes of taking part in rehearsals with the Musical Fund Society Orchestra. Because his diaries for 1847 end in early September,[52] it is very likely that Winner began playing with them either just before or around the time of his marriage. His marriage may have even been a catalyst for taking on the extra work. It is likely Winner played violin in the orchestra (his seating in that group is unknown) as the repertoire in his diary indicates:

January 8, 1848
Afternoon at rehearsal, Musical Fund Hall, played Beethoven's Symphony.

January 22, 1848
Went to the Musical Fund Society rehearsal, played one of Beethoven's symphonies and an overture by Lindpainter[53] called *Lichenstew.*

By February 2, Winner writes of being elected to membership in the Musical Fund Society. This would probably have been of some comfort to Septimus, as it would not only have given him something of a steady income as a performer but also provide for his family should anything happen to him.

Septimus also frequently took extra work in pickup orchestras around the city. He wrote of playing at several events and balls in 1848 and beyond:

March 20, 1848
Play'd at the National Guard's Ball at the Museum, very fine indeed, came home 4 1/2 o'ck.

March 27, 1848
Played at Fairmount's Ball.

Winner makes several notes in his diary about playing with the Philadelphia Brass Band. Given the instruments on which he gave lessons and with which he had some facility, it is likely that he played banjo with the group. A portrait later in life cites Winner as being the leader of this group for five years although Winner's diaries provide no corroborating evidence to support this claim.[54]

Winner's diaries of these early years also make mention of the Cecilian Musical Society. Winner became a member as early as May 5, 1849. It is possible that he joined this group in order to secure additional performance opportunities (although there are no diary entries that indicate any performances were part of belonging to this group). It may also have been that he saw this as an opportunity for advancement in Philadelphia's music circles. While, by 1852, Winner had become secretary of this organization, if it did advance his career in any way, there is no mention of it in either his diaries or correspondence.

According to some diary entries, it appears that Winner was not immune to the potential pratfalls of a musical life:

January 6, 1849
Playing at the ball on Monday night I was much embarrassed for a while, having violin to use; whilst playing most intensely

in a forte passage off flew the neck! and having not yet received my cash I went in search of another and luckily, as fate
would have it, borrowed one from Mr. Carles in Chestnut
Street. By the way, that was a glorious ball for the Irish population, they danced the *"Bowl'd Sojor Boy"* till the room was
filled with steamy brath [*sic*] and the lights grew dim.

The economic downturn of the late 1840s was almost certainly a
factor in Winner's taking on extra work. It must have been on his mind
as Septimus and Hannah's first child, a daughter, Emily Hawthorne,
was born on August 27, 1848. His diaries of the time reflect these concerns but they also feature his trademark sense of humor, a trait, according to family lore, inherited from his father:

October 5, 1848
Delightful out of funds, came to the conclusion to go to the
poor house by request of a gentleman friend, took me there,
didn't like it much and concluded I'd come home, got back
about 5 o'clock, found home to be the better place.

October 14, 1848
All things fine except pocket . . .

December 7, 1848
Times are very hard at present, everybody seems to be complaining. I have but 10 pupils which is about one half the
number I had this time last year. I think of moving from this
old neighborhood to some more bustling neighborhood. Even
though business should be no better, I have cold comfort of
knowing that it cannot be worse. Some persons say they have
"the blues," my principal pastime is that of nursing the baby,
and smoking cigars. Somebody sent me a very pleasant note
the other day politely requesting me to try my luck in the lot-
tery, but I concluded that it was better to use my money for a
certain purpose than an uncertain one. I therefore paid for gas
to light an empty stove.

I don't think I was born for riches tho I'm far from being poor.
Well "all in all" I consider I'm as happy as most men, I'm
thankful for what I get, and sometimes happy for that which I
only anticipate getting, in other words what doesn't come.

Winner finished the entry with a poem:

Heaven makes not matters unto man's desire,
For storms arise when prayers for sunshine fail,

And torrid hearts distract his fevered brain,
Whilst hope keeps waiting for a cooling draught.

The wants of man are many, and he sighs
For much that is unto his life denied;
His needs are few, compared to his desires,
For mankind never can be satisfied.
God only knows what for his life is best
And often proffers more than he deserves.

He prays from heaven only what he craves,
And asks not for the boon he truly needs;
Then sighs, that he forsaken seems to be,
Because no answer cometh to his prayer.

He cries: "Oh, Lord, hast thou forsaken me,
That I no favor in thine eyes behold?"
Not realizing in his truant heart
That he, in fact, from Him hath gone astray.

Let those so prone to find a fault with heaven
Give daily thanks for what to them is given,
The crimes of man's neglected duty calls
For punishment more justly than his sins;
Is this not why prayers of many fail
And die unanswered as they leave the lips?

Winner's 1849 diaries make no mention of any more dire financial straits save one entry:

September 10, 1849
I was thinking about the cost of building a house, but came to
my senses when I found I was too poor to pay for the digging
of a foot of cellar! What a state of affairs.

While it is possible that Winner's financial situation had improved by the summer of 1849, it might also be the case that he was distracted by the events of the day. In the summer of 1849, Philadelphia suffered a horrifying cholera epidemic, one that Winner, like so many other Philadelphians, recorded meticulously in his diaries. The daily newspapers were filled with reports of the epidemic and hospital reports were frequently front-page news. Winner may have also been distracted by the considerable excitement concerning the rush to California following the discovery of gold at Sutter's Mill.

In general, Winner's business must have been doing better. His

The Cholera Epidemic

According to the June 18, 1849, edition of the *Philadelphia Public Ledger*, the epidemic of Asiatic cholera started in New York, spread to many parts of the northeast, and began to infect Philadelphians in the beginning of that month. Winner's diaries accurately recount what must have been on the minds of many of his fellow residents. Fortunately, it would seem the Winner family was spared.

June 5, 1849
The Cholera is increasing in the city of New York, averaging 40 cases a day, people are getting frightened in this city as two cases of late have terminated in death. Such a cleaning of streets and cleaning of houses never was known before.

June 16, 1849
There is no popular excitement except the Cholera, people are mighty careful of their "alimentiary canal" refusing even the delicious strawberry, peas, and new potatoes.

June 22, 1849
Ten cases of cholera in the city, some people very much alarmed.

June 27, 1849
Twenty cases of cholera and several deaths.

June 28, 1849
40 cases, 10 deaths.

June 29, 1849
48 cases, 13 deaths.

June 30, 1849
48 cases, 18 deaths.

July 1, 1849
23 cases, 20 deaths.

July 5, 1849
The cases vary from 50 to 80, deaths from 20 to 30.

July 15, 1849
73 cases, 29 deaths.

The California Excitement

With the exception of the Civil War, arguably one of the most famous events of the nineteenth century was the "California excitement," better known today as the gold rush. Thousands of men, women and families traveled west in hopes of finding riches following the call of "Gold!" at Sutter's Mill.

While the rush itself began in 1849 (spawning the famous term the forty-niners, for those who went west), there was still a great deal of interest in what was happening in the untamed west in later years. The growth of new cities and the promise of untold riches would fill the dreams of many an eastern resident.

Winner noted the initial events with what was probably the same level of interest as many of his neighbors:

May 3, 1849
Went to the river with the Band [presumably the Philadelphia Brass Band] to play for the passengers departing to California, in the ship Susan Owens.

May 16, 1849
The California excitement is wearing away inasmuch [*sic*] all who intended to go seem to have gone.

While the initial excitement may have worn away, the impact on average Americans of this time was significant and even Winner was not immune to the lure of the West. It was still on Septimus' mind in 1857 as he grew increasingly frustrated in business and began to think of leaving Philadelphia.

December 18, 1857
Think of going to California, wouldn't hesitate for a moment if I had the means. I hate Philadelphia above all places.

December 22, 1857
Have more serious thoughts of leaving Philadelphia either for Wyoming or San Francisco and am satisfied that this city is not the spot for me. Everybody of my own level seems to look with contempt on my endeavors because I am gaining a little popularity outside this great mass of brick and mortar.

When the Winner family ultimately did leave, their travels took them less than 5 percent of the distance Septimus considered.

diaries indicate that he was playing for more and more events in the
city and his teaching roster was growing every month. In addition,
Septimus and Hannah, on March 26, 1849, moved to a new home and
business location at the corner of Seventh and Callowhill (this address
is often given as 257 Callowhill but is also cited as 267 Callowhill).
Winner was also able, on January 8, 1850, to buy a new violin from his
father.

If Septimus and Hannah were still concerned about their financial
condition in 1849, it is unlikely they would have made the decision to
have another child. To the contrary, their second child, Ella Guyer (initially named Helen) was born on March 26, 1850. On that day, Winner
wrote the following entry in his diary:

March 26, 1850
Quite an eventful day, another daughter born. Begin to feel
rather old. Hannah very well considering all, I really love her
though she may have faults. Emily felt lost all day, rather fret-
ful, tho cakes and candys [sic] cure all her troubles.

A third child, James Gibson, was born February 15, 1852. Winner's diaries on the topic of his newborn son are too humorous not to
include here:[55]

February 15, 1852
Had to rise early. Hannah had the "fidgets," had to dress
quick, had to run for the "family physician" and the nurse, had
to –to –to, never cared a "pig," not because it was a boy but
because there weren't two.

February 16, 1852
Felt fatherly when I knew it was a "jockey," bless his soul,
was happy all day somehow or other because it wasn't twins.
Hannah doing well – very well, has done extremely well for
one her size.

The name of Winner's first son is significant and deserves a brief
sidebar here. As most sons of the time would very likely have been
named for a family member, Winner persuaded Hannah to name their
first son in honor of his dear friend, James Gibson. Little is known
about Gibson but his friendship with Winner was significant. When he
died, three years earlier on August 13, 1849, Winner made the following diary entry:

August 16, 1849
Gave a few lessons and did some work. Ankle [previously
sprained] growing much better. Went to J. Gibson's funeral,

spent the afternoon and got home around 6 1/2 o'clock. Went to bed as soon as possible, tired and sad. I have not for a long while lost a friend that I prized so highly. I would have given much to see him once before he died, but something made us distant, for a year back, some misunderstanding, some mystery, that makes me sad. I never felt for any young man the same kind of regard that I felt for him, he was indeed the dearest companion of his sex, I feel that I can never forget him nor think of him without an earnest sigh, there is no one like him, no one that I can feel the same for, how I shall ever remember how I loved him. Alas, poor Jim.

For the next several years, Gibson's wife would be a frequent visitor in the Winner home.

Building a Business

As the 1850s began, Winner took specific steps to give himself every possible opportunity for success. His diary entries from the time indicate that Winner was in the process of his first serious expansion, from simply being a music teacher to selling sheet music and instruments at the Callowhill address.

November 17, 1849
Sold my Melodeon. Felt richer than ever, had $80 in my hands which were actually my own!! A lot of dirty hateful rotten banknotes. What a world! Expect to spend it mighty soon, however, plenty wanted "all around."

March 13, 1850
Since I sold my piano I have added much to my small stock, which increases slowly, but surely. I find Callowhill St. quite [*sic*] and I hope it may continue so, a respectable place for business.

March 15, 1850
Bought a lot of accordians [*sic*] and musical instruments generally . . .

It is also in 1850 that we have the first evidence that Winner had begun to arrange popular songs of the day for publication as sheet music. This represents a significant expansion of his musical activities at the time and leads the way for future events.

October 16, 1850
Received an edition of my first publication of music, *Village Polkas*.

Winner's diaries for 1851 and 1852 give mixed indications of the relative success of his new business activities. Some entries describe business as "dull" while others indicate that things had improved. One diary entry of 1852 indicates that he had, at some point, engaged his younger brother Joseph, who by now would have been fifteen, in the store:

June 10, 1852
A quiet day, made new arrangements with Joseph, concluded to take him back again in the store. Things going on much better than of late.

Whether Joseph's return to the store was the result of settling some form of family squabble or of improved business following hard times is unclear. It is clear, however, that by 1853, Winner was not only expanding his business more but also feeling quite positive about his future:

January 8, 1853
Was busy repairing all kinds of instruments and engraving *No. 7 of a Collection of Music for the Violin.* Began to do a very fair business and am in hopes of someday living without so much anxiety and exertion.

February 15, 1853
Feel myself "some" now as I get twenty dollars a quarter for teaching, hold my head rather higher and act more "dignified" of course.

February 16, 1853
Made arrangements with Charley Davis to have my *Winner Collection* sterotyped which I hope may prove to my advantage.

Beyond the *Village Polkas*, these were clearly not the first arrangements that Winner had published.[56] If his *No. 7* is to be taken at face value, then numbers one through six must have preceded it. Unfortunately, these publications are now lost although one might consider the notion that Winner published a *No. 7* to give the *impression* that earlier editions existed and give his new publication more credibility in the market place. While this may seem like a far-fetched thing to do to ensure sales in the marketplace, Winner's savvy as a businessman should not be underestimated. It is central to the man, and ultimately the woman, who would be one of Philadelphia's best-known composers during the nineteenth century.

Notes

1. Robert A. Gerson, *Music in Philadelphia* (Philadelphia: Theodore Presser, 1940), 23-24.
2. Charles Hamm, *Yesterdays: Popular Song in America* (New York: W.W. Norton, 1979), 2.
3. Gerson, *Music in Philadelphia*, 25.
4. None of the research sources used for this study cite a specific reason for the lifting of the ban. However, one might surmise that the continuing activity of American musicians was at least one factor. It is unlikely that the Continental Congress could maintain such a conservative, puritanical stance for very long.
5. Hamm, *Yesterdays*, 3-5. The term "pleasure gardens" refers to the outdoor garden areas frequented by London's elite starting in the seventeenth century. These musical performances featured popular airs of the day outside of an operatic or storytelling context. Not surprisingly, the first popular songs to emerge from these settings were rustic pastorals, designed to preserve the character of the overall experience. The tradition that started with the *Beggar's Opera* was taken up by such English composers as Thomas Arne (1710-1778), James Hook (1746-1820?), and Charles Didbin (1745-1814).
6. Hamm, *Yesterdays*, 26-27.
7. Gerson, *Music in Philadelphia*, 51. This magazine bears no relationship to the journal of the same title that Winner created and published in 1867.
8. Gerson, *Music in Philadelphia*, 52-54. Only two fragments from the opera survive: a rondo from the Overture and the song "Why, Huntress Why?"
9. Gerson, *Music in Philadelphia*, 53. The church, formerly at Pine between Third and Fourth Streets, no longer exists.
10. William White Bronson, *The Inscriptions in St. Peter's Churchyard, Philadelphia* (Camden, N.J.: Sinnickson Chew, 1879), 376.
11. Gerson, *Music in Philadelphia*, 73.
12. Sigmund Spaeth, *A History of Popular Music in America* (New York: Random House, 1948), 88-91.
13. The Virginia Minstrels consisted of Dan Emmett (fiddle), Billy Whitlock (banjo), Frank Brower (bones) and Dick Pelham (tambourine). First performing on February 6, 1843, at the Bowery Amphitheater in New York City, the structure of the show—songs, jokes, dances and instrumental numbers—set the pattern for all minstrel shows to come. The format, with the men on either end known as Mr. Bones and Mr. Tambo and one of the middlemen, Mr. Interlocutor, as the sad-faced burnt-cork foil and master of ceremonies, was a mainstay in American popular entertainment for years to come.
14. The majority of the information on the Musical Fund Society comes from Gerson, *Music in Philadelphia*, especially pages 54-66. The remainder comes from the document *Musical Fund Society of Philadelphia: A Brief History* (no credited author) published for internal research purposes by the Keffer Special Collections division of the University of Pennsylvania Libraries.
15. It should be noted that the various musical societies responsible for Philadelphia's cultural growth frequently performed what from a modern perspective would be called both classical and popular music. Little distinction was made between the two genres (unlike today) among the music-going public.

16.   Gerson, *Music in Philadelphia*, 64. Malibran was supposedly so delighted with the acoustics of the Musical Fund Hall that she improvised songs
while walking up and down the aisles of the theatre while her accompanist
from the Paris Conservatoire assisted at the piano.

17.   A very thorough description of the growth of the piano in American
musical culture can be found in two sources: Daniel Spillane, *The History of
the American Pianoforte* (New York: D. Spillane, 1890) and Arthur Loesser,
Men, Women and Pianos: A Social History (New York: Simon and Schuster,
1954).

18.   Gerson, *Music in Philadelphia*, 44. An Albrecht pianoforte dating
from 1789 was on display at the Pennsylvania Historical Society until at least
the 1930s. When this author visited the society in 2000 and 2001, the instrument was not in immediate evidence.

19.   Irwin Silber and Jerry Silverman, *Songs of the Civil War* (New York:
Dover, 1995), 1.

20.   Nicholas E. Tawa, *The Way to Tin Pan Alley: American Popular
Song, 1866-1910* (New York: Schirmer Books, 1990), 12.

21.   Charles Eugene Claghorn, *The Mocking Bird: The Life and Diary of
Its Author, Sep. Winner* (Philadelphia: Magee Press, 1937), 1-2. Much of the
information on Septimus' lineage was graciously provided in personal correspondence with Charles Eugene Claghorn, Septimus' great-grandson and
Melissa Claghorn, Claghorn's granddaughter.

22.   Some attempts to find information on Septimus the songwriter mistakenly list him as a comb-maker which, as we know, was the occupation of
Septimus, the uncle.

23.   Howard L. Myers, *The Music of Septimus Winner* (Master's thesis,
University of North Carolina at Chapel Hill, 1950), 8. When Myers wrote his
thesis on Winner, he was fortunate enough to be able to examine one of Joseph
Winner's violins as a result of contacts with Winner's descendants. He described it as "an example of good workmanship. It has the earmarks of a
'cheap' violin: the purfling is not made of separate strips of wood but is fixed
by grooves and varnish. The back is of two pieces, and the seam between these
is made too obvious by contrasting grain directions for the violin connoisseurs
ever to claim much beauty for it. . . It was probably good enough to satisfy the
demands of the amateur violinist of the nineteenth century."

24.   Winner's diaries are currently housed as part of the Septimus Winner
collection at the Historical Society of Pennsylvania.

25.   *The Drunkard* was a popular temperance play of the 1840s and 1850s
written by William Henry Smith (1806-1872). Despite Barnum's lifelong resi-
dency in New York and Fairfield County, Connecticut, Barnum's Museum
(formerly Peale's Museum) in Philadelphia had been purchased in either 1849
or 1850. Barnum ran the establishment for a little over a year. The museum
later burned to the ground.

26.   Claghorn, *The Mocking Bird*, 2. This story, representing only one in a
long series of family apocrypha, was passed down to Charles Eugene Claghorn
by his father, Winner's grandson.

27.   Claghorn, *The Mocking Bird*, 2.

28.   The North Liberties area was the district bordered by Vine and Sixth
Streets, Comden Creek and the Delaware River. Modern Philadelphians sometimes refer to the area as Old City.

29. Claghorn, *The Mocking Bird*, 3-4. These stories were passed down through the family.

30. Not only did Winner use his mother's name to create his most famous pseudonym but he would also pen many songs about the importance of mothers in the home. This is made even more significant given that there are no song lyrics about fathers.

31. Claghorn, *The Mocking Bird*, 3. This story was also recounted by family members. While Molidore Spiegel seems plausible as the name for a classmate of German descent, Theopholus Bopholus seems unlikely.

32. George Birdseye, "America's Song Composers, No. VI: Septimus Winner," *Potter's American Monthly* (June 1879): 433.

33. William C. Claghorn, foreword only to *Cogitations of a Crank at Three Score and Ten*, by Septimus Winner (Philadelphia: Drexel Biddle, 1903), 7. The identity of the author of the introduction is not included in the book itself. It was provided by Charles Eugene Claghorn, the author's grandson and Winner's great-grandson.

34. Claghorn, *The Mocking Bird*, 3.

35. The First Central High School of Philadelphia was located on Juniper Street below Market. The exact name of the school is a source of some confusion. Claghorn and Gerson call the school Philadelphia Central High School and the High School of Philadelphia alternately. According to Philadelphia records, however, First Central High School was the official name. Built in 1838, the school remained at its location for decades until being torn down and replaced by a Wannamaker's Department Store.

36. Robert A. Divine, et al., *America Past and Present, Vol. 2, From 1865* (New York: HarperCollins, 1995), 586.

37. This notebook is part of the Septimus Winner collection at the Historical Society of Pennsylvania in Philadelphia.

38. Birdseye, "America's Song Composers, No. VI: Septimus Winner," 433-434.

39. "Friends Pay Tribute to Septimus Winner," *The North American Philadelphia*, May 12, 1901.

40. Claghorn, Charles Eugene. *Whispering Hope: The Life of Composer Septimus Winner* (unpublished manuscript, 1977), 3.

41. Claghorn, *The Mocking Bird*, 4.

42. "Men and Things: Philadelphians Who Set the World Singing," *Evening Bulletin Philadelphia*, May 12, 1937.

43. This information comes from family records and was kindly provided by Melissa Claghorn. Hannah's brothers and sisters included Charles (1810-?), Rebaca (1813-?), Catharine (1819-?), Jacob (1821-1822, died in infancy), Benjamin (presumably "Benjamin Jr.," 1823-?), Caroline (1828-?), Sarah (1837-1838, died in infancy) and Emma (1840-1927).

44. The references to "Hattie" and "Laurie" are most likely to girlfriends. Gib, as he was known, married Florence E. Heiner in August, 1874.

45. Myers, *The Music of Septimus Winner*, 12. Myers interviewed Florence Claghorn, the composer's granddaughter, as part of his thesis research.

46. William Arms Fisher, *One Hundred Years of Music Publishing in the United States* (Boston: Oliver Ditson, 1933), 89.

47. Myers, *The Music of Septimus Winner*, 10.

48. Claghorn, *The Mocking Bird*, 4.

49. "A Chat with the Author of the 'Mocking Bird'," *The Philadelphia Press*, May 17 1901.

50. Jean Hournstra and Trudy Heath, *American Periodicals 1741-1900* (Ann Arbor, Mich.: University Microfilms, 1979), 95.

51. Myers, *The Music of Septimus Winner*, 14.

52. Winner's diaries for 1847 end on September 7. This last entry discusses having his daguerreotype taken. This is most likely the photograph on the cover of this volume. It is interesting to note that the entries around his wedding date are missing, having been removed either by Winner himself or by a family member wishing to protect his privacy. Winner also makes mention of another daguerreotype, taken January 16, 1850. It is possible that the picture on the cover dates from this time instead.

53. The reference here is to German composer Peter Joseph von Lindpainter (1791-1856).

54. Birdseye, "America's Song Composers, No. VI: Septimus Winner," 434.

55. Clearly there was some level of concern that this pregnancy would result in twins. Winner's diary entries indicate some level of relief but this is probably in a humorous vein, especially given his pride over having had a son.

56. Myers, *The Music of Septimus Winner*, 139. Myers has a citation for the 1851 original instrumental song, "Gentlemens' [*sic*] Bloomer Waltz." It seems unlikely that this is an original song as it would then represent Winner's first original composition—which we know to be incorrect. The Keffer Collection at the University of Pennsylvania currently owns a copy of another 1851 song, "Grafulla's Favorite Waltz," that was also an arrangement of a popular song.

Chapter Two (1853-1860)
Alice Hawthorne Emerges

Portrait of a Composer

In his own research on nineteenth-century composers, Nicholas Tawa extrapolates a composite of the typical songwriter, his origins and training:

> Popular song composers active in the last third of the nine-teenth century usually came from lower-middle-class families: they were children of shopkeepers, barbers, printers, farmers, artisans and the like. Usually no other family member had a strong inclination toward music making, nor was there evi-dence of musical talent in their ancestry. They did not nor-mally display prodigious musical gifts during childhood. Of none of them could one say "hats off, a genius!" For some, entry into a songwriter's life seemed accidental rather than deliberate. For a majority, the hunger to perform music and to create songs did not produce a desire to undergo extensive musical training. Their backgrounds and early attitudes did not predict what they would become.
>
> If we drew a composite picture of the typical songwriter, we might find that his parents were unsympathetic to a musical career and urged the child to take up a trade. What musical knowledge the songwriter had was self-taught . . . or picked up fortuitously . . . Because of [a] yearning to make music, the fledgling songwriter left home and accepted any available job as an entertainer, a job that often involved singing, and thus learned how to carry out their vocation and almost by happen-stance commenced songwriting. Quite a few songwriters then led disorderly personal lives, entered unstable marriages, sometimes drinking heavily, spending money freely when they

had it, and learning to go without when they didn't – not an unusual state of things. Impermanence accompanied them on the road, whether as salesmen (the employment of several fledgling songwriters) or as performers with a traveling entertainment troupe.[1]

From Winner's perspective, this description is only about one-quarter accurate. Winner came from a family with at least some musical background, and his brothers Joseph and C. Sivori followed him into the business. While Winner may not have been as prodigious as Mozart, he clearly had poetic abilities that manifested themselves by his late teens. He also must have had some early training on the violin.

Additionally, we have no evidence that Joseph and Mary Ann discouraged their son's intended profession. The fact that two other brothers also entered the musical profession may be indicative that they weren't strongly against it. The later distress that seems to have befallen many of the composers in Tawa's study seems to have eluded Winner. Where many appear to have led something of a vagabond, itinerant lifestyle, Winner, to the contrary, was the consistent family man. While he may have had a restless nature, as exhibited by his almost effortless changes in business addresses and partners, he stayed the course from a career perspective. His personal habits seem to stand in an almost diametric opposition to Tawa's portrait. Late in life, Winner was known to say that he kept "regular and strictly temperate habits" and that his only stimulant was "the cup that cheers but not inebriates"—tea.[2]

Conversely, a posthumous portrait of Winner written for the publication of his late poetry in *Cogitations of a Crank at Three Score and Ten* provides a very different picture than Tawa's:

> He would compose in solitude upon his violin, transpose to the piano, write the words of his song, and then taking up his engraving tools, work far into the night until the plates of his compositions were complete. The next day he would present to the public through his own store, his work of the previous night.[3]

Certainly this portrait is overly romanticized. The implication that Winner (or any other songwriter) was that prolific is almost certainly a fabrication. Beyond that, the portrait allows little time for the actual printing of the music not to mention the lithography for the covers.

While it is possible that Winner may have picked up at least some skills fortuitously, he also was smart enough to realize his own shortcomings in terms of musical knowledge. In the beginning of 1853, Winner began studies in the "art and science of music" with Leopold

Meignen, the conductor of the Musical Fund Society Orchestra at the time. Winner enjoyed these studies, as his diaries make clear:

February 3, 1853
Went to Meignen's in the afternoon to take a lesson and never enjoyed myself better. It is the most amusing and interesting study on earth.

Winner's notebooks indicate that his first lesson with Meignen occurred on January 6, 1853. Winner's notebooks from these lessons consist of what from a contemporary perspective would appear to be a college level first-year harmony course. Subjects include triads and seventh chords, voice leading, nonharmonic tones, chromatic chords and modulation (a technique Winner would rarely use). Winner's notebooks indicate that these lessons continued until May 4, 1853, although few further diary entries exist on the subject.

Winner had already written a few songs and had completed some arrangements by this time. But it wasn't until after his studies with Meignen that these songs would reach.

Leopold Meignen (1793-1873)

Called Philadelphia's "most influential teacher [of the] early nineteenth century,"[4] Leopold Meignen was a mainstay in Philadelphia musical circles during his lifetime.[5] In additional to Winner, his students included Philadelphia composers Michael Hurley Cross, William Henry Fry and Charles H. Jarvis. A graduate of the Paris Conservatory and reputedly a bandmaster in Napoleon's army, he conducted the Musical Fund Society Orchestra from 1846 to 1857, where he led Beethoven's symphonies as well as the overtures to Weber's *Oberon* and Mendelssohn's *Midsummer Night's Dream*. In addition, he also served as conductor for both the Handel and Haydn Societies during the 1850s.

Born and raised in Paris, Meignen had a reputation for a "profound musical knowledge" and his European training clearly influenced his students. A composer of a variety of music, his most notable works include the *Grand Military Symphony* (premiered by the Musical Fund Society Orchestra in 1845) and an oratorio, *The Deluge*. Meignen was also a partner in one of antebellum Philadelphia's more successful publishing concerns, the Fiot-Meignen Company (with Augustus Fiot). When it was dissolved in 1839, Meignen continued to publish music under his own name until 1859. His one collaboration with Winner was an arrangement of Hawthorne's "Chimes of the Monastery" (1854).

Stephen Collins Foster (1826-1864)[6]

Born July 4, 1826, Stephen Collins Foster was raised in Lawrence-ville, Pennsylvania, just outside Pittsburgh. Foster was arguably the greatest songwriter of his time. He penned more than two hundred songs that are now considered American folk songs including "Oh! Susannah," "Jeannie with the Light Brown Hair," "Old Folks at Home" (known by the lyrics "Way down upon the Swanee River"), "Camp-town Races," "My Old Kentucky Home" and "Beautiful Dreamer".

Tawa's description at the beginning of this chapter resonates strongly with Foster's life. Although he grew up in a moderately afflu-ent middle-class family, Foster's parents had no inherent musical abili-ties. In fact, they were frequently surprised by Stephen's abilities as a child. It is said that he could pick out melodies on the flageolet or guitar at an early age. As a young man, Foster began to write songs but, as his family wished that he learn a trade, he worked as a bookkeeper in the Cincinnati offices of his brother, Dunning. There, he began a relation-ship with the publisher W.C. Peters who would publish the majority of his works throughout his lifetime.

Wishing to distance himself from the "Ethiopian ballads" that, although popular, were dismissed in serious musical circles, Foster often sold the rights to his works and collected few royalties. In one notable instance, Foster agreed to be paid $15 for the composition of "Old Folks at Home." E.P. Christy, of the Christy Minstrels, paid Fos-ter and was credited as composer on most publications. Foster received no royalties for the song until years later when he reclaimed the rights.

As a result of selling his songs, a certain amount of carelessness with his money and frequent creative slumps, Foster often lived on the brink of poverty. Foster was regularly asking for (and receiving) ad-vances on future works. He began to drink, most notably during slumps, and lost touch with his family. It is said he could not even af-ford music paper and sketched songs on the brown paper bags used to conceal alcoholic beverages in public.

In January of 1864, Foster was staying at the American Hotel in the Bowery area of New York City. According to Spaeth, Foster was severely ill with influenza (and not drunk) when he fainted and fell across a sink in his room. The sink broke and slit Foster's throat. His friend and collaborator, George Cooper, found the composer naked and bleeding some time later. Miraculously alive, he was taken to the char-ity ward at Bellevue Hospital where he died two days later. His wallet contained exactly thirty-eight cents and a slip of paper bearing the in-scription "dear friends and gentle hearts."

The Birth of Alice Hawthorne

With the publication of Winner's first original songs, we witness the birth of Alice Hawthorne. The use of this pseudonym would continue for over thirty years and would ultimately come to define a genre of nineteenth-century music, the Hawthorne ballads. The first publication would also launch a career that would ultimately eclipse Winner's own successes as a composer and pedagogue. At the time, Winner could never have predicted his own reactions to that success.

From 1853 to 1860, virtually every original song Winner penned appeared under the Hawthorne name, whereas arrangements and original instrumental works were published under Winner's own name. Why would he choose to use pseudonyms at all and perhaps more significantly, why would he, at least initially, make the decision to publish under a woman's name?

The use of pseudonyms in the nineteenth century was not only frequent among artists and writers, it was almost de rigueur. Victorian sensibilities demanded a sense of modesty in which artistic achievement of too high an order (as opposed to amateur ability) was concealed so as to maintain the "humility" of the creator. Well known examples from the nineteenth century abound: Artemus Ward (Charles F. Browne), Mark Twain (Samuel Clemens), Josh Billings (Henry W. Shaw), Mr. Dooley (Finley P. Dunne) and many others.

With that in mind, it is conceivable that Winner had something of a pecking order in mind with regards to the types of pieces he was writing and, therefore, the name under which we would publish it. Arrangements of others' work would not constitute an overt demonstration of creative prowess and could, therefore, be published under his own name. Likewise, instrumental works such as his numerous quicksteps, schottisches and marches might also have appeared less demonstrative, especially as these works may have been based on original tunes by other composers. Original songs, however, would have been more of a direct creative statement, thereby requiring the disguise or, better put, the façade of a pseudonym.

However, Winner also would have had a much more important reason for choosing to publish under pseudonyms. As the proprietor of an increasingly successful music store, Winner may not have wanted to be put in the position of pushing his own original works on his customers. An arrangement or instrumental work might have been more acceptable to plug to his customers, but judgment of an original work may have been more than Winner's ego was capable of managing, especially at the outset of this part of his career.

Beyond that, Winner may have genuinely hoped for honest feedback especially as he embarked on composing original songs. By using a pseudonym, he would be able to solicit such feedback without concern that others might be trying to spare his feelings or without having to suffer the brutality of direct criticism. Certainly this rationale seems plausible enough to suggest that Winner was motivated not to publish original material under his own name.

This rationale is at least partially confirmed by Birdseye in his portrait of the composer from 1879:

> This [the song "How Sweet Are the Roses"] was published under the name of "Alice Hawthorne," adopted from his mother's maiden name, and it must be admitted, a very pretty one. Most of his songs that came after it bear the same name upon the title page, as it seemed to him that it would be scarcely consistent with modesty for him to recommend and "push" songs from his own counters with his name upon them. Besides, in this manner he was enabled to test his capabilities as a composer, and his powers of pleasing the public, without in any way compromising himself. If he failed, it was merely left for him to be silent. But he did not fail.[7]

Having determined some plausible reasons to use a pseudonym in general, we are led to the far more interesting question of why Winner would choose a woman's name for the publication of his original songs and specifically the sentimental ballads. The origin of the name itself comes from Winner's mother, Mary Ann Hawthorne, although the origin behind Winner's use of the Christian name Alice remains unclear. Family records and Winner's own diaries make no mention of any woman named Alice. As a result, the source of Winner's choice will almost certainly remain a mystery. Given his family history, it's not surprising that Winner chose to honor his mother. It is also very likely that Winner made a practical business decision, capitalizing on the Hawthorne name so potential customers might make a connection to the famous author.

Family records cite only that Mary Ann, Septimus' mother, was a "distant relative." While the exact genealogy is unknown, we do know that there was no contact between Alice's namesake and the famous author. Interestingly enough, if Winner had known Nathaniel Hawthorne in any way, he might have opted against naming his creation after him. Despite some support for women authors in his circle and the fact that he praised his wife's writing as some of "the most perfect pictures that ever were put on paper," Nathaniel Hawthorne expressly forbade his wife from publishing her own works.[8]

In choosing the name Alice Hawthorne, Winner may have genuinely wanted to acknowledge his mother, especially given their strong emotional connection. At the same time, however, what we know about Winner the businessman, even a moderately nascent one, leads to some other possible theories behind his decision.

The Rise of the Lady Amateur

The evolution of women's roles in music begins with what Tick calls the lady amateur of the late eighteenth and early nineteenth centuries. Socially desirable and accepted, the lady amateur was judged based on her "accomplishments"—i.e., demonstrating skills in those nonacademic subjects that were part of a young woman's upbringing.[9] Tick thereby equates musical accomplishments for women and the romanticized nineteenth-century notion of femininity.

Prior to 1830, the Victorian image of the musical lady amateur was firmly held throughout America. As Tick notes, it is not until the 1840s that women composers actively published under their own names—in limited circles—and were acknowledged by their contemporaries.[10] Since the goal of middle- and upper-class women in American society was to have accomplishments that would attract a potential husband—accomplishments that included dance, embroidery and painting—music was "seen as the medium in which the role of a lady could be acted out."[11] Professional accomplishments, or anything beyond amateur status, were strongly frowned upon from a societal standpoint. "Correct" women of the time were seen as performing in amateur or domestic circles, with limited training, usually singing or performing on a "feminine" or domestic instrument such as piano or harp—everything her male counterpart would not be, e.g., professional, well-trained, performing on "male" instruments such as the banjo or guitar.

From 1830 to 1870, an evolution occurred in the relationship between women and music in America. Tick defines this evolution as the "replacement of the ideal lady with that of the true woman."[12] Accomplishment for female musicians shifted from an upper-class social milieu to a middle-class home environment. The emphasis of musical training was more on domesticity versus elegance in a social context. Despite this change, many of society's positions on music and women remained the same, especially with regards to professional accomplishments. However, the increasing presence of professional women in the periodicals and literature of the time, according to Tick, supports the notion that women were increasingly moving out of the domestic musical sphere and into the professional one.[13]

Having already been in business as a private teacher for six years and as a shop owner for at least three, Winner would have clearly recognized that his primary customers were women and that they were responsible for music-making in the home. It is also possible that, as a result, Winner concluded that an "amateur" woman composer writing for amateurs might be highly appealing to the customers in his own store and, therefore, to customers at large.

Winner was almost certainly influenced by the fact that the precedent for women publishing music (albeit largely under pseudonyms) had already been established. At minimum, the increasing presence of women's magazines, many of which featured poetry and songs by amateurs, might have confirmed the notion of publishing under a woman's name with Winner.

What is almost certain, though, is that the decision to publish under the Hawthorne pseudonym was originally a short-term measure. It is tempting to speculate on what happened next given the success of the first original songs and the subsequent christening of the Hawthorne ballads genre. One might conclude Winner was trapped into continuing to use the name in order to ensure ongoing sales and income. Equally likely though is that Winner knew a good thing when he saw it and, at least at first, continued to use the Hawthorne moniker to guarantee a successful future.

As something of a sidebar, it should be noted that Winner was not the only male composer who adopted female pseudonyms—especially in the context of the women's magazines. The use of pseudonyms (male, female or anonymous) was not a means to avoid discrimination. Instead, it was a way to deter accusations that an individual was seeking fame or personal glory. Tick[14] cites at least three examples of men using women's pseudonyms in the nineteenth century including Benjamin Carr, discussed in Chapter One, who published the popular song "The Little Sailor Boy" under the frequently used pseudonym A Lady. The motivation behind this ascription is unclear. It may have been because the text was written by a woman, Susanna Rowson, or it may have reflected the growing acceptance of female composers beginning to publish their music, even if under a pseudonym.

Another example concerns the publication of "My Hopes Have Departed Forever" (1851) also under the pseudonym A Lady. Royalties for the song were paid to none other than Stephen Foster, the song's composer. Tick notes that the tune was not original but had been borrowed from "The Valley Lay Smiling Before Me," originally published as part of *Moore's Irish Melodies*. Tick theorizes that Foster adopted the pseudonym for the publication of an arrangement rather than publish under his own name and give the impression that it was an original composition. She also theorizes that Foster felt that a female pseudonym might have been more appropriate given the nature of the text.

Closer to home, Winner's own brother, Joseph Eastburn Winner, allowed an 1869 pirated edition of his best known song "Little Brown Jug" to be published under the pseudonym Betta. From the date of this publication, we know that this occurred after Joseph had seen the spectacular success of his brother's publications as Alice Hawthorne. Despite these other examples of men publishing under a female pseu-

donym, Winner remains the only composer who published under what
we might call a "full" pseudonym, i.e., Christian name and surname.

Whatever the rationale, the first Hawthorne ballad would set a series of events in motion—events over which Septimus would have little
control and that would shape his entire professional life.

The First Publications

As Winner's career begins to take shape, it becomes increasingly clear
that, even at this early stage, Winner understood several important factors that would define his place in the American musical sphere. As an
astute and sensitive observer of his world, Winner could not help but
notice that American society was changing, and changing rapidly. As
part of the growing merchant class himself, he could see how this new
middle class was changing the social and cultural landscape of his native Philadelphia.

As a musician, he was clearly aware of developments in American
popular song. The impact of works by such composers as Stephen
Foster was shaping a new American cultural landscape. Given that
Winner sold sheet music in his stores as well as the fact that he performed with so many local orchestras and bands, Septimus must have
been not only cognizant of but also absorbing the new style of American popular song that was taking shape as early as the 1840s.

As a shop owner, Winner must have seen the changing role of
women in antebellum America. Given the growth of the middle class,
he must have increasingly seen the role of women in creating what
many writers on American popular culture have called the domestic
sphere. Women, increasingly relieved from the burden of work, were
able to focus exclusively on the family and the raising of children.
Where young girls were concerned (and to some extent young boys),
musical ability became increasingly important. This knowledge must
have influenced his decisions as a composer and arranger, both in terms
of the texts he wrote and the relative difficulty of his music.

As a teacher, Winner would have recognized that there was an
opportunity to capitalize on the public's growing desire for musical
education. It is not beyond the realm of possibility that his own customers would have asked him for teaching materials that could be used
in the home on an amateur level (as opposed to undertaking the more
serious endeavor of private study).

Lastly, as a fledgling composer and arranger, Winner would have
had each of these factors prominent in his mind as he set out to establish himself. Given this knowledge, Winner clearly capitalized on the
opportunities that presented themselves to him—opportunities that did
not make themselves as apparent to his contemporaries.

Probably the most significant realization Winner had concerned the
increasing importance of musical ability as an indication of status in

American society. It would be this realization that would strongly influence his output as a composer, author and pedagogue, arguably for
the rest of his life.

Winner's diaries around the time of his first original publications
are sporadic at best, featuring entries early in the year and a scant few
late in the year. It was during this hiatus from his diaries that Winner
must have entered into his first partnership and published the first of
the original songs. The earliest extant publications, all arrangements,
were published under the name S. Winner at the Callowhill address.[15]
But by the end of 1853, Winner's new business was fully operational,
spurred either by his own initial successes or by the need to gain additional capital to support his fledgling endeavors.

Very little is known about William H. Shuster, Septimus' first
publishing partner. Philadelphia business records provide little information on what Shuster may have done prior to his partnership with
Winner or after. He clearly had some musical aspirations, as one published instrumental, "Kane's Funeral March," is ascribed to him (it was
originally published under the pseudonym Elisha Kent). However,
these aspirations must have been even more short-lived than their partnership. Lasting until early 1856 (with the publication of "Listen to the
Mocking Bird"), the partnership appears to have ended amicably, as the
men stayed friends for several years.

Winner's diary entries indicate his excitement about the possibilities as well as his faith in their partnership:

> *December 1, 1853*
> Feel as if I really would get along somewhat better now since
> we have opened the new store, business is quite promising,
> and I have every confidence in Shuster and hope I may always
> feel that same reliance as I now enjoy.

> *December 2, 1853*
> "My Cottage Home" sells rapidly, which I am proud of be-
> cause it is such gratification to Shuster, business was very
> good all day. Sold another piano and melodeon[16] making two
> pianos this week.

> *December 5, 1853*
> Was busy all day engraving "How Sweet Are the Roses."

It is clear that the partnership with William Shuster held promise
and was exactly what Winner needed at this point in time. These diary
entries also represent the first mention of Winner's original songs.
Published by Winner & Shuster and under the Hawthorne name, "My
Cottage Home" and "How Sweet Are the Roses?" represent Winner's
first foray into original songs. While it is likely that Winner began to

compose as early as 1850, it is notable that he waited until after his studies with Leopold Meignen before publishing any original works.

Winner sold these first original songs both in his own store and through other Philadelphia music dealers. It is also possible that he had some distribution beyond his native city. Either way, the songs became popular enough, in Winner's estimation, to continue down this nascent path.

For his next effort, Winner returned to familiar stomping ground and wrote the highly sentimental Hawthorne ballad "What is Home without a Mother?" (which he dedicated to Shuster's daughter Ann Eliza). Birdseye wrote that this one piece established Winner as "the *father* of all Mother-songs" (emphasis his).[17] The story of how this song came to be is recounted by Claghorn and was verified by Winner's surviving grandchildren.[18]

> It appears that there was a woman living near Winner who took her baby out on her back porch each evening to hear the song of a bird which they had caged there. Two or three years later as Mr. Winner was passing by he noticed the child standing there all alone, and he asked her what she was doing. She replied that she was waiting for her mother to come home to hear the "birdie" sing. As it happened, the little child's mother had died the week before. Mr. Winner was deeply moved by the incident and he took the child to his residence where he entertained her with some music until a servant called for the little girl to take her home. That evening, Septimus wrote his piece *What is Home without a Mother?*

If this story is true, it is one that very well might inspire a composer in the way it inspired Winner. However, one might also view it as exactly the kind of story Winner would have told later in life to bolster the song's popularity. While it might be cynical to take such a view, Winner lived during the time of the greatest showman to ever walk the earth, P.T. Barnum. Is it possible that Winner was as great a showman as the mastermind who coined the phrase "there's a sucker born every minute?"

"What is Home without a Mother?" handed Winner his first significant hit as a songwriter. It was performed and popularized throughout the northeast and very likely spread to other parts of the country as well. Spawning the Hawthorne ballads genre, the song was unquestionably a resounding success. Hamm provides one important reason why:

> Its success may be measured in part by the flood of imitations, parodies and "answers": "What is Home Without a Baby" (Gilmore), "What is Home Without a Brother" (Haynes), " . . .

Without a Father" (Rees), " . . . a Husband" (H.C.P.), " . . . a Sister" (Haynes again), " . . . a Wife" (Fiske), and " . . . Without the Children" (Keller) were only some of them.[19]

From the perspective of Hawthorne's career, probably the most significant publication was the ballad "Our Good Old Friends" (1855) which, for the first time, featured the image of Alice Hawthorne shown on page 122 and signed in Winner's unmistakable hand. With at least ten Hawthorne Ballads issued by the time of "Our Good Old Friends," Winner clearly intended to capitalize even further on the Hawthorne name by creating an image of the composer as a romantic woman, perhaps even a chaste one.

The image (shown both on the cover and in the photospread) is striking, not just because it bears such a strong likeness to Winner in his youth, but also because of the choices involved in "presenting" Hawthorne to the musical public. Her skin is clear and pure, her hair conservative yet stylish. Her dress, while also stylish, isn't revealing in any way and tapers to the waist; she is a woman who cares for herself well. While we cannot see her hands or ears, the absence of jewelry is noticeable, as if to say that Alice Hawthorne is a conservative middle-class woman, maybe even a mother, and certainly never "flashy." Because professional women musicians were often frowned upon by the musical public (frequently they were thought of as being "loose"), it must have been important to Winner to present her as being a "gifted amateur." What is also striking is that Winner chose not to use his by now regular lithographer, George Swain, to create this cover. Instead, he chose to hire the firm of Sarony and Company in New York.[20]

It is interesting to speculate on this decision. Did Winner wish to conceal his double identity as Hawthorne? Every indication is that he did for it is rarely mentioned in his diaries. If he did wish to conceal it, from whom would he need to do this? Certainly the lithographer George Swain (for reasons that seem minor at best) but perhaps also from his business partner William Shuster. It seems implausible that Shuster would not have known that Winner and Hawthorne were one and the same, but at the same time it may explain why Winner's partnerships were always so short-lived, e.g., if someone got too close to the truth, Winner would move on. Certainly Winner wished to conceal Hawthorne's true identity from his customers and the music-buying public at large, but it would seem that engaging a New York firm to create this image would be exceeding the boundaries of what was necessary unless he wished to conceal his dual identity from Shuster as well. With no evidence to the contrary, one might even speculate that Winner told Shuster that Hawthorne lived in New York and, therefore, that the image could only be produced there.

A Matter of Influence

Musically, the early songs are strikingly similar (as they are to many other songs of the day). As products designed for an amateur audience, they had many musical qualities in common:[21]

Sound. Piano and vocal instrumentation featuring a solo voice for the verses and four-part refrains to accommodate group performance. Strophic songs feature solo voice only. Rarely did these songs feature any extremes either of range, dynamics or contrapuntal techniques. Their overall effect was one designed to be pleasing and harmonious.

Harmony. Almost always diatonic (within a given key) with emphasis on the key's primary chords (referring to the tonic, subdominant and dominant triads). In addition, major keys that are, theoretically, easier to play (i.e., no more than two sharps or flats) are much more prominent. Dissonance and chromaticism is used for special effect only (as compared to Winner's European contemporaries Mendelssohn, Schubert or Schumann). Modulation is extremely rare.

Melody. Diatonic, often pentatonic, highly predictable melodies were the norm. Nonharmonic tones and chromaticism were featured rarely and reserved for special effect. Ornamental devices (e.g., trills) were infrequent and melismatic settings (e.g., more than one pitch per syllable of text) uncommon. These melodies were often accompanied by steady, predictable piano textures (Alberti figures, "oom-pah-pah" textures, broken chords or arpeggios).

Rhythm. Steady, simple duple or quadruple meters (e.g., 2/4 or 4/4) were most common. Triple meter exists in the earlier works but becomes much more popular in the 1870s as waltzes gain increasing popularity in the United States (according to Hamm, Winner was among the first to recognize this trend). Compound meters (e.g., 6/8, 12/8) were rare. Syncopation is rare in sentimental ballads and was more often reserved for "Ethiopian" style songs.

Form. A four- or eight-bar piano introduction (i.e., prelude) is almost always present. Its purpose was to establish the primary melody of the song. Verse and chorus structures are most common, with four-part choruses a regular presence (an outgrowth of the singing families that were so popular at the time and to accommodate group singing in parlor settings). Strophic structures (i.e., several verses set to the same or similar music) are also common. Regular phrasing is a prominent feature in both verses and chorus, most often in four bar units. Text that is sufficient for at least three verses. Postludes or closing sections that reiterate the primary melodic material are common.

"My Cottage Home" (Example 2.1) is a song very typical of this model, conforming in many ways to other popular songs of the day. In quadruple time, the "easy" key of D major, a vocal range of an octave and a strophic structure, the only anomaly is the harshness of the G# in the melody against the G-natural in the harmony. One might best view this anomaly as rising from inexperience; Winner was very likely still developing a stronger sense of harmony to accompany such melodic chromaticism. All in all, however, the character and simplicity of the song strongly indicates that Winner was already catering to the type of clientele who shopped in his store.

Example 2.1

Surprisingly, or perhaps not surprisingly, "What Is Home without a Mother?" (Example 2.2) is also in D Major, in quadruple time, and features a limited vocal range suitable for amateurs. It would seem that Winner considered these to be the three ingredients for successful performance in the home. Where this song differs from its predecessors is in the rhythmic complexity of the melodic line as well as the expressive notations indicated by the several fermatae in the score. At the same time, Winner's harmonic naiveté is still in evidence as he clashes the same G# in the melody against the G-natural in the harmony.

Example 2.2

"How Sweet Are the Roses?" (Example 2.3) follows a similar pattern to "My Cottage Home." Also strophic and in D major, but in waltz time, the range of a ninth would again have been completely suitable for performance in the home. In the case of both songs, the piano accompaniment is designed for amateur performance.

Example 2.3

There is virtually no syncopation and the range required for a pianist consists of no more than an octave at any given point, thereby
falling easily within the span of even a small hand. As with its prede-
cessor the song is in strophic form featuring rhythmically similar verses
set to the same music. The song is harmonically simple, limited almost
completely to the primary chords of the key (D major and A major).

Why were these musical elements so similar? Where songs of this type, i.e., sentimental ballads, are concerned, it was unquestionably the impact of three critical influences that shaped America's music for decades to come. The first, as described earlier, was the nationwide popularity of the songs of Stephen Foster. The remaining two are discussed in the sidebars that follow.

Moore's Irish Melodies

In 1808, the American musical public witnessed the publication of one of the most important influences on nineteenth-century American music. The multivolume *Irish Melodies* arranged and fitted with new texts by Thomas Moore (1779-1852), having already had a powerful impact in Great Britain, was published in its entirety in Philadelphia (1815) and had subsequent printings in New York, Salem (Mass.), Boston, Hartford (Conn.), Columbus (Ohio) and Exeter (N.H.).

According to Hamm, one reason for the phenomenal success of the *Irish Melodies* was that Moore succeeded where many of his American and English predecessors failed.[22] He was able to touch upon a mood of nostalgia that was typified by the themes of childhood, lost home and friends that were highly popular among post-Revolutionary War Americans. At a time when Americans were struggling to create a political, social and economic infrastructure upon which they could build a new country, it is not surprising that the "simplicity" represented by the *Irish Melodies* would endure for more than half a century.[23]

The Irish, known throughout Europe as balladeers and with a rich store of songs, had already influenced American song as early as the 1780s. With such Moore-enhanced songs as "The Last Rose of Summer" (tune: "The Groves of Blarney"), "The Harp That Once Through Tara's Halls" (tune: "Gramachree") and "The Minstrel Boy" (tune: "The Moreen"), the *Irish Melodies*, according to Hamm, "share the distinction with Stephen Foster of being the most popular, most widely sung, best loved and most durable songs in the English language of the entire nineteenth century."[24]

While the musical style would influence countless songs throughout the nineteenth century, the popularity of the texts was just as influential. Sentimental and nostalgic texts would be a feature of the most prominent American songs through the turn of the century. Many of those songs featured Irish themes such as "Sweet Rosie O'Grady," "Down Went McGinty," "My Wild Irish Rose" and "I'll Take You Home Again Kathleen." The enduring popularity of the *Irish Melodies* and their descendants was no doubt a factor in the later popularity of such performers as Harrigan and Hart and George M. Cohan.

The Hutchinson Family[25]

At virtually the same time that minstrel groups swept to popularity in the United States, there was something of a backlash against the ribald and occasionally off-color humor that characterized these shows. Singing families (or groups posing as families) were formed not only for entertainment purposes but also to address the sociopolitical issues facing America in the 1840s and 1850s. Nowhere was this merging more complete than with the Hutchinson Family, also called the Tribe of Jesse.

The early Hutchinsons had come to America in the 1630s, settling first in Salem, Massachusetts. Later generations then moved to Milford, New Hampshire in 1799. Elisha and his fifteen-year-old bride, Mary Leavitt, had sixteen children—thirteen survived to adulthood. Almost all the children were involved with the group at one point or another.

Inspired by the early success of the Rainer Family in 1839, John Hutchinson (the oldest child) trained his brothers to perform in a similar way. The program consisted of solo songs, ensembles and instrumental works but it was the close vocal harmonies that were most popular with audiences and from the beginning.

The most enduring line-up of the family was Asa (child number fourteen), Judson (number eleven and an exceptional violinist), John (number thirteen and the composer of many of their songs as well as their manager), and Abby (the youngest, who first performed with the group before she was a teenager).

Perhaps the best-known Hutchinson song was "The Old Granite State" which introduced each member of the family in turn. Gerson credits Jesse (number nine) with the composition although John initially copyrighted the work. Their 1843 concert tour of every major East Coast city was a spectacular success and established them as one of the most popular singing families in the country. Beyond their musical success, however, the Hutchinsons were best known for the variety of causes they supported, often following conferences and meetings to perform in support of them.

The first of their causes was temperance. After some of the brothers experienced trouble with the bottle and inspired by some of their contemporaries, they each took a temperance pledge and incorporated temperance songs into their repertoire—the most famous of which was "King Alcohol." (Given that, it's not surprising that Septimus would have gone to see them.) Later in their careers, they would also take up the growing cause of women's suffrage, traveling as early as 1851 to a women's rights convention in Akron, Ohio, to lend their support.

(Continued on next page)

The Hutchinson Family—Continued

Probably their most important cause was the abolition of slavery. In their early years, they performed at the opening and closing of every meeting of the Boston Anti-Slavery Society. While the family felt strongly about the growing abolitionist movement, they were also smart enough to exclude some of the more inflammatory materials they wrote for their paying audiences. One song, "Get off the Track" (an adaptation of "Old Dan Tucker"), was so inflammatory that no publisher would initially issue it. A later concert at Musical Fund Hall was canceled because the owners refused to admit "persons of color," in stark contrast to the Hutchinson beliefs. In an introduction to "Get off the Track", they wrote "words composed and adapted to a slave melody, advocating the emancipation of the slaves and illustrating the onward progress of the anti-slavery cause in the United States."[26] By 1846, the *Philadelphia Courier* had had enough of the Hutchinsons' politics, writing: "It is really time that someone should tell these people in a spirit of friendly candor, that they are not apostles and martyrs, entrusted with a mission to reform the world but only a company of common song-singers."[27]

The Hutchinsons however were undaunted. A poster advertising one of their concerts made their sentiments clear: "Many new songs . . . such as awaken the deepest emotions of the heart, OPPOSITION TO SLAVERY and OPPRESSION, and a desire to elevate WOMAN TO HER EQUAL RIGHTS . . . Women half-price because her wages are but half the price paid men . . . Fugitive slaves not only free, but every one who will prove himself such, shall be presented with a DOLLAR AND A QUARTER" (emphasis theirs).

By the early 1860s, each member of the family had a family of his or her own and the original group split into splinter groups, some of whom recruited other members of the family, while others recruited outside musicians. Despite some continued successes (they campaigned vigorously for Lincoln in 1860), the real heyday of the family (1841-1849) was over. While they continued to campaign vigorously for the issues that mattered to them, they were turned away from performing for Union troops in support of the war because their abolitionist stance was considered too radical. Brigadier General Franklin is reported to have said that their performance would "demoralize the army." The matter ultimately went all the way to McClellan (who silenced them) and then to Lincoln for a final decision (he allowed them to perform).

Hamm's summary of their influence is appropriate here: "It may well be that the Hutchinsons altered the course of American history,

(Continued on next page)

The Hutchinson Family—Continued

that their music hastened the confrontations and conflicts that led in-
exorably to the Civil War, that their songs fanned passions and created
the sense of togetherness and resolve necessary to convert ideas and
ideals into action, that their singing of John Brown's Body converted
more people to the antislavery cause than all the speeches and sermons
of the time. There is no mistaking their sincerity, their deep and genu-
ine concern for human misery . . . and there is no mistaking the fact that
they made a deliberate choice, at a critical point in their career, to state
their political and social views in public concerts, whatever the damage
to their professional career."[28]

From a lyrical perspective, several authors provide insight into the
general character of poetry and song texts written by women in this
period as the social conventions of Victorian America dictated restric-
tions on content. The primary characteristics of most nineteenth-
century songs, as defined by Tick, Hamm and others, include limitations on what were considered suitable emotions or affections, including love, piety and friendship. Frequently, these emotions were expanded through melancholic devices.[29] Many of these songs feature a
first-person point of view suggesting that the emotions stemmed from
the author's own feelings and, therefore, by extension from the singer.

Many of these works feature a language of sorrow that, according
to Hamm, typified the sentiments of the time. As the United States approached, lived through and experienced the aftermath of the Civil
War, this type of language may be have held an unusual resonance for
war-weary Americans.[30] In addition, it most likely fostered a fondness
for nostalgia that would become prevalent in poetry of the day. Hamm
notes that most Americans in the first part of the nineteenth century
were immigrants. While this would have been a bond to begin with,
their common experiences in the New World would create a sense of
nostalgia for home that brought these new Americans together. Songs
avoided such topics as "political scandals, emotional adjustments of
widowed women, orphaned children, crippled ex-soldiers, the plight of
freedmen in the South," etc., resulting in what Hamm calls a thirst for
escapism on the part of the American musical public.[31]

From a gender perspective, many of the lyrics expressed a point of
view that steered away from the male adoring an idealized female (as in
Foster's "Jeannie with the Light Brown Hair"). Rather, they moved
toward a more "female" point of view either in relation to men or, more
significantly, to other women. The celebration of friendship between
two women was a common theme, as are personal tributes or shared
mourning or loss in this context.[32] This would have been cou-

pled with a lack of idealized men as opposed to the reverse that was so often true in works by male lyricists.[33]

Lastly, many of the lyrics of these sentimental ballads were shaped by an attitude best described by Henry Tuckerman, a nineteenth-century critic, who described female poetry by saying that "men *do not* expect extensive knowledge and active logical powers from a female poet. They *do* expect to feel the influence and power of affections" (emphasis mine).[34]

Even in his early works, several themes emerge that strongly characterize Winner's original lyrics. These themes include:

Nature. Clearly an influence of his boyhood in the Wyoming Valley, many of Winner's songs focus on the joys and wonders of nature. Flowers, fields, insects, animals—all are featured prominently in many of his songs (just as they were featured in the children's books). These aspects of nature were often used as a metaphor for life and death.

Home. As has been discussed, the common experience of nostalgia for home bonded new Americans together.[35] A great many of Winner's songs revolve around the comforts and shelter of home. Beyond that, the horrors of war would almost certainly have influenced popular sentiment.

Parents and specifically mothers. Mothers and their importance in the home are a prominent feature of Winner's lyrics. Much of this would not only have stemmed from Winner's own attachment to his mother but also from the growing importance of women in the domestic sphere of the nineteenth century. It was key to creating the mystique around motherhood that persisted well into the twentieth century. Winner's reluctance to write any lyrics praising the father and his place in the family are, as discussed earlier, understandable given his upbringing. In fact, not one of Winner's songs extols the virtues of fathers (in comparison to the songs of his brother, Joseph Eastburn Winner, which occasionally do praise fathers and their importance).

Nostalgia. This theme has been cited above as part of nostalgia for home but there was also another important aspect of this nostalgia: a love of the way things were in one's childhood. The technological, social and economic changes taking place in American society were significant enough. The events of the Civil War, for many Americans, only served to fuel the desire for "the way things were." It is not surprising that so many songwriters focused on a longing for the past as a means to create an emotional connection with the American public.

Death, especially the death of a loved one. Given the upbeat nature of Winner's songs, their major keys and occasion-

ally jaunty rhythmic settings, it is surprising to modern students of music that Winner would use this type of setting to
discuss elements of death and dying (see "Listen to the
Mocking Bird" for an excellent example). However, a strong
feature of many of Winner's sentimental ballads is the redemption that comes from death. Regardless of Winner's religious leanings—or non-leanings—this was a subject he felt
needed to be addressed with honesty and directness in his lyrics.

   Old friends. In several songs, Winner's poetry treats old
friends with a reverence similar to first loves. This ties
strongly into the theme of nostalgia.

Other lesser themes in Winner's works include love between men
and women, religion, political songs and children's songs. Notably absent from his output are topical songs that attempted to capitalize on
trends of the day (as in, for example, "A Bicycle Built for Two").
   In "My Cottage Home," Winner wrote lyrics highly sentimental in
nature and full of reminiscences that combine many of the themes
mentioned above including nostalgia, home, nature and even parents, to
some extent:

My home, my home, my cottage home,
Thou fair and lovely spot,
How sad and lonely is my soul
When I can view thee not.
The vines may blossom in my path,
And flow'rs I most adore,
But what are all their charms to me,
If not beside my door

Home is a name we ne'er forget,
Like other names of earth;
We never grow too old to love
The spot that gave us birth.
And when in dreams of faded years,
Of all our youthful pride,
How sweet to dwell beneath the roof
Where our dear parents died.

When Winner republished the song in or around 1886, he added an
additional verse.[36] Interestingly enough, it contains one of the few references to a father's place in the home found in his lyrics:

My home, my home, my cottage home,
I'll love thee ever more,
And ev'ry heart that greets me,

When I reach thy humble door;
And though my mothers smile be gone,
My fathers watchful care,
I love to dwell beneath thy roof,
For home was always there.

"How Sweet Are the Roses" also uses the theme of nature, here combining it with the theme of death and loss of friends that would predominate his work:

How sweet, how sweet are the roses,
And how we watch for their bloom;
We gather them in their glory
And scatter them over the tomb.
But weeds unheeded lift their heads,
And in their stillness wave,
Like better friends in silent hours
Beside the lonely grave.

How fair, how fair are the lilies,
How dear to the heart and the eye,
And how we wait for the beauty,
And gather them 'ere they die.
But weeds, alas, how said it seems
To pass them coldly by
For they have buds and blossoms too
And flower 'ere they die.

Again, on republication sometime in or after 1886, Winner added a third verse:[37]

Alas, alas, how they perish,
And pass with summer away.
The rose, the weed and the lily,
Beside each other decay.
But weeds must bud and blossom too,
And flower 'ere they die.
Then pluck them not in cold disgust,
And cast them from the eye.

In "What Is Home without a Mother?" the programmatic origin of the song may have been his only inspiration (even though it conveniently combines the themes of mother and lost loves so prevalent in his work). However, the words may also have concealed a tribute to his mother and a testament to her importance in his life. Given that Winner had his own father arrested less than twelve months prior to the publi-

cation of this song, the words carry a special resonance not typical of
Winner's lyrics:

> What is home without a mother?
> What are all the joys we meet?
> When her loving smile no longer
> Greets the coming, coming of our feet!
> The days seem long, the nights are drear,
> And time rolls slowly on.
> And oh! How few are childhood's pleasures
> When her gentle, gentle care is gone.
>
> Things we prize are first to vanish;
> Hearts we love to pass away,
> And how soon, e'en in our childhood,
> We behold her turning, turning gray;
> Her eyes grow dim, her step is slow,
> Her joys of earth are past,
> And sometimes ere we learn to know her
> She hath breath'd on earth, on earth her last.

The Growth of an Entrepreneur

The publication of Winner's first three songs and the remarkable success of at least one of them either demonstrates that Winner clearly
understood and was sensitive to the market that he was writing for, or it
may be evidence of his incredible luck. This success was followed by a
flurry of additional Hawthorne releases in 1854. Each of these releases
achieved modest sales and only served to enhance both the reputation
of Alice Hawthorne and the business of the newly formed Winner &
Shuster publishing house and music store. Interestingly, it would appear that it did little to promote Winner's own name as a creative artist.

Winner's 1854 publications included "I Set My Heart upon a
Flower," "Mercy's Dream" (dedicated to the Misses Gibson, family
friends and the inspiration for the name of his first son), "Come Gather
'round the Hearth," "The Pet of the Cradle," "Rebecca at the Well"
(published by Lee & Walker) and "The Song of the Farmer" (dedicated
to Shuster). Also published in 1854 was the adaptation of the song "Les
Cloches du Monastere" ("Chimes of the Monastery"). This song represents the only collaboration between Winner (writing the words under
the Hawthorne moniker) and his teacher Leopold Meignen (who arranged the tune after Wely).

All of these sentimental ballads were published under the
Hawthorne moniker and it is here that we begin to see the first split
between Winner's career and Hawthorne's. Winner published two additional works in 1854, both of them instrumental pieces, and both un-

der his own name. "The Fireside Schottische" and "The Wyoming Waltz," both published by Winner & Shuster, represent a clear decision on Septimus' part: to isolate particular genres of published songs and create a clear distinction between his two personae.

Further evidence of this decision is provided by the only remaining publication of 1854, an "Ethiopian ballad" entitled "Hop De Dood'N Doo," published by Winner & Shuster under the pseudonym M.A.I. This additional early pseudonym is authenticated by the only other song to be published under this name, "Aunt Jemima's Plaster" (1855), which was later released under Winner's own name. In this particular case, the choice of a new pseudonym was very likely motivated by the fact that "Ethiopian ballads" or "coon songs" as they were often known, were seriously frowned upon by established music critics (and in some cases, the musical public). Just as Stephen Foster avoided using his name on early songs of this type, Winner may have elected to do the same, not just for the sake of his own career but also to protect the Alice Hawthorne name. It is interesting to note that both Winner and Foster initially avoided such an association. While Southern songwriters were prevented from absorbing the considerable Negro influence around them due to class distinctions and societal conventions, Northern composers were able to take advantage of this influence to forge what is now recognized as one of the few distinctly indigenous musics of America. While Winner would later return to these influences on some levels, Foster would not live to try in later years.

Having established himself comfortably as both a musical entrepreneur and a composer (albeit not by his own name), Winner continued the breathless pace that he established in 1854. In 1855, Winner fueled Alice's career by publishing at least one new Hawthorne ballad per month and no arrangements or instrumentals under his own name. Most were published by Winner & Shuster as they capitalized on good sales and a growing business. Others were published to forge new relationships (or capitalize on existing ones) with Lee & Walker in Philadelphia and the Oliver Ditson Company in Boston.

These new relationships with other publishers began as a result of Winner's membership on the Board of Music Trade. In June of 1855, Winner recorded his new activities in his diary:

June 5, 1855
Went to New York with Uncle Wm. Hawthorne to attend the formation of a board of Music Trade.

June 6, 1855
Met Mr. Peters of Cincinnati, Willig of Baltimore, Ditson Reed of Boston and nearly all music publishers of the Music Trade held our first meeting.

This networking would continue after he returned home.

June 11, 1855
Very fine pleasant day. Mr. Peters from Cincinnati and Mr. Willig from Baltimore called at the store.

These relationships would prove extremely advantageous to Winner. Many of his later songs would be published through these new connections, as would many of the pedagogical works. This would provide amply for Winner and his family in his later years.

In 1855, Winner published "Cast Thy Bread upon the Waters," Hawthorne's first religiously oriented song and a harbinger of later religious-oriented works. He also issued "Our Good Old Friends" that brought the image of Alice Hawthorne to the public. Also published that year were "Dreams That Charmed Me When a Child," "The Golden Moon," "The Happiness of Home" (continuing Winner's fondness for nostalgic songs), "Let Us Live with a Hope," "My Early Fireside" (a moderate hit that was dedicated to Miss Louisa Carr) and "Why Ask If I Remember Thee?" Also published that year were the aforementioned "Aunt Jemima's Plaster" (under the M.A.I. pseudonym and the only other "Ethiopian ballad"), as well as "Fond Moments of My Childhood" (Lee & Walker) and "The Days Gone By" (Ditson).

In 1856, Winner dissolved the Winner & Shuster partnership but not without publishing more Hawthorne ballads with Shuster or through other publishers earlier that year including "Am I Not True to Thee?," "To Him That Giveth Let Us Sing" (another sacred ballad) and "Years Ago." It also produced the first Hawthorne instrumental, "The Hiawatha Polka" (which capitalized on the vogue for things American Indian). But it was one song that would catapult Winner, or perhaps more accurately Alice, into the national spotlight.

"Listen to the Mocking Bird"

In late 1855, Winner wrote and published the first of the several songs that would solidify Alice's reputation as an American songwriter. While the songs that had been previously published all enjoyed respectable sales and firmly established both Alice Hawthorne and the Hawthorne ballads in the minds of the American musical public, it was not until this song that Winner could truly claim to have a serious hit on his hands.

As would seem to be de rigueur, there are many variations on the same story as to the origin of "Listen to the Mocking Bird" (first published in 1856). Perhaps the best-known of these stories follows:

Mr. Winner reiterated that the melody came to him through the whistling of a colored boy, named Dick, who ran errands for the store. Dick Milburn, who was known as "Whistling Dick" had been a beggar, collecting pennies, nickels and dimes from persons on the streets of Philadelphia, where he whistled and played upon his guitar. At various times he imitated the warble of the mocking bird, and on one of these occasions Winner heard him and was attracted by the pleasantness of the tune. It was with this inspiration that he composed his famous piece, while the colored boy was given a job in the store.[38]

An interview with Hannah Winner following her husband's death provides a little more detail on this same story (and contradicts some of the "facts" stated above):

He was twenty-six when he wrote the words and music of *Listen to the Mocking Bird*. How he came to compose the song his wife told recently in a voice that quivered a little. "In 1852," said Mrs. Winner, "we had a music store down near the Delaware River, in Philadelphia. A young colored man of the name of Richard Milburn used to clean up for us occasionally, and this young man was called "Whistling Dick" on account of his powerful and sweet whistle.

Mr. Winner liked Dick, liked to hear him whistle, and liked to hear him sing. "If you only had a song that you could sing and whistle both," he would say, "that would be a fine combination." And Dick would agree that it would and he would ask Mr. Winner why he didn't fix up such a song for him. "Well, Dick, I will" my husband said one afternoon, and he wrote the words and music of *Listen to the Mocking Bird* that evening—wrote them in about three hours and showed them to me before we went to bed.

The next morning Mr. Winner ran over *Listen to the Mocking Bird* with "Whistling Dick," and the latter had soon learned both the melody and the words. And thereafter "Dick" was always singing and whistling his new song, and before a week had gone by it seemed as if all Philadelphia had learned the song from him, for, wherever you turned, the strains of *Listen to the Mocking Bird* fell on the ear."[39]

While Hannah had the year wrong, the story is plausible enough. However, it is the only anecdote that makes mention of Milburn as a store employee, even an occasional one, prior to the composition of the song. One post-death account tells a slightly different version of this same story:

Listen to the Mocking Bird is now 50 years old. One September day in 1852, Winner sat in his parlor listening to the notes of a mocking bird belonging to a neighbor across the way. Suddenly, the song became a duet when another bird joined in. Winner dashed to the street in order to better follow the music and found there to be a diminutive Negro boy upon the gutter's edge, who added a beautiful whistling to the bird's song. All this was inspiration to Winner, and the mockingbird's song was written the next day. The little barefoot Negro was the first to sing it. In a few days, it had swept over the entire country.[40]

An entirely different version of the story was published in an interview late in life:

His [i.e., Septimus'] father was manager of old Temperance Hall at Third and Green streets, and, while still young, the future composer became a member of the orchestra at the old Arch Street Theatre. It was while a member of this orchestra that he composed *Listen to the Mocking Bird.* The idea was suggested to him one evening when a little boy in the gallery suddenly emitted a loud, shrill whistle and the actor exclaimed, "He whistles like a mocking bird."[41]

Some of these facts were confirmed in yet another interview but changed the locale:

It was while playing in the Walnut Street Theatre orchestra that he composed *The Mocking Bird.* It had its origin in a little boy whistling in the gallery and the remark was made that he "whistled like a mocking bird."[42]

Ultimately, it may be that none of these stories are true, as the only consistent aspect of the story seems to be that it was based on a whistle of some kind, whether from Milburn, a child in an audience, a bird or some combination thereof. As the most famous of these stories focus on Milburn, it might be plausible to assume that the Milburn story, in some form or another, has at least some basis in truth.

The real origin of Mr. Milburn may never be known. There seems to be some confusion over whether he worked at the store initially or was rewarded with a job there after the song was published. In addition, it is unclear as to whether he previously knew Winner or only met him when the song was written. The first publication of the song, by Winner & Shuster in 1856, credits Milburn with the "melody" for the song while giving Alice Hawthorne the credit for the music and words. Subsequent publications make no mention of Milburn and there is no record of his being paid any royalties for his contribution to its success. One might theorize that Milburn never existed at all or that if he did, his contribution was minor at best. Myers has theorized that this may, in fact, have been the case:

> It may be that Winner did not actually compose any of his most famous melody, but on the other hand he may have composed all of it that is usually remembered to day. The cause of this state of uncertainty is that the *Mocking Bird*, in its original form, consisted of three distinct melodies, all based on the same harmonic progression. The first two of these are the verse and chorus of the song as we usually remember it, while the third is an instrumental interlude that is imitative of bird calls and very whistlable. It is quite possible that this last section was Milburn's only contribution, except, of course, for the harmonic basis of the other sections, and that Winner decided to give him credit for the whole melody, since to do so would be slighting no one but the imaginary Miss Hawthorne.[43]

The origin of the ubiquitous Hallie is also a matter of some conjecture. Given that both Hallie and Hally were used as spellings in the song, two possibilities exist. One possibility is that Winner's use of the name came from Winner's nickname for his sister, Julia Winner Rapson.[44] Family lore tells that when Julia was a child, she was unable to fully pronounce her name and would say "Hallie" instead. We know that this nickname stayed with her for the rest of her life and Winner may have chosen to immortalize his sister in this manner.

Equally likely, however, is that Winner chose to capitalize on the rising popularity of Harriet Lane (later Harriet Lane Johnston, 1830-1903), who was the orphan niece of President James Buchanan. Buchanan adopted Hal, as she was known, in 1841 when Harriet was only eleven. Buchanan referred to her as a "mischievous romp" at the time.[45] By all accounts, Harriet was a headstrong, lively and exceptionally poised young woman. She accompanied Buchanan to Washington when her uncle was secretary of state in the Polk administration and grew familiar with Washington social circles despite her relatively young age. She then accompanied her uncle to London, in 1854, when Buchanan served as the United States minister to Great Britain. Harriet was a favorite of Queen Victoria, earning the honorary rank of ambassador's wife. When Buchanan moved in to the Oval Office in 1857, Harriet, now twenty-seven, took on the role of official hostess (Buchanan was the only president who never married). She was an immediate hit in Washington society, especially after the dreary years of the Pierce administration (Jane Means Appleton Pierce spent her White

House years in virtual seclusion, writing letters to a recently deceased son).

When "Mocking Bird" was written in late 1855, it is very likely that Harriet Lane's reputation was known to Septimus Winner. So whether he meant to immortalize his own sister or Buchanan's niece may never be fully known—it may have been a combination of both or, for Winner, a fortuitous happenstance.

The song itself (Example 2.4) is highly similar to his other output of 1853-1856. Easy to play, comfortable for most voices, the verse and refrain structure of the song allowed everyone to join in the merriment. The song also featured an additional section that could be whistled rather than performed on the piano. It is this section that Myers theorized was Milburn's only contribution. Where this song differs from its predecessors and what may, in fact, have set it apart is the highly rhythmic nature of the melodic line.

Most people probably don't remember the lyrics to the song with the exception of the opening of the chorus (Example 2.5). For such an upbeat, dare we say happy song, the lyrics reveal a surprising sadness, completely consistent with the themes Winner liked to exploit in the Hawthorne ballads:

I'm dreaming now of Hally,
Sweet Hally, sweet Hally,
I'm dreaming now of Hally,
For the thought of her is one that never dies.

She's sleeping in the valley,
The valley, the valley,
She's sleeping in the valley,
And the mockingbird is singing where she lies.

[*Refrain*]

Listen to the mockingbird,
Listen to the mockingbird
The mockingbird is singing o'er her grave
Listen to the mockingbird,
Listen to the mockingbird,
Still singing where the weeping willows wave.

Ah! Well I yet remember,
Remember, remember,
Ah! Well I yet remember,
When we gather'd in the cotton side by side.
'Twas in the mild September,
September, September,

'Twas in the mild September
And the mockingbird was singing far and wide

[*Repeat refrain*]

Example 2.4

"Listen to the Mocking Bird," was, in short, a phenomenon. It enjoyed continued publication through the rest of the nineteenth century
and it inspired numerous new publications and arrangements (many by
Winner himself). One set of sales statistics reports that the song sold
more than twenty million copies; 14.5 million in the United States,

Example 2.5

3.275 million in Great Britain, and another 2.225 million in continental Europe.[46] While this number might seem high, it isn't, given the huge number of arrangements and subsequent publications. One moderately difficult piano arrangement, "The Mocking Bird Variations," by Edward Hoffman, "greatly increased the sale and popularity of the original song."[47] Other arrangements (and a further indication of the song's popularity) included a quickstep, waltz, fantasia, galop, quickstep for four hands, polka, polonaise, quadrille, redowa,[48] barcarolle, variations, schottische, easy quickstep, march, mazurka, nocturne, minuet, and rondo.[49] Perhaps the most virtuosic was Grobbe's "The Mocking Bird Fantasia for Violin and Piano," which includes cues indicating that at one time it was available for orchestral performance.[50] In a 1931 article, Thompson wrote:

> *Listen to the Mocking Bird* was not slow in coming to popularity. It swept over the country as a popular song. The south

in particular went wild over it. The mocking bird is a native southern bird, and that was an added reason for the song's popularity in that section of the country. Many southern ladies of mother's time can thank this song for the fact that their given name is Hally. Their mothers and fathers sang the old song, and when the doctor said "It's a girl," they just naturally agreed upon calling the baby girl Hally.[51]

Two quotes are frequently mentioned that only add to our understanding of the song's popularity. King Edward VII of England is reported to have said, "I whistled *Listen to the Mockingbird* when I was a little boy."[52] Abraham Lincoln is reputed to have said, "It is a real song. It is as sincere and sweet as the laughter of a little girl."[53] There were reports that people danced to the song on the White House lawn when news came of Lee's surrender. Lincoln's reported attachment to the song might also have come from his beloved stepmother, whose name was Sally (thereby being reminiscent of Hally).

One well-reported story concerning this song has also turned out to be a complete fabrication on Winner's part. In an interview late in life, Winner reported:

"Sung as badly as it was, imagine my astonishment when a few weeks later, I heard the song wherever I went. Its success was instantaneous and I sold the song" adding after a moment's pause, "for a song—sold it outright, and notwithstanding the tremendous sale it had in after years I never received a cent in royalties."[54]

Winner reputedly sold the copyright for the piece to the publishing house of Lee & Walker (the second publisher to issue the work) for five dollars. This has been reported in numerous places, notably in Claghorn's 1937 biography of Winner.[55] The facts, however, must be that Winner assigned Lee & Walker limited rights to use the piece, as they were among the first to exploit its success, issuing a series of successful derivatives.

The supposed sale of the work to Lee & Walker was, in fact, a fabrication. Winner never sold the song to anyone. Why Winner chose to do this may hark back to the "modesty" behind choosing not to publish his compositions under his own name. If he reported that he had sold the song, he would be also be spared any accusations of ostentation or of flaunting his successes. Regardless of what he said, Winner collected royalties from the song for his entire life, which most probably assured him a real level of comfort from year to year. Margaret Ferguson Winner, Septimus' youngest child, continued to collect royalties after her father's death.[56]

Just as had "What Is Home Without a Mother?," "Mocking Bird" also spurred numerous parodies. Perhaps one of the most significant was the use of the melody as a basis for a song (albeit poetry of a fairly low order) commemorating the battle of Vicksburg:

> 'Twas at the siege of Vicksburg,
> Of Vicksburg, of Vicksburg.
> 'Twas at the siege of Vicksburg,
> When the parrot shells were whistling through the air.
> Listen to the parrot shells,
> Listen to the parrot shells,
> The parrot shells are whistling through the air.[57]

Despite its amazing success and popularity, "Mocking Bird" did nothing to promote Septimus' personal career. Certainly it helped Alice's immeasurably. It was almost certainly the success of this song that would ultimately create a rift between Winner and his creation in the years to come.

The Children's Books

Winner's diary entry concerning Charley Davis has already been cited but it bears repeating here:

February 16, 1853
Made arrangements with Charley Davis to have my *Winner Collection* sterotyped which I hope may prove to my advantage.

Charley Davis was, in fact, Philadelphia publisher and engraver Charles H. Davis. He and Winner were friends and neighbors, Davis' store located at 62 North Eighth Street (Winner was currently at 110 North Eighth Street). Septimus, in his ongoing efforts to promote Alice's career, clearly struck a deal with Davis. This deal would further broaden and seal Hawthorne's reputation among not only the musical public but among the literary public as well.

In 1854, Winner published a series of children's books authored by Alice. Little is known about the origin of these books, how they came to be published or of their relative success in terms of returns (although the fact that many of these books were republished in 1868 by New York publisher Allan Brothers is indicative of at least some success). There is no mention of these books in Winner's diaries nor were his descendents, it would seem, aware of them. Even the chronology of their creation and publication is, to date, unknown.

Because they are simply too interesting not to repeat in certain cases, several excerpts are provided below (the drawings are the original, uncredited illustrations that appeared in each book).

The Elephant[58]

The elephant is as remarkable for his size and mild disposition as the lion is for his strength and ferocity. His thick skin, slow motions, his large tusks, and that very curious contrivance, his trunk, which is at once a hand, a lip, and a weapon of defiance, make him a most curious and extraordinary production of nature.

Elephants were formerly used in war, but the invention of gunpowder has dismissed them from service, except as beasts of burden. They are still, however, used for purposes of state in the East, and in tiger hunting. It is an admirable swimmer. When domesticated it is the most gentle, obedient, and affectionate of animals; it soon conceives an attachment for its keeper, and appears even anxious to anticipate his wishes; but while grateful for favors, it is no less indignant at insults. The story of the tailor of Calcutta is well known, who having been accustomed to give an Elephant an apple as he passed to the water, one day, when hurried, pricked his proboscis with a needle, and the Elephant retired; but filling his trunk with the foulest water, on his return, flooded the poor fellow off his board, by discharging upon him the dirty deluge.

By and large, the books were probably quite easy for Winner to write. Six of the seven titles feature brief anecdotes describing an example of the topic at hand. A few days of reading in his local library would have very likely provided the necessary information. The remaining book, a continuous story, was very likely a tale Winner told his children. In and of themselves, the books are harmless although they contain a great deal of misinformation and stereotypes. They may have been in process for several years although, once again, one would expect at least some mention of them in Winner's diaries. It is even plausible that William Shuster collaborated with him, as it is a considerable output for such a short period of time. In 1854 alone, seven short volumes were issued: *The Book of Curiosities; The Book of Adventures; Our Jenny—A Story for Young People; Stories of Asia; Stories of Africa; Stories of Remarkable Birds for the Amusement of My Young Friends* and *Stories of Wild Animals.*

Even a modest level of success would have furthered Alice's career at just the point when the Hawthorne Ballads were beginning to gain widespread recognition. The books also feature a level of exoticism that will be repeated in Alice's next writing endeavors.

The Hoopoe[59]

The Hoopoe is remarkable not only for the crest on his head, which he raises and depresses at pleasure; but also for his familiarity and playfulness. Mr. Bechstein says, its grotesque grimaces are very amusing. It distinguishes itself peculiarly by a constant movement of its head, every time touching the ground with its beak; and at the same time jerking its crest forward and giving a catch with its wings and tail; when thus advancing onwards, it looks as if it were walking by the aid of a stick. I have kept several in my chamber and amused myself with their strange demeanor. When looked steadily at they immediately begin their pantomime. M. Von Schauroth writes to me as follows: "Two young Hoopoes which I had taken from the summit of a loft oak I reared with difficulty. They would follow me everywhere, and if they only heard me at a distance they made a twittering cry of joy, and would spring towards me; they did not fly much, but with apparent facility when they did so; if I sat down they climbed up my clothes. They always looked in my eyes to see if I was at leisure, and would suit their conduct accordingly.

Morocco[60]

(Continued on next page)

Morocco—Continued

The Moors inhabit the cities of Barbary, and the country in their immediate vicinity. The term Moor, derived from the ancient Maurt, is applied throughout Africa in a very vague manner. In Central Africa it is made to comprehend all Mahometans who are not Turks. In Barbary, however, the wandering tribes are distinguished by the name of Arabs, and the term moor is applied chiefly to the inhabitants of cities. Mahometan cities in general, present a uniform scene. The inhabitants drag a recluse, gloomy, and monotonous existence. They are strangers to social assemblies, to public amusements, to the arts, and to any thing that animates life. Their time is chiefly spent in a retired manner, in the interior of the house. The females, according to the invariable Mahometan customs are strictly excluded from general society, and must see none of the male sex, except their husbands; they are immured like slaves in the apartments of the harem. That aspect of apathy and gravity, however, which a Moor presents at first view, is, in a great measure, fallacious, and he is easily roused from it to the most outrageous acts of bloodshed and violence. In Barbary, the habits of seafaring and piratical life have rendered these occasions more frequent, and have produced a character more habitually turbulent and disorderly, than is usual in Turkish states. Indeed, European travelers have usually described the Moors as a race devoid of all good qualities, and combining every sort of depravity; but the relations between the parties have usually been of a very hostile nature, embittered both by religious and political rancor.

The harem, that favorite and almost sole seat of Oriental luxury, is, of course, inaccessible, and can only through some peculiar chance be seen by Europeans. Lempriere, however, in his character of a physician, was admitted into that of the Emperor of Morocco. It consisted of a wing of the palace, entirely separated from the rest, and communicating only by a private door, of which the emperor had the key. The edifice was divided into a number of courts, communicating by narrow passages, round which were ranged the apartments of the wives and concubines, who were sixty to a hundred in number, besides their domestics and slaves. There was a principal sultana, who had a general superintendence, over the establishment, but enjoyed not the same influence with the emperor as some of the younger favorites. There were several European captives, who appeared to the traveler the chief ornament of the harem, both as to personal and mental accomplishments. The Moorish ladies were enormously fat, and utterly stupid and ignorant.

Winner the Pedagogue

Leaving the sentimental ballads and the children's books to Hawthorne, Winner was already publishing instrumental compositions and arrangements under his own name. Seeking other outlets to promote his own name, he turned to his background as a teacher to provide not only a new source of income but also a new source of notoriety. Although it may not have been the kind of notoriety he hoped for artistically, he would now put that background to good use from a publishing perspective.

In 1854, Winner published the first of what would ultimately become an astounding array of pedagogical books for the amateur musician. The first of these, *Winner's Improved Method for Violin*, is significant not only in that it was for the instrument he knew best (and by all accounts, still played professionally), but also in that he chose to attach his own name to the product.

This decision is important in that as a shop owner who dealt directly with this particular niche of his musical public, Winner was, theoretically, able to safely publish pedagogical materials under his own name. It's very likely he dispensed pedagogical advice to his customers from behind the counter of his store. It would, therefore, be a logical next step to do this on a larger scale. As a pedagogical product as opposed to a creative one, he would not feel so modest about selling this type of product to his customers. It also spared him any critical judgment, as pedagogical books, then as today, do not necessarily require any aesthetic appreciation; they are judged solely on whether or not they achieve the desired result.

The success of his first book for violin must have been significant enough to warrant continuing down the pedagogical path, just as Winner had followed his Hawthorne successes down the path of sentimental balladry. In 1854, he also published *Winner's Improved Accordion Method*, thereby attempting to capitalize on this initial success.

In subsequent years, Winner would author and publish pedagogical books for at least twenty-three instruments including flute (first published in 1857), piano (also in 1857), guitar (1858), voice (1860), melodeon (also first appearing in 1860), clarinet (1861), drum, fife, and flageolet[61] (also in 1861), banjo (1864), organ (1865), concertina (1869), cornet and piccolo (1870), violoncello (1872), mandolin and zither (1884), trombone and ukulele (probably in 1892, although the first publication dates found by this author are 1905 and 1924 respectively) and double bass (1894). By his death, he had authored over 150 separate books for these instruments, the last of which, the *Eureka Series*, was still in publication as late as 1949, selling 422 copies.[62]

Winner's Improved Method became something of an initial brand name for his pedagogical publications. This series was followed by other series including *Winner's New Primer*, *Winner's Easy System*,

Winner's New School, Winner's Ideal Method, Winner's Eureka Method (among the most popular), *Winner's Self-Instructor, Winner's American School* and *Winner's Perfect Guide*. Each of these series of publications helped to solidify his reputation as a pedagogue. Winner was also able to leverage the considerable connections he had made through the Board of Music Trade. Among the many publishers to publish the pedagogical works were Oliver Ditson in Boston, Lee & Walker in Philadelphia, Wulschner & Son in Indianapolis, Phillips & Crew in Atlanta and S. Brainard in Cleveland. These relationships would also benefit Hawthorne as many of these publishers would re-publish Alice's songs as well.

As part of his continuing work as a pedagogue, Winner also developed and ultimately patented what he called an "instructing scale for pianos" (Figure 2.1). Sold under his own name, this would have only increased his reputation as a pedagogue.

To Williamsport and Back

In 1857 Winner, now firmly established as a pedagogue, publisher, arranger and somewhat anonymous composer, entered a new partnership with local businessman E.M. Kerk. The partnership is notable in that it was the first of Winner's many enterprises to publish a sentimental ballad that would appear under Septimus' own name, "Kissing Thro' the Bars."

As with William Shuster, little is known about E.M. Kerk. Winner makes a few notations in his diary that give an indication of how the partnership worked but precious little information on the man himself:

> *March 23, 1857*
> Took E.M. Kerk as a partner this day. He is to invest $1000 and receive one fourth of the profits. I am to retain all the copyrights of my own productions.

And, it would seem, Septimus was still pursuing new ventures:

> *April 23, 1857*
> Another trip to New York City, saw Uncle Hawthorne, met with Firth Pond and Co. on other productions.

As quickly as Winner's partnership with E.M. Kerk began, it seems to have ended. Winner was unhappy with his new business partner but the relationship may have survived (Winner later dedicated a series of violin and piano arrangements, *Solos from the Opera*, to him):

The Self-Instructor for Piano

In December 1863, Winner arranged to patent a new invention designed to assist amateur performers at the piano. Made of wood and beveled so as to fit snugly over the piano keys while fitting firmly against the back of the keyboard, the *Self-Instructor for Piano* provided note names and notation for each of the pitches. Ingenious for its time, it is only surprising that it had not been previously invented.

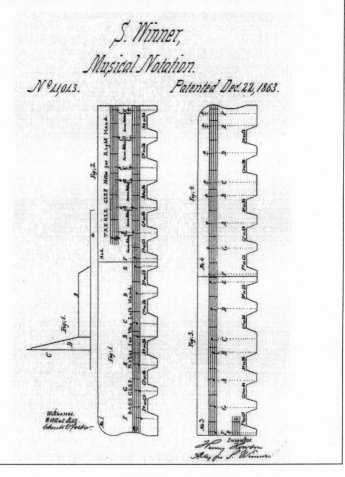

Figure 2.1

November 23, 1857
Suspended with the services of E.M. Kerk this day, found him
more of a "drawback" than a propeller. Can't abide an ignorant associate. Think I will dispense with partnerships hence-
often unless I get one of the right sort. Feel quite relieved
when I found myself once more hanging out my "own hook."

With the panic of 1857, Winner began to allow other publishers to
issue new works under both the Hawthorne and Winner names. With
two dissolved partnerships behind him, Winner may have been happy
to let others handle the publishing end of his business while he continued to work on pedagogical materials and original compositions.

The Panic of 1857[63]

With the end of the Crimean War, Russia increased its exports of
wheat and grain to other countries in an attempt to assist its faltering
economy. As a result, U.S. farmers were forced to lower their prices to
compete. With farmers able to buy fewer goods, the situation created a
ripple effect throughout the country that impacted manufacturers, rail-
roads and other related business.

Banks whose business depended on these businesses ultimately
collapsed, notably the Ohio Life Insurance and Trust Company. Hundreds of rural banks followed. The notable exceptions to these failures
were in the Southern states, able to stay solvent through cotton sales.
Ultimately, the panic gave the South renewed confidence in the viabil-
ity of a slave economy and was among the factors that ultimately pre-
cipitated the Civil War. In his diaries, Winner commented on the impact in Philadelphia:

October 17, 1857
All the banks in New York, Boston, Philadelphia and everywhere
else, North, South, East and West have closed or suspended.
Thousands of people are out of work, business intolerably dull,
nothing doing anywhere, dark prospects all around.

In 1857 Winner & Kerk, while still using the 110 North Eighth
Street address that had been used by Winner & Shuster, published only
two more songs. The first was a Hawthorne ballad, "The Flower
Fadeth." The other was a Winner instrumental, written for one of
Philadelphia's great actors, the "Edwin Forrest Quickstep."
Winner then made a brief attempt to go it alone as a publisher.
Under the company name Sep. Winner, he published the instrumental

"Drama March" (under his own name) that was also dedicated to Forrest. It would be the only work he would self-publish for the next eighteen months.

Edwin Forrest (1806-1872)[64]

Edwin Forrest, a native Philadelphian, had something of a strange introduction to the acting world. He volunteered to play a female captive in a Turkish prison at age eleven and this experience provided him with enough of a taste for life on the stage that he became determined to become a star. At age sixteen, he became part of a traveling company that toured throughout the Midwest and ventured as far as New Orleans in its performances of both Shakespeare and modern works.

Within one year of his New York debut (at age twenty, playing Othello), he had become one of America's most popular actors. One leading critic of the day reviewed Forrest's performance with the headline "He came – We saw – He Conquered!" Within one year, he went from being paid twenty-eight dollars a week to two hundred dollars a performance.

Known as a health fanatic, Forrest was meticulous about his physical regimen and was known for his impressive physique (causing Fanny Kemble, a leading actress of the day, to exclaim "What a mountain of a man!"). While he would eat a light meal before each performance, he would return to his hotel afterwards to gorge himself on cream or buttermilk and a mixture of cold cornmeal mush, oatmeal and brown bread.

Forrest continued to act throughout the Civil War, but by that time his star had begun to fade. Eclipsed by younger actors like John Wilkes Booth, Forrest continued to work, determined to earn a living on the stage. He continued to work almost nonstop until his death in 1872. Whether he and Winner knew each other at all is purely speculative. The song named for him and the dedication of the march were more likely an attempt to capitalize on Forrest's popularity than a tribute to a friend.

In 1857, Winner also allowed himself a little bit more of the limelight as a composer. Additional Hawthorne ballads of this year include "As We Gathered in the Hay," "Home and Friends (When the Sun Goes Down)" and "The Summer of the Heart" (all published by Firth Pond & Co., New York), "The Heart's Mission" and "This Land of Ours" (published by Lee & Walker).

Winner the composer, on the other hand, ventured into the genre of comic and humorous songs, his first foray into this arena. Also published by Lee & Walker in 1857 were "No One to Kiss" and "Nothing to Wear" as well as the instrumentals "Nothing to Wear Polka" and the "Annie Laurie Schottische." Oliver Ditson also published Winner's "Widders Beware, Maidens Take Care," another in this first group of comic songs.

With the coming of a New Year and with the pressure of the financial panic weighing heavily on him, Winner appears to have grown tired and/or frustrated with the musical circles of Philadelphia. He continued to compose but published almost exclusively through other companies. The Hawthorne ballads of 1858 include "Away From Home" (Henry McCaffrey, Baltimore), "Good-Night But Not Good-Bye" (W.C. Peters of Cincinnati, Foster's lifelong publisher) and "I Have Tidings" (Miller & Beacham, Baltimore). Other Hawthorne Ballads of the year include "Gentle Maggie (I'm Coming Home from Sea)" and "Netty Moore" (Lee & Walker), "Motherless Kate" and "The Old Red Cent" (Oliver Ditson) as well as "The Shepherd Boy," "There Is Wealth for Honest Labor" and "The Wicket Gate" (publishers unknown).

Winner also published songs under his own name this year as well. He ventured into the arena of popular ballads with "I'll Kiss You Quick and Stay," "Juana, Cuba's Fair Isle" and "Winner's Banjo" (Lee & Walker) while continuing to compose comical songs like "The Red Petticoat" and instrumental works such as "The San Francisco Schottische."

Despite his continuing activity, Winner's financial frustrations must have been considerable as he began to actively look to move his family out of the city. On September 10, 1858, Winner, accompanied by William Shuster (evidently they were still friends although no longer business partners), traveled northwest to Williamsport, Pennsylvania, where he rented a house and store. His diaries express his feelings at the time:

December 23, 1857
Think I smell the green field afar off. Oh, how I would like to live where I could only embrace the heavens of nature and behold the mighty work of God instead of man. May come to it some day, I am determined to, if I live and of course I shall if I have my health and strength, do it while you're young!

September 7, 1858
Closed my store at 148 North Eighth Street, too dull to stand it any longer, properly disgusted with Philadelphia.

The move must have been extremely unpopular with Hannah. She had no opportunity to see the house before the family moved there. With five children and a household to pack up and move (both Mary Ann, known as Chick, and Francis Dixey had been born, in 1854 and

1857 respectively), the long trip to Williamsport some 175 miles away by train would have been unpleasant. As it so happened, Winner recorded that almost all of the children became sick:

> *October 22, 1858*
> The hardest days work I have ever done was accomplished this day, moved the goods from the car to the house. All the family arrived safely this day and we all took tea together for the first time in Williamsport at Mr. Banger's. 'Twas a good thing Sarah Jane came along with Hannah for they [i.e., the children] were all sick in the car.

As a sidebar, the naming of Winner's second son should be commented on here. Francis Dixey Winner, born in 1857, was clearly a favorite of Septimus. He is mentioned in many of the letters he wrote to Hannah, as Frank (as he was known) seems to have accompanied her on many of her "vacations." The covers of many of Winner's editions of music bear dedications to an E.F. Dixey or note that they were introduced or sung by this same man. These songs, almost all comic ballads, include "Der Deutscher's Dog" (1864), "He's Gone to the Arms of Abraham" (1863), "The World is Topsy Turvy" (1864), "The San Francisco Schottische" (an 1858 instrumental) and the arrangement "That Lady in the Cars" (1868). Clearly, a composer-performer relationship existed between the two men; one that was strong enough to suggest the name when his second son was born in 1857.

Once settled in Williamsport, Septimus and Hannah sought to establish themselves in the musical and social circles of the town. Hannah may have been more successful in this regard, as she continued to make several trips to Williamsport in later years. Septimus, on the other hand, was most likely frustrated by the lack of any real business opportunity in the area. He may have also been reminded of his own relocation as a child, when his father moved the entire family to the Wyoming Valley. According to Myers, "it took only a few months for him to realize that in spite of the spiritual advantages of being close to nature, 'the country is no place for the music business.'"[65] Shortly thereafter, Winner wrote in his diary:

> *September 1, 1859*
> Began to pack up for Philadelphia again. It is as much pleasure to do it as it was to come. Hannah is doing well and is quite elated with the prospects of going home.

> *September 2, 1859*
> Business is very dull and no prospects for fall so I think the best thing to do is to return, having now become satisfied that the country is no place for the music business.

On October 1, the family, now augmented by one more (a daughter, Jennie, was born on August 28), ventured back to Philadelphia. Winner then moved into new stores located at 716 Spring Garden Street. Spring Garden Street would figure in Winner's life for the next twenty years.

Ultimately, the move did more than just uproot the family; it also seriously impeded Winner's compositional activities. Only two songs were published in 1859, neither of which achieved any real success. The Hawthorne ballad "Jenny, Darling Jenny" was a lackluster effort at best—its only significance being that it forever would immortalize the birth of his daughter. Winner's only instrumental for the year, "The Williamsport Schottische," seems to have been an obvious attempt to endear himself to the "locals." Once home, Winner was anxious to get back to work.

Notes

1. Tawa, *The Way to Tin Pan Alley*, 23-24.
2. Birdseye, "America's Song Composers, No. VI: Septimus Winner," 436.
3. William C. Claghorn, Foreword to *Cogitations of a Crank at Three Score and Ten* by Septimus Winner, 8.
4. Gerson, *Music in Philadelphia*, 101-2.
5. John Bewley, "Philadelphia Composers and Music Publishers: Leopold Meignen (1793-1873)," Keffer Collection of Sheet Music, ca. 1790-1895, Annenberg Rare Book and Manuscript Library, University of Pennsylvania, http://www.library.upenn.edu/special/keffer/meignen.html (accessed September 10, 2001).
6. Spaeth, *History of Popular Music in America*, 103-22. The majority of the information on Foster used in this volume comes from either Spaeth or Hamm.
7. Birdseye, "America's Song Composers, No. VI: Septimus Winner," 434.
8. Autumn Stephens, *Wild Women: Crusaders, Curmudgeons and Completely Corsetless Ladies in the Otherwise Virtuous Victorian Era* (Berkeley, Calif.: Conari Press, 1992), 41. Hawthorne tried to lend his support to Delia Bacon's circuitous seven-hundred-page volume, *The Philosophy of the Plays of Shakespeare Unfolded,* but was apparently unable to finish reading it despite writing the foreword. He also praised the "angry young woman" novel, *Ruth Hall,* praising its lack of "female delicacy" (see same, pages 133, 137).
9. Judith Tick, *American Women Composers before 1870* (Rochester, N.Y.: University of Rochester Press, 1979), 1-2.
10. Tick, *American Women Composers before 1870,* 4.
11. Tick, *American Women Composers before 1870,* 15. It is important to note that class as a cultural distinction is equally important to issues related to gender. Because Winner's family was distinctly middle-class (or upper-middle-class) and it was specifically this class in American society where the majority of these changes occurred, other issues related to class have been purposely

excluded. Any discussion herein should be thought of, therefore, as relating exclusively to the developments of middle-class women in nineteenth-century America.

12. Tick, *American Women Composers before 1870*, 21.

13. Tick, *American Women Composers before 1870*, 31.

14. Tick, *American Women Composers before 1870*, 63, 74-75, 255. Tick's analysis of this event is particularly interesting in that she cites the cliché that anonymous was a woman but revels in the irony that "in this case, the 'lady' turns out to be a man."

15. The specific street number on Callowhill varies from source to source and no confirmation can be found in Winner's diaries or in Philadelphia business records. Alternately numbered 257 or 267 Callowhill, both addresses seem to have been places of business at one point or another. Barring yet another move or an expansion to a location down the street, the only other explanation for the multiple addresses might be a re-numbering of streets.

16. The melodeon was, at the time, a popular name for a type of home organ.

17. Birdseye, "America's Song Composers, No. VI: Septimus Winner," 433.

18. Claghorn, *The Mocking Bird*, 20.

19. Hamm, *Yesterdays*, 259-60.

20. Sarony & Company was one of the many business incarnations of Quebec-born Napoleon Sarony (1821-1896). After working for Nathaniel Currier in New York, he began the first of his many businesses in 1843. The Keffer Collection shows no record of a Sarony & Company—instead they cite the business name Sarony & Major which lasted from 1845 to 1857, when the firm became Sarony, Major and Knapp.

21. Jan LaRue, *Guidelines for Style Analysis* (New York: W.W. Norton, 1970). LaRue's model provides an excellent vehicle for discussing music with musicians and laymen alike.

22. Hamm, *Yesterdays*, 61. Sentiment was widely seen not only in musical texts but also in the fiction and poetry of the time.

23. While this notion is well supported by Hamm, it has been debated by numerous musicologists including Gerson and Tick.

24. Hamm, *Yesterdays*, 44.

25. Hamm, *Yesterdays*, 141-61. Hamm provides an excellent history on the Hutchinson Family, only some of which is summarized here. Spaeth's *History of Popular Music in America*, 95, also provides some insights.

26. Silber and Silverman, *Songs of the Civil War*, 272.

27. Hamm, *Yesterdays*, 153.

28. Hamm, *Yesterdays*, 156.

29. Tick, *American Women Composers before 1870*, 93.

30. Hamm, *Yesterdays*, 51.

31. Hamm, *Yesterdays*, 254.

32. Tick, *American Women Composers before 1870*, 93. This type of friendship predates speculation that such friendships involved lesbianism.

33. Tick, *American Women Composers before 1870*, 94.

34. Tuckerman, Henry, Introduction to *The Works of Felicia Hemans*, edited by Rufus Griswald (Philadelphia: John Ball Co., 1850). As quoted in Tick, *American Women Composers before 1870*, 93.

35. Hamm, *Yesterdays*, 54.

36. While there is no corroborating evidence to support this conclusion, the author's copy of this song, published after the *Hawthorn* [*sic*] *Leaves* collection of 1886, features an extra verse, typed above the staff, in a font clearly different from the original plates.

37. See previous note. The same criteria apply.

38. Claghorn, *The Mocking Bird*, 28-9.

39. "Septimus Winner Dead; Wrote 'Mocking Bird,'" *The New York Tribune*, February 14, 1902.

40. "Noted Composer Dead; Septimus Winner Author of many Popular Songs," *Philadelphia Record*, November 23, 1902.

41. "Friends Pay Tribute to Septimus Winner," *The North American*, May 12, 1901.

42. "Songs That Won Fame for Winner," *The Times* (*Philadelphia*), May 16, 1899.

43. Myers, *The Music of Septimus Winner*, 23.

44. Claghorn, *Whispering Hope*, 21.

45. Beatrice Gormley, *First Ladies: Women Who Called the White House Home* (New York: Scholastic, 1997), 34-37.

46. "Songs That Won Fame for Winner," *The Times* (*Philadelphia*), May 16, 1899.

47. Birdseye, "America's Song Composers, No. VI: Septimus Winner," 435.

48. The *redowa* was a Czech dance that gained popularity on the European continent and ultimately, in America in the 1840s and 50s. It was typically in 3/4 time and bears at least some similarity to the mazurka.

49. Myers, *The Music of Septimus Winner*, 24.

50. Myers, *The Music of Septimus Winner*, 24. Myers notes that the copyright date on the orchestral arrangement was 1891, yet another indication of the song's longevity.

51. Dave Thompson, "Songs That Mother Used to Sing," *The Prairie Farmer*, March 7, 1931.

52. Claghorn, *The Mocking Bird*, 30.

53. Claghorn, *The Mocking Bird*, 30.

54. "A Chat with the Author of the 'Mocking Bird,'" *The Philadelphia Press*, May 17, 1901.

55. Claghorn, *The Mocking Bird*, 30.

56. Charles Eugene Claghorn to the author in a letter dated July 6, 2001.

57. Silber and Silverman, *Songs of the Civil War*, 231.

58. Alice Hawthorne, *Stories of Wild Animals* (Philadelphia: Charles H. Davis, 1855), 26-29. Illustrator unknown.

59. Alice Hawthorne (Septimus Winner), *Stories of Remarkable Birds for the Amusement of My Young Friends* (Philadelphia: Charles H. Davis, 1855), 24-27. Illustrator unknown.

60. Alice Hawthorne (Septimus Winner), *Stories of Africa* (Philadelphia: Charles H. Davis, 1855), 22-29. Illustrator unknown. Several entries in this volume seem almost purposely designed to give the impression that Ms. Hawthorne may have traveled to Africa herself (a fact we know not to be the case).

61.   The flageolet appears to have been something of a clarinet and re-corder hybrid. If one were to take a recorder and affix a rigid sharp edge (as opposed to an open hole) or potentially even a reed to the end, one would get a rough idea of what a flageolet may have looked like. The instrument appears to have fallen out of use after the nineteenth century.

62.   Myers, *The Music of Septimus Winner*, 1.

63.   John A. Garraty, *1001 Things Everyone Should Know about Ameri-can History* (New York: Doubleday, 1989), 183-4.

64.   Lester S. Levy, *Picture the Songs: Lithographs from the Sheet Music of Nineteenth-Century America* (Baltimore: Johns Hopkins University Press, 1976), 134, 136.

65.   Myers, *The Music of Septimus Winner*, 25.

Chapter Three (1861-1865)
A Civil War

Two Careers Resume

With new stores on Spring Garden Street and the family now safely relocated back to Philadelphia, Winner resumed as full an operation as he could and immediately got back to work. The year 1860 was, in many ways, though, a transition year for Winner. The disruption of moving his family and business coupled with the recovery from hard economic times must have been difficult for Septimus and his family, especially as they watched the country prepare for war.

Initially, however, Winner took advantage of his newfound energy. Under the Hawthorne name, Winner published three new ballads, "New Friends True Friends," "Look With Thy Fine Eyes Upon Me" and "What Shall I Offer Thee?," each of which achieved modest sales.

It is after 1860, though, that we begin to see Septimus' and Alice's careers diverge. To date, almost all of Winner's successes had come under Alice's name and he devoted the lion's share of his energy to her career. In 1861, a marked shift begins to take place and Winner begins to publish much more often under his own name. The motivation for this change is central to understanding the dynamics that existed between Winner and his creation.

One motivation may have been the onset of war. As we have seen, Winner made a deliberate decision to limit his creation to a specific type of song (i.e., the sentimental ballads). As war songs gained increasing popularity and as Winner felt increasingly pressured or obligated to provide those songs, he may have felt it was inappropriate for Alice to partake in topics that would be unsuitable for a "woman of her standing." If this was Winner's motivation, it was short-lived. As we shall see, Alice would become as involved as any other songwriter of her day in contributing to the war effort.

The numbers themselves clearly demonstrate that a shift was taking place. The first chart (Figure 3.1) clearly shows the extent to which

Winner focused on Hawthorne's career. In only one year between 1854
and 1858, did Winner's published output match Hawthorne's. (This
should be seen in the light of the fact that most of Winner's output was
instrumental works and that this chart does not take into account either
the children's books or the pedagogical studies.) In most cases,
Hawthorne's output vastly outnumbers Winner's.

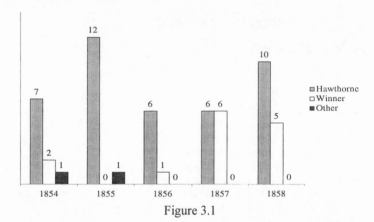

Figure 3.1

A scant three years later (1859 and 1860 are omitted due to the
personal circumstances in Winner's life), a trend begins to take shape.
Winner's works start to outnumber Hawthorne's, in one case (1864) by
almost as wide a margin as Hawthorne outnumbered Winner (Figure
3.2). Why?

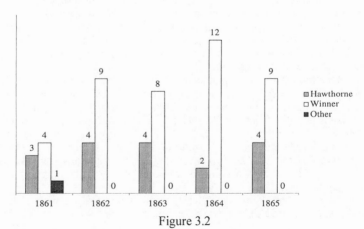

Figure 3.2

The answer to that question lies less in Winner himself (at least initially) and more in how Winner and Hawthorne were perceived by the outside world. The critical reaction to Alice Hawthorne was very positive—Winner himself was not as fortunate, as a story the composer retold later in life describes:

> Once I had written something under my own name and a literary and musical journal called the "Round Table," published in New York, pitched into me most savagely. It compared my music to that of "Alice Hawthorne" and suggested that "gifted lady" should be represented by a publisher other than Sep. Winner, through whom, for some unaccountable reason, she usually gave her works to the musical world.[1]

At least initially, Winner probably laughed off this review. As someone who enjoyed good humor throughout his life, it is very likely that the irony of this review was not lost on him. However, another story Winner told in a 1901 interview struck much closer to home:

> I was spending an evening in which Matthias Keller[2] was a member. Turning to me during a lull in the conversation, he launched into a mild criticism of my work and ended up with the suggestion that I would do better if I were to take Alice Hawthorne as my model.[3]

For Winner, this event was probably not as easy to dismiss. It would be one thing for a New York-based journal to compare him unfavorably to Hawthorne, but it would have been quite another for a member of his own circle to do the same. Taking place sometime between 1856 and 1860 (and likely towards the latter of these dates), Keller's comments must have been particularly stinging (especially in light of the fact that Keller himself penned one of the many parody songs of "What Is Home without a Mother?"). Winner had deliberately kept his alter ego a secret—a decision he may have been beginning to regret.

Given the dramatic shift in his use of pseudonyms, several explanations are possible. First, Winner very likely began to resent Alice's success, especially as it came at his own expense. Second, as the composer of several nationwide hits, he must have yearned, contrary to Victorian social mores, for at least some of the recognition he was rightly due as a composer. From his standpoint, being known as an arranger, a pedagogue and as a composer of instrumental ditties must have paled in comparison to the success of, to cite only one example, "Listen to the Mocking Bird." It is here, at the outset of the war, that the two careers diverge and something of a Civil War occurred between Septimus and Alice.

In 1860, Winner introduced a new but short-lived pseudonym. The motivation behind this may have been simply to keep Alice quiet but it may have also been to prove to himself that he could duplicate Alice's success with another pseudonym. Under the name Marion Florence, Winner published the instrumental "Tit-Tat-To Schottische" (some sources mistakenly give the publication date as 1855). Only used once, this pseudonym gives an indication of things to come. Not to ignore his previous activities, Winner returned to his pedagogical books, publishing *Winner's Melodeon Primer* and *Winner's Singing Method* in 1860, with further publications to follow. Winner also began to develop a series of songs (all published in 1861) that would enhance his own name as a composer (although at this early stage, he still published the sentimental ballads under Alice's name). It would only be one year before Winner began to encroach on Alice's previously hallowed territory.

The Onset of War

There is no record that Septimus Winner saw military service during the war years. With the onset of the Conscription Act in 1863, it may have been that Winner was able to partake in what was being called the "rich man's war and the poor man's fight" by paying the $300 fee to avoid service. The same can't be said for Winner's father. At well over age sixty, Joseph found himself enlisted (although not enscripted, as he would have been well past the age limit). While there is no direct evidence, it is interesting, given their past relationship, to theorize that Septimus may have been unwilling to help his father. However, it is just as likely that Joseph chose to serve in aid of his country.

The Conscription Act spurred a number of popular songs including "Wanted—A Substitute," "The Substitute Broker" and Work's "Grafted in to the Army."[4] Winner also commented on the state of affairs in his "He's Gone to the Arms of Abraham" (1863), which was written to the tune of the popular Confederate ballad, "Bonnie Blue Flag":

> He tried to be exempted
> A red head was his plea
> It was the same as being lame,
> In hollow tones said he;
> The surgeon "couldn't see it" –
> He said it was "no go,"
> But many say he might have passed,
> A greenback did he show.[5]

During the war years, Winner worked to maintain his business and support his family. Without doubt, 1861 was a difficult year for both Septimus and Hannah as their youngest daughter, Jennie, born in 1859, died aged eighteen months.[6] Winner kept almost no diaries during the war but this event is noted in detail:

April 4, 1861
Jennie is an awful looking object, has not been able to see for eight days, think is getting better slowly.

April 5, 1861
Jennie pretty much the same, opened one of her eyes partially at intervals.

April 8, 1861
Jennie no better yet.

April 12, 1861
Jennie died at 12 o'clock this night. Stormed all night. Gibson, Chick and Frank very sad.

April 14, 1861
Buried Jennie this morning in Old Fellow's Cemetery. Mother, Father, Cad and Jule went with Hannah and I, Emily and Ella. Frank, Gib and Chick still very sad.

No doubt, the effect on Hannah was significant and did little to alleviate her "nerves." During the Civil War, when travel was unsafe at best and Pennsylvania a site of some of the war's significant battles, she undertook several trips to visit family and friends. Even after a year, Winner's letters indicate that their daughter's death may still have weighed heavily on Hannah, as both his concern about her and his desire that she know she was missed at home is emphasized throughout.

August 22, 1862
We have made out very well since you left. Ella is like a lost lamb. I was about to say lost sheep but I don't want to insinuate that I am a ram for all. Gibson is in the peach-stone trade and Chick is perfectly herself in Days of Absence. Septimus [an obvious reference to himself] is about the same, old two and sixpence like a cat in a strange garret. I tried to fill up the bed last night but it was too big. I find the mosquitoes trouble me now since they can find nothing <u>sweeter</u> [emphasis his] to eat.

August 23, 1862
The first thing the children said this morning was, "only twelve more days" and "mom will be home" . . . Now, Han, I want you to try and enjoy yourself as much as possible while you are away and stay just as long as you conveniently can . . . although I would be glad to see you home tomorrow, yet I am willing for you to stay until you are perfectly rested and satisfied . . . I envy you up there among the mountains. Oh! For a lodge in some vast wilderness just at such times for "*What is home without a mother, when so hot we almost smother. Nothing but a plague and bother, from one long day until another, turn one way or turn the other* . . . " Now I've got to writing nonsense again!

September 3, 1862
We were all exceedingly glad to hear from you and the children, especially Ella, felt very bad when they found you would not [return] tomorrow but you know I told you to stay as long as it was pleasant for you, so I have made up my mind to be easy until you arrive, when no one in the world will be more glad to see you.

Despite any grief over Jennie, Septimus forged ahead with his multiple careers as composer, publisher, pedagogue and teacher. In 1861, Winner (through either Oliver Ditson or Lee & Walker) released a variety of *Method* books to meet the ever-increasing demand for amateur instruction in music for the home. With the advent of the Civil War, music became an increasingly important way for people and families to come together. Music education, as a result, became increasingly important. Winner issued a string of his *Perfect Guide* series for accordeon [*sic*], clarionet [*sic*], fife, flageolet, flute, guitar, melodeon and piano, all in 1861. As the sales for these began to wane, Winner issued his *New Primer* series in 1864 for accordeon [*sic*], banjo, guitar and piano, the more popular instruments used in the home. This was followed by his *Easy System* series that began publication in 1865 with the first set for piano and melodeon.

The Hawthorne ballads continued to be very popular among Americans even though they rarely addressed the issues of the day. Instead, they continued to focus on the themes of nostalgia that were featured in earlier works. Hawthorne Ballads of 1861 included "The Cozy Nook," "My Mother's Kiss" and "Snow-White Rose." These were followed in 1862 by "As Dear Today As Ever," "Friend of My Heart" and the instrumental works "Le Solitaire Schottische" and the "Jovial Schottische."

Despite these works, the Winner name was appearing with an ever-increasing frequency. In 1861 and 1862, Winner, under his own name,

published new works in a variety of genres. Instrumentals of these
years included "Colonel Ellsworth's Funeral March" (the first of many
works composed for fallen soldiers), "The Contraband Schottische,"
"The Reveille," "General Halleck's Grand March," the "Rondo Polka,"
the "Ruby Schottische" and the "Trab-Trab Galop."

More importantly, however, Winner began to publish sentimental
ballads under his own name. This was his first foray into Alice's territory—a clear breach from the self-imposed limits of the past decade.
The motivation was clear but the results were probably not what he had
hoped for. While he clearly hoped to capture some of the limelight
away from Alice, these new efforts couldn't match the success of her
previous works. The first of these ballads, issued in 1862, included the
songs "Away, Away the Morn is Brightly Breaking," "There's Not a
Sorrow on My Heart" and the somewhat popular "There is No One
Like a Mother" that returned to very familiar stomping grounds.

Winner also continued to write humorous or comical songs. "Bully
For You (Oh, I'm a Single Man)" was among the earliest of the many
comic songs Winner would compose, although not necessarily publish,
under his own name.

Lastly, there were the patriotic songs. Spaeth describes the first of
these as a bona fide hit for Winner in the Union states. "Abraham's
Daughter" or "Raw Recruits," published in 1861, was a pro-Union song
designed to promote the burgeoning war effort.[7] It was also among the
many songs published during the Civil War that began to actively promote Lincoln as the symbol of a unified America and use his name as a
metaphor for the Union cause.

One source on Winner cites that Tony Emmett wrote the text for
this song. However, Winner copyrighted the song upon its publication.
It may be that Emmett is a figure lost to history. It may have also been
a new pseudonym.

In either case, the song was written to praise one of the many
regiments in the Union army that, rather than wear Union blue, wore
distinct and colorful outfits. Modeled after the Zouave Corps of the
French army, these regiments wore bright red pantaloons, blue shirts
and white turbans. Winner must have seen the 114th Regiment Pennsylvania Volunteers, organized in Philadelphia at the beginning of the
war, who wore similar outfits and chose to immortalize them in song.[8]
The chorus of this song is enough to demonstrate the sentiment:

> And I belong to the Fire Zou-Zous
> And don't you think I oughter?
> We're goin' down to Washington
> To fight for Abraham's daughter.
> The volunteers are pouring in
> From every loyal quarter.
> And I'm goin' long to Washington

To fight for Abraham's daughter.

"Abraham's Daughter" appears to have enjoyed a considerable popularity on the minstrel stage. Silber and Silverman note a variety of printed versions that made use of "black face" dialect.[9] The mention of Johnny Bull in the fourth stanza of the song was a direct reference to English support of the Confederacy, a situation that caused increasing concern in the early years of the war. The song, however, was quite successful, spurring numerous parody songs, most notably "Abraham's Daughter II" that was sung nightly by Ben Cotton in the music halls of San Francisco.

By all accounts, Winner was no abolitionist. Instead, his politics were more Unionist in that he supported the aims of the North to bring the Southern states back into the Union, a viewpoint that would have labeled him a Northern Democrat. However, he was also not immune to the fervor of the war. One notable example of this is shown in Winner's answer song to the highly popular Confederate ballad "Maryland, My Maryland."

The original ballad, first published on April 26, 1861, as a poem in the *New Orleans Delta*, was written by Baltimore native James R. Randall. Randall was fiercely Confederate and had high hopes that his home state would secede from the Union. He penned the poem (ultimately set to the tune of "O Tannenbaum") hoping to convince his fellow statesmen to join their southern brothers. When Maryland didn't secede, Randall wrote another poem, "There's Life in the Old Land Yet," hoping to further fuel the fires of secessionism that raged in the border state.[10]

Randall's words spawned many parodies, of which Winner's was only one. Turning the pro-Confederate stance on its ear, Winner changed the lyrics to reflect the feelings of many in the North:

> The rebel horde is on the shore,
> Maryland, my Maryland!
> Arise and drive him from thy door,
> Maryland, my Maryland!

Winner's other well-known patriotic song of the early war years was "The Rally for the Union" (1862, words by C.M. Tremaine). But no other song emerging from Winner's pen caused him or his politics as much controversy as "Give Us Back Our Old Commander, Little Mac, the People's Pride." To fully understand the details of this story, it is necessary to recount some of the events of the Civil War.

Little Mac, the People's Pride

In 1861, one of the most significant battles of the early war took place at Manassas Junction in Virginia, a battle better known by the name Bull Run. The current commander in chief of the Union forces, General Winfield Scott, had been too ill to completely lead in battle, and command fell to General Irwin McDowell. McDowell's tenure as leader of the Union army was tenuous at best. His defeat at Bull Run further convinced Abraham Lincoln that he needed a charismatic and effective leader to lead the armies into battle if the Union was to be victorious.

Desperate to find a man who could equal the military leadership capabilities of Confederate Generals Robert E. Lee or Thomas J. "Stonewall" Jackson, Lincoln turned to George Brinton McClellan (1826-1885). McClellan was a graduate of West Point (second in his class) and had achieved at least one military victory, having successfully led the rout of the Confederate army from the western part of what was then the state of Virginia. That part of Virginia was later admitted to the Union as the state of West Virginia. While his background and this victory might seem impressive on the surface, McClellan was really only a facilitator. That part of the state had largely been loyal to the Union cause and, therefore, eradicating the Confederacy from that part of the country was accomplished with relative ease. His background too was only somewhat up to the task. At the time, West Point was much more of an engineering school than the standard-bearer for military training that it is today.

Despite his lack of any real experience, at the age of thirty-five McClellan was placed in command of the Army of the Potomac on July 25, 1861. He was subsequently appointed commander in chief of the Union armies on November 5, 1861, largely because Lincoln could find no one else suited to the task. With limited training and abilities, McClellan suffered from a consistent lack of initiative in advancing the Union troops against the Confederacy. One reason for this may have been the fact that he was firmly opposed to the abolitionist cause. The other was an overinflated ego that couldn't bear the notion of defeat. Given the nickname The Young Napoleon due to some early successes as a junior officer, McClellan often refused to inform his civilian superiors of his plans and, on one occasion, refused to see Lincoln when summoned.

While in command of the Potomac army, McClellan waited month after month to attack the Confederate forces, consistently overestimating the strength of their army. McClellan's plan was to advance by way of the peninsula between the James and York Rivers, and lead a march on Richmond meeting McDowell's army to coordinate a joint attack. Despite Lincoln's fears of battles so close to Washington, McClellan was able to move within five miles of the Confederate capital. Once again, he overestimated the forces of the Confederate army, led by Johnston, and when McDowell failed to join him, he retreated. On their return to Washington, the Confederate army followed and McClellan's army suffered brutal losses. The battles are historically seen as Union victories because they managed to prevent an attack on Washington. However, at the time, morale in the Union was low and McClellan's reputation was suffering. McClellan was characteristically egotistical in the face of these events and blamed the defeat on Lincoln, Edwin Stanton (the secretary of war), and the War Department. McClellan even went so far as to say that Lincoln was unfit "to have any general direction over military men."[11] Now dubbed "Mac the Unready" and "The Little Corporal of Unsought Fields" in the press, McClellan was relieved of his command by Lincoln on March 11, 1862.

Shortly thereafter, the Union suffered a disastrous defeat at the second battle of Bull Run. With men streaming back to Washington and residents of the capital fearful that an advancing army was on its way, Lincoln again called on McClellan to lead the Union forces in battle. McClellan, who had always been held in high esteem by his troops, welcomed back the man they affectionately called "Little Mac."

George Brinton McClellan (1826-1885)[12]

By no means was native Philadelphian George Brinton McClellan's notoriety limited to his battles in the Civil War. McClellan remained an outspoken figure in American history for the rest of his life.

After Lincoln fired McClellan (for the last time), McClellan returned to his Trenton, New Jersey home, confident that Lincoln would recognize his folly, return McClellan to his former position and issue new orders. Those orders never came. In 1864, McClellan would use both his former position and his notoriety to mount an unsuccessful run for the presidency. It initially appeared that McClellan's Democratic platform calling for an end to the war would win him the presidency. However, several significant Union victories reenergized the war-weary Union, and McClellan was only able to win victories in three states (Delaware, Kentucky and his home state of New Jersey). He lost the vote by a 212 to 21 margin in the electoral college and a 2,330,552 to 1,835,985 margin among the general populace.

Resigning his commission in the army when he lost the election, McClellan later became governor of New Jersey (1878-1881). History, it would seem, has not been kind to McClellan; the military historian Kenneth P. Williams described him as "merely an attractive but vain and unstable man, with considerable military knowledge, who sat a horse well and wanted to be President."[13]

With Lee moving toward Pennsylvania from Maryland, McClellan advanced his troops. The two opposing forces met at Antietam, one of the bloodiest battles of the war. Initially, McClellan moved with an uncharacteristic swiftness, as members of his command had determined Lee's plans. But later McClellan's hesitancy got the better of him. While Lincoln considered Antietam enough of a victory to issue the Emancipation Proclamation, he was furious with McClellan for allowing Lee to escape.

This was probably McClellan's biggest mistake. Given that Lee had inferior forces and was trapped against the Potomac, McClellan should have advanced toward Richmond. If he had followed Lee, he would very likely have gained valuable ground, might possibly have captured Richmond and might well have made significant inroads toward ending the war. Following this debacle, the Confederate cavalry was able to ride completely around the Federal army, doing over $250,000 in damages and embarrassing Lincoln. Despite McClellan's protestations, the War Department ordered him to relinquish command of the armies. Lincoln now appointed General Ambrose Everett Burnside to take his place.

On orders from Lincoln, Burnside began a December 1862 march on Richmond by way of Fredericksburg, a strategically important town on the Rappahannock River. Reaching their position quickly and with a commanding army some 115,000 strong, Burnside was delayed not only by a small band of Confederate soldiers but also the river itself, when materials he had ordered for pontoon bridges were delayed. The three-week delay gave Lee time to regroup his army, ultimately able to meet Burnside with a force some 78,000 strong.

The Confederacy had developed two key strategic positions. The first, in abandoned buildings on the coast of the Rappahannock, severely delayed the Union army's ability to cross the river. The second was just south of the city along a sunken road protected by a stone wall. From these vantage points, the Confederacy was able to inflict heavy losses (some 13,000 men) as the Union made fourteen separate attempts to charge the Confederate stronghold. Burnside's retreat and ultimate defeat resulted in a new low for Union morale. The South, bolstered by the win, used their newfound confidence to launch their invasion of the Northern states in the summer of 1863.

With the disastrous defeat at Fredericksburg, there was a strong sentiment to return McClellan to command. He *had* suffered heavy losses and was seen as a victim of his own ego-inflated insecurities, but McClellan had the support of the troops and, so it seemed, the ability to learn from his mistakes.

The pro-McClellan sentiment appears to have been strong in Winner as well. On a chance trip to Washington, Winner witnessed a stirring event. He saw and heard thousands of Union soldiers shouting "Give us back our little Mac" at a rally. When he returned to Philadel-

phia, Winner immediately set about writing the lyrics that would result
in one of the most difficult times of his career:

Give us back our old Commander,
Little Mac, the peoples' pride,
Let the army and the nation
In their choice be satisfied.
With McClellan as our leader,
Let us strike the blow anew,
Give us back our old Commander,
He will see the battle through.

[*Chorus*]
Give us back our old Commander,
Let him manage, Let him plan;
With McClellan as our leader,
We can wish no better man.

Men may fight for fame and glory,
Some may fight just "for the tin";
Give us then our noble leader,
Let us fight, but fight to win.
Uncle Sam has lots of money,
Mighty stores and many men,
Yet the people 'think it funny'
We should be repulsed again.

[*Repeat chorus*]

Pope he made a dash for Dixie,
Said he'd set the darkies free,
But he hasn't done a'ready,
What we did expect to see.
Down upon the Rappahannock,
Burnside went with army bold;
Says he tried to do his duty,
Acting not as he was told.

[*Repeat chorus*]

Congressmen may plan and twaddle
How the fighting should be done,
Bull Run taught them to skedaddle,
Ely took too slow to run.
Editors! Our men of wisdom?
Lay the plan for Richmond's fall,

Greely knows, just how McClellan
Could have bag'd the rebels all.

[*Repeat chorus*]

Down in Dixie he may lead us,
We will follow any route,
Till the silly war department,
Gives the order, RIGHT ABOUT.
Lincoln's great on Proclamations,
Stanton councels [*sic*] Uncle Sam,
Halleck does as their adviser,
Fremont is a perfect sham

[*Repeat chorus*]

In writing these words and the music that went with them, Winner must have known that the song had all the makings of a popular hit. Whether it was fueled by Winner's desire to capture some of the limelight away from Alice or simply because Winner thought that his alter ego should avoid politics, Septimus published the song under his own name and through his own publishing house. It was a decision that Septimus may have lived to regret.

Once published, the song was an almost immediate sensation, sweeping through the Union states at what even today might be considered a brisk pace. Family reports indicate that some eighty thousand copies were sold within the first few days.[14] According to Claghorn, it was "sung by nearly every soldier of the Army of the Potomac, during their day's work and at the camp fires in the evening."[15] The impact of the song should not be discounted. One account some forty years later called it the "famous song that stirred the nation and almost disorganized the Union army during the dark days of 1863."[16] One of the country's best-known actresses, Julia Mortimer, sang the song regularly, often at Ford's Theatre in Washington, where sentiment was at its strongest.

Further proof of both the popularity and pervasiveness of "Little Mac" can be found through the regular documentation of popular songs by the news media. During the Civil War, many of America's newspapers, responding to the overwhelming demand for information about soldiers on the front, published information about the most popular songs sung by Union soldiers. In a variety of instances, "Little Mac" was cited as being among the most popular (most often paired with "When This Cruel War is Over" by Charles C. Sawyer and Henry Tucker).[17] The text was certainly a big part of this but the tuneful refrain helped popularize the song as well (Example 3.1).

Ambrose Everett Burnside (1824-1881)[18]

Burnside's failure at Fredericksburg, partially due to mitigating circumstances, was also due on some levels to lack of training. Citing his own inexperience as a commander, he turned down the leadership of the Army of the Potomac on two separate occasions: following his successful expedition down the North Carolina coast at Roanoke Island and again after the second battle of Bull Run.

A native of Indiana and, like McClellan, a graduate of West Point, he followed his disastrous performance at Fredericksburg with a series of lackluster military encounters. Despite his success at Knoxville, his performances under Ulysses Simpson Grant at Wilderness and again at Spotsylvania were unspectacular, largely because of his *own* reluctance to advance in battle, following the nightmare of Fredericksburg. Later, he bungled a mine explosion that followed the battle of Petersburg. Given his performance, Burnside was sent on leave and never recalled to active military service. The real failure came on the part of the military leadership which did not recognize that Burnside simply wasn't ready to take on the job. He resigned his commission on April 15, 1865, one day after Lincoln's assassination.

Burnside often found himself heavily lambasted in the song literature of the day. The song "Richmond Is a Hard Road to Travel" (E.P. Christy) was very publicly dedicated to Burnside despite the fact that it satirized the difficulties many Union commanders had in capturing the Confederate capital.

Returning to civilian life, Burnside held numerous directorial positions in the railroad industry and then turned to politics, successfully running for governor of Rhode Island in 1866. He was reelected in 1867 and 1868 and then became senator from Rhode Island in 1874 and served in that position until his death in 1881. After a career marked by both successes and failures, Burnside is best remembered today for the distinctive coiffure to which he lent his name, sideburns.

The popularity of the song didn't escape the notice of either Abraham Lincoln or Secretary of War Edwin Stanton. Both of them vigorously opposed the reinstatement of McClellan and were infuriated by the song's popularity. Its continued performance by troops and entertainers alike only served to fuel their fire. Ultimately, Stanton had enough. He issued a general order declaring further performance of the song to be treasonous and authorized the arrest of anyone heard singing it. But it is at this point that the stories, like so many in Winner's life, diverge.

One account, which we now know to be false, has it that Stanton ordered Winner's arrest and imprisonment at Fort Lafayette. According to the story, Winner's release from Fort Lafayette was contingent on his promise to discontinue publication of the song and on the destruction of any existing copies. The origin of this story is unclear—whether it came from Winner himself or from an overzealous newspaper reporter anxious to heighten the dramatic circumstances of Winner's life may never be known.[19] If Winner did make it up, he may have been inspired by the plight of other composers and publishers. A.E. Blackmar, the New Orleans publisher, was arrested and fined by General Benjamin F. Butler during the Union occupation of New Orleans for continuing to publish the song "Bonnie Blue Flag" despite an official Union ban.

Example 3.1

Other accounts are far less dramatic but at the time were probably no less frightening for the humble father and businessman. One later account describes an agent from Secretary Stanton's office arriving on the doorstep of Winner's store (then located at 933 Spring Garden Street) to inform him that further publication "would result" in his imprisonment.[20] No records exist to verify it, but most accounts and family lore indicate that Winner was brought before a hearing or tribunal, at which he promised to cease publication of the song. Winner informed the tribunal that the song had been "innocently written" and that he had "no thought of treason when he composed the piece."[21] Having

Secretary of War Edwin McMasters Stanton (1814-1869)[22]

A native of Ohio, Edwin Stanton built a successful legal career in both Pittsburgh and Washington, D.C., and was among the first lawyers to successfully argue a temporary-insanity defense in a murder case. His reputation led to an offer to join the lame-duck Buchanan administration as attorney general in 1860. Stanton later returned to political circles when he agreed to be legal advisor to Simon Cameron, the secretary of war in the Lincoln administration.

Stanton replaced his boss when Cameron refused to remove a passage in his annual report stating that freed slaves should be armed and used against the Confederate army. Lincoln dismissed Cameron and, as his assistant, Stanton rose to hold the position. What Lincoln did not know, and never would, was that Stanton had written the offending passage in the report.

Stanton was highly critical of Lincoln and once told a friend that he could find "no token of intelligent understanding of Lincoln or the crew that govern him." During the war, Stanton doubled the size of the war department, censored the press and took over the nation's telegraph lines.

Following Lincoln's assassination, Stanton uttered the famous line, "Now he belongs to the ages." But as head of the nation's armies, he found himself blamed for the lack of security that contributed to the assassination itself and the events leading up to it. Later, it was discovered that he had personally withheld and was probably responsible for excising passages from John Wilkes Booth's diaries so that the distinction between the earlier kidnapping plot and the ultimate assassination plot would not be entered into evidence at the trial of Booth's co-conspirators. This excision is almost certainly responsible for the first hanging of a woman in the United States, Mary Surratt.

Stanton had ongoing conflicts with Andrew Johnson, Lincoln's replacement. Stanton worked with congressional Republicans to implement more radical Reconstruction policies in the South, a stance that put him in direct opposition to Johnson's more lenient approach. Johnson suspended Stanton in August 1867 and then fired him in February 1868. In protest, Stanton locked himself in the offices of the war department, claiming job protection under the Tenure of Office Act.

Stanton's greatest desire was to be appointed to the Supreme Court. He had been overlooked for an appointment once, Lincoln believing that Stanton could be of greater value in his cabinet position. Ultimately, President Grant appointed him to the high court in 1869. Stanton died four days after his confirmation by the Senate.

given his word, one he no doubt kept, he destroyed any existing copies of the song. Some accounts report that thousands of copies were ultimately destroyed and Winner, most likely having been sufficiently scared to agree, published no more. Since it was wartime and Winner was probably shaken by the entire proceedings, it is unlikely he felt he had any other options.

Another apocryphal story concerning "Little Mac" arises directly from Winner's supposed imprisonment. Family legend has it that Abraham Lincoln, knowing that Winner and Alice Hawthorne were one and the same person, had supported Winner's release from prison. As Septimus was never imprisoned as a result of the song, it is unlikely that Lincoln had any knowledge of the proceedings following Stanton's original orders. Even if Lincoln knew of the proceedings, it is highly unlikely that he would have known of Winner's dual identity. Such a sequence of events is, therefore, highly improbable.

"Little Mac": A Postscript

McClellan's connection to "Little Mac" didn't end with his Civil War service. As governor of New Jersey in the late 1870s, McClellan made a well-publicized appearance at which the song was sung some fourteen years after the war.

It is surprising that a song considered treasonous during the Civil War should become, only a few years later, a rallying cry in support of one of America's more popular presidents. After two terms as president, Ulysses S. Grant had retired and returned to private life. After the unpopular presidency of Rutherford B. Hayes, the Republican machinery favored Grant as their delegate for president at the upcoming convention of 1880. While there was a great deal of opposition to any president serving a third term, even a nonconsecutive one, Grant entered the convention with 306 firmly committed delegates from New York, Pennsylvania and Illinois. While Grant led initially, he could never achieve a full majority. Vote after vote was held with Grant's supporters chanting "Little Mac" in unison before every ballot. The effort never paid off. On the thirty-sixth ballot, James A. Garfield was nominated for the presidency.

Other Civil War Efforts

Winner's brush with the law was almost certainly very disturbing to both him and his family. Once the shock of the circumstances wore off though, it is very likely that the episode brought him a great deal of notoriety as well. One might even conclude, given the publication records, that Winner decided to use this notoriety to his advantage. In the remaining years of the Civil War (1863-1865), Winner published a total of thirty-nine new vocal and instrumental compositions. Of these thirty-nine publications, twenty-nine were published under Winner's own name while only ten new Hawthorne ballads appeared. While the opportunity may have come from the worst possible circumstances, Winner was able to capitalize on his newfound fame and sell as many of his new compositions as he could while the fires of his fame were still bright.

Significant Hawthorne ballads from these closing years of the war include "Down upon the Rappahannock" (one of only a few Hawthorne patriotic songs), "Parting Whispers," "Did You Think of Me Today?," "Pretty to Me," "I Am Dreaming of the Loved Ones," "Just as of Old," "Pray Tell Me the Wish of Thy Heart " and "T'were Better That Words Were Unspoken." A remaining Hawthorne ballad, "Lost Isabel (Isabel, Lost Isabel)," was best known at the time from the sentimental melodrama *East Lynne*.

"Down upon the Rappahannock" must have earned considerable sales for both Winner & Co. as well as for William R. Smith, who published later editions. One advertisement endorsed the song with the tag line: "A hearty welcome is always extended to this eminent composer's productions."[23] The only other Hawthorne patriotic ballad beyond "Rappahannock" was also a considerable success. As mentioned earlier, one of the favorite songs of the Union soldiers in the heyday of the war was the sentimental ballad "Weeping Sad and Lonely" also known as "When This Cruel War Is Over" (written by Charles C. Sawyer and Henry Tucker). The song was a tremendous success for its authors, and Winner, capitalizing on its success, penned the Hawthorne ballad and response "Yes, I Would the War Were Over." The song became a great success during the Civil War, equaling Winner's other hits in sales and notoriety (something he may not have intended, given his emphasis on his own name career). On one edition, it was advertised as follows:

> The immense sale of this answer song to the popular song "When This Cruel War Is Over" is enough to recommend it without further notice. It has been sung nightly at the Eureka Theatre in San Francisco by the popular vocalist Sig. Abecco amid unbounded applause. The sentiment is good and the melody beautiful.[24]

Winner, as we know, was much more prolific at this time. Songs from 1863-1865 include the ballads "Pretty Sally," "Our Sweethearts at Home," "Eyes Will Watch for Thee and the "Farewell Song of *Enoch Arden* (I'll Sail the Seas Over)," which was based on the Tennyson poem, and, according to Birdseye, became more popular than the poem itself in its time.[25] These songs show Winner stepping further into Alice's territory and achieving some measure of success at it.

Figure 3.2

Winner was also busy issuing a steady stream of instrumental selections. In addition to several arrangements, he also composed the "Comet Waltz" (dedicated to his brother Joe and advertised as, "A first class composition . . . in the composer's own familiar style. One of those peculiar melodies that make a permanent impression upon the mind and which we sing at times unconsciously."[26]), the "Flash Scottische," "Love's Chiding's Waltz," "Passing Thoughts," the "Rebus Polka," the "Rosine Waltzes," the "Sunshine Polka" and the "Scaley Polka." In addition, he composed several instrumental works intended to tie in to the military and/or political events of the day including the "Drummer Boy's March," "General Hancock's Grand March," the "Cruel War Quickstep" (an arrangement of Hawthorne's "Yes, I Would the War Were Over"), the "Greenback Quickstep," "Rosencrans Military Schottische," and "Secretary Chase's March and Quickstep" (dedicated to Salmon Chase, secretary of the treasury).

Comic songs from these years included the aforementioned "He's Gone to the Arms of Abraham," as well as "The Rubber Man," "Kissing in Fun," the "Song of Jokes," the "World Is Topsy Turvy" and "Tobias and Biancos."

Winner's patriotic songs included "Our Flag o'er Georgia Floats Again" (dedicated to his lithographer, George Swain), "Our Nation Calls for Peace Again," and what may have been the most difficult for him to pen, "A Nation Mourns Her Martyr'd Son (An Honest Man's the Noblest Work of God)," written to commemorate the death of Lincoln. Another somewhat patriotic song that Winner claimed as of 1865 was the well-known tune "Ellie Rhee" or "Carry Me Back to Tennessee" (Figure 3.2). Winner's song was an arrangement of the song "Ella Ree" written by C.E. Stuart and James W. Porter and first published in 1853. However, it was Winner's version that became the popular hit and, according to Spaeth, remained a favorite of the "hill-billy set."[27]

Clearly Winner was taking advantage of his newfound notoriety to establish himself as Alice's equal, on every front. However, it was one additional song, a song he would never have anticipated, that would bring Winner the fame he wanted for himself, not only for the rest of his life but well beyond.

"Der Deutscher's Dog"

How Winner became acquainted with the German folk song repertory in general and with the tune "Im Lauterbach Hab'Ich Mein' Strumpf Verlorn" in particular will never fully be known. Certainly, the immigrant German population in eastern Pennsylvania was significant and Winner, as a retailer and performer, was aware of developments in the German art song repertory. Winner eventually took "Im Lauterbach" and wrote a children's ditty that, from a contemporary standpoint, may have resulted in his best-remembered song. While today the lyrics are remembered quite differently, the original lyrics are shown below and the tune, one might imagine, is familiar to almost anyone (Example 3.3):

> Oh where, Oh where ish mine little dog gone;
> Oh where, Oh where can he be.
> His ears cut short und his tail cut long:
> Oh where, Oh where ish he.
>
> [*Chorus*]
> Tra la la la la la la la la la la,
> la la la la la la la la la la,
> Tra la la la la la la la la la la,
> Tra la la la la la la la

Example 3.3

I loves mine lager'tish very good beer,
Oh where, Oh where can he be.
But mit no money I cannot drink here.
Oh where, oh where ish he.

[*Repeat chorus*]

Across the ocean in Germanie,
Oh where, oh where can he be.
Der deitchers dog ish der best compagnie.
Oh where, Oh where ish he.

[*Repeat chorus*]

Un sasage ish goot, bolonie of course,
Oh where, Oh where can he be.
Dey makes um mit dog und dey makes em mit horse,
I guess dey makes em mit he.

[*Repeat chorus*]

The German influence here is obvious (Winner often joked in a
kind of German dialect in letters to his wife and in his own diaries). It
is also probable that Winner was influenced by the tide of European
immigration that began after the Civil War. According to Silber, this
influx of Germans (and similar ethnic groups) gave rise to what was
known as the stage Dutchman, a "thickly accented, beer drinking, sau-
erkraut-slurping nincompoop as lovable as he was dumb."[28] This character was a feature not only of Winner's song but also of such songs as
Henry Work's "Corporal Schnapps."

Sales figures for this song in its initial release are unknown. While
almost anyone with an ear for music would admit to the allure of both
the tune and the words, it is unclear whether this song was as hugely
popular in Winner's lifetime as opposed to its ubiquitous presence
since.

Of course, there were derivations of the song (as in "The Little
Wee Dog" and "The Dutchman's Lee-tle Dog"[29]) but it did not spur the
kind of answer songs that "What Is Home without a Mother?" or many
others did. It might, therefore, be safe to conclude that the song enjoyed
respectable sales but was not an instant hit. Advertised on other Winner
publications as "one of the funniest comic songs every issued," it bore
the tag line couplet "a little nonsense now and then is relished by the
best of men."[30] It is far more likely that its success was achieved over
time. Many obituaries from the turn of the century and Claghorn's 1937
biography make mention of the song—thereby acknowledging it as one
of the better known works—but do not provide great detail on it—as
they do on several of Winner's other hits.

A Matter of Growth

Given that Winner spent much of the Civil War branching out into so
many different styles of music, one might assume that the style of the

songs would branch out in as many directions. This is partially true in that the children's songs (as shown in "Der Deutscher's Dog") retained a simplicity that on some levels is reminiscent of the earlier works.

At the same time, though, Winner was starting to expand his compositional choices. As he became increasingly comfortable with his ability to write what many would call a simple ditty, he looked for new means of expression. No doubt much of this search was inspired by the music he saw around him not only in the work of fellow Americans but also in the German art song repertory that was gaining an increasing foothold in the United States. Composers such as Schubert, Schumann, Beethoven, Mendelssohn and potentially even Brahms would have been familiar to Winner, and their influence would increasingly show in his work.

Winner began to write what might best be termed a "concert song"—a song that would not have been intended for performance in the home and that would require more artistry from the singer. Winner started writing these concert songs during the Civil War and, even on the surface, they are markedly different from the sentimental ballads that typified his output in the 1850s.

The concert songs would often stretch the limits of phrasing and formal structures. In the 1870s, others would be through-composed. The melodic material, though still largely triadic, would indulge in a greater level of chromaticism. It would also require more agility from the singer, starting to exploit vocal leaps beyond the primary chords of the key. The harmony changed as well. Gone was the dependence on the primary triads of a given key. Instead, they were replaced with more secondary chords and, on occasion, secondary dominants (we are still far away from such chromatic devices as the Neapolitan chord or augmented sixth chords).

To best illustrate the onset of this development, compare two songs from roughly the same time (albeit written for different purposes). The first, the Hawthorne war song "Yes, I Would the War Were Over" (Example 3.4), starts to feature some level of new melodic and harmonic development but still exists within a framework of the primary triads and a regular formal structure.

Compare this to the stage song "Lost Isabel" ("Isabel, Lost Isabel"), from the play *East Lynne* (Example 3.5). While not written for professionals (it would have been sung by a nonsinging actor), Winner clearly required a greater level of musical craftsmanship. The fact that the song also became a hit may have been an indication of the rising level of performance ability in the home. After all, amateurs in the 1840s would probably have been very different from the musical amateurs during the war (and beyond).

Winner was clearly expanding his compositional vocabulary in this song. Melodically, the song shows a greater level of chromaticism than previously seen and also specifies a certain number of ornaments that are rarely seen in the earlier works. Harmonically, the song is also more demanding. Incorporating secondary dominants, Winner uses extended harmonic passages to articulate the phrases and veers away from the tonic-dominant-tonic structure that predominates in so many of the 1850s works.

Example 3.4

Example 3.5

Example 3.5—*Continued*

Structurally, Winner also expands on the traditional eight- or six-teen-bar structure. This affords him opportunities for expanded expressive devices—opportunities that he would take advantage of in later works. By examining the music here (presented as originally published) we also see Winner taking greater care with his expression marks. Winner's careful notation of dynamics, tempo indications and expressive markings reveals a composer beginning to spread his musical wings. In later works, Winner would take full advantage of his new skills to full compositional fruition—not only in the concert songs of this time but in all of his songs in future years.

Lyrically, the themes of sentimental ballads didn't change much during the war. Winner, like most other composers, continued the primary themes that were seen in the 1850s. An excerpt from Winner's "Away, Away the Morn Is Brightly Breaking" provides an example of this lack of change:

> Away, away,
> The morn is brightly breaking,
> Away, away!
> All care and toil forsaking,
> Away, away, away, away, away,
> For the merry morn is telling
> Of a bright and joyous day.

For the sunny fields are fair,
With their beauty ev'rywhere,
And how bracing is the air,
And how bracing is the air.
Let us wander far away,
On this happy holiday,
Let us wander faw away, away, away,
Away, away, away, away,
For the merry morn is telling
Of a bright and joyous day.

The major difference in this period occurs with the sentimental war ballads. While these ballads echoed many of the themes popular in pre-war ballads, they came with a new twist. Certain themes were augmented to make them more appropriate to the feelings many felt during the war. The key themes or perhaps better put, gimmicks, of many Civil War songwriters included the use of a soldier's supposed dying words to create a song text. This was often paired with the supposed "true story" of their battlefield heroics. This particular ploy to sell songs was evidently so popular that the public began to approach these songs with a noticeably raised eyebrow. To overcome what was no doubt a healthy skepticism, one songwriting team even obtained the services of a priest to "verify" the authenticity of the text.

Other significant themes in sentimental wartime ballads included absent limbs (this maudlin practice had probably no greater example than George Root's "Will You Wed Me Now I'm Lame, Love?"). Also ever present, according to Silber, were the unfortunate "drummer boys" who, if their number in song is to be taken as representative, would appear to have died in staggering numbers during the course of the war.[31] Additionally, songwriters increasingly turned to posing questions as the titles of their songs, a trend whose origin is unclear. Some of the songs cited above as well as those from Winner's pen attest to the frequency of this practice.

Winner certainly wasn't immune to these themes but it appears that he didn't pander to them either. Certainly a popular theme of the war, the ever present mother, or more specifically, mother waiting at home for her boys to return from war, or dying soldiers passing last words to their mothers, or dying soldiers seeing their mothers at the moment of death (and so on), was well-represented by Winner (and countless others). While many of these themes might seem either maudlin or even amusing to us in the present day, Silber offers an important rebuke:

These overly dramatic, tearful songs, each shedding rays of glory in a glowing halo of noble sentiment, appear to us as ridiculously naïve. But if the stylized lyrics and saccharine melodies strike us as cliches today, let us remember that these

were new and fresh when they were written and that constant
imitation and parody over the years have dulled the creative
sparkle of this music . . . These songs tell us of the mood and
ethic and idiom of the people of Civil War America . . . Let us
remember that the Civil War claimed the lives of some
700,000 Americans, a sum figure larger than the total of all
American deaths in all other wars in our history combined.
And these were the songs of the men who fought and suffered
and died.[32]

New Partners and Increasing Competition

The later war years find Winner continuing to run his music publishing
and retail businesses but it was also a time of great hardship. Although
he had recently sworn them off, in 1864-1866, Winner formed new
publishing partnerships (both under the name Winner & Co.) with
M.A. Smith and later with James F. Ferguson. Nothing is known about
either of these men except that it seems likely that Margaret Ferguson
Winner, Septimus' youngest child, was named after the latter. It is
likely that these partnerships were undertaken to offset the ever-
increasing costs of staying in business at the time. Winner was also
probably tired of maintaining a business on his own and, being the astute businessman that he was, was constantly seeking out new sources
of revenue (no matter what he said in his diaries). He may have also
hoped to devote a larger portion of his time to his musical endeavors, as
they had been bringing substantial reward and recognition to him for
several years.

At the same time, Winner was facing increasing competition from
a new generation of songwriters who were coming into their own in the
1860s and 1870s. While this new competition certainly didn't impede
Winner's own productivity, it likely spurred new business decisions.
Winner very likely saw that many of these composers were published
by separate businesses, a situation that may have appeared very appealing to him after more than fifteen years of going it alone. This insight would also spur new business decisions going forward.

In combination with the increasing presence and influence of his
American and European contemporaries, Winner's new outlook would
also trigger a series of compositional choices that become increasingly
prominent in his later works. These choices would ultimately lead to
his most significant growth as both a composer and lyricist. As Winner
begins to reconcile his relationship with Alice, Septimus' growth as a
composer can be seen not only in the works of both Septimus and Alice. These are aspects of musical growth that can also be seen in the
many who would join Septimus and Alice in the pantheon of America's
first generation of songwriters.

George Frederick Root (1820-1895)[33]

Born in Sheffield, Massachusetts, in 1820, George Frederick Root published over five hundred original songs from 1852 until his death and was most active during the Civil War years. Like Winner and Foster, Root initially avoided associating himself directly with minstrel songs, publishing them under the name *Wurzel*, German for "root."

Root studied music as a child and was reportedly, at thirteen, delighted that he could play as many instruments as his years. After studying in New York briefly, Root went to Paris for one year to continue his musical education. Finishing what Birdseye described as "severe study and diligent application," Root returned to the United States and began his professional career.

Root settled in Chicago and worked at the publishing firm of his brother, Root & Cady, and began to issue a steady stream of new works. Probably his single greatest success was the "Battle Cry for Freedom" (1862)—better known by the opening lyrics "Rally Round the Flag Boys"—which premiered July 24, 1862, and was sung regularly by the Hutchinson Family. Root's strong abolitionist politics underscored many of his successful works. In 1862, Root would sign a petition to the president calling for a decree of emancipation as "a sign of national repentance as well as a military necessity."[34]

Root's success with the "Battle Cry for Freedom" was equaled by "Tramp! Tramp! Tramp!" or "The Prisoner's Hope" (1863). Root wrote the song when Northerners were increasingly concerned about the fate of family members in Confederate prison camps (a condition that by most account, *should* have caused significant alarm). Root's musical version of those concerns was so immediately successful that he developed his own sequel, "On, On, On, The Boys Came Marching" or "The Prisoner Free." Root also wrote a song for those soldiers who had died in prison and never returned to their families, "Starved in Prison" (1865).[35] Other songs that placed Root firmly at the forefront of nineteenth century American composers include "There's Music in the Air" (1857, with lyrics by Fannie Crosby, a.k.a. Mrs. Alexander Van Alstyne), his arrangement of "Flee as a Bird" (1855, lyrics by Mary S.B. Dana), "Just before the Battle Mother" (1862, which capitalized on the mother theme so prevalent at the time), as well as its parody songs "On the Field of Battle Mother" (1863) and "Just after the Battle" (1863), as well as what would arguably become one of the most popular songs of the Reconstruction era, "The Vacant Chair" or "We Shall Meet But We Shall Miss Him" (1864?).

Root was awarded an honorary doctorate in music from the University of Chicago in 1872. He died on Bailey's Island, Maine, on August 6, 1895.

Henry Clay Work (1832-1884)[36]

Closely associated with the firm of Root & Cady, Henry Clay Work was born in Middletown, Connecticut, and began his career as a printer. Work was a strong abolitionist, unionist and prohibitionist and, according to Spaeth, sported a most luxuriant beard. His strong politics came from his father, convicted in Quincy, Illinois, for helping slaves escape via the Underground Railroad.

Work's first compositions begin to appear during the Civil War, most notably with the comic song "Grafted into the Army" and the much more serious work, "Kingdom Coming," also known as "The Year of Jubilo" (a song that still attracted attention some seventy years later in an arrangement by Jerome Kern). The popularity of both of these songs established Work in the minds of the American musical public.

Work issued a steady stream of war-related ballads, several of which achieved popularity. Some of his memorable titles include "The Song of a Thousand Years," "God Save the Nation" and "Marching Though Georgia" (1865) which was written to commemorate Sherman's triumphant march through that Southern state.

Two of Work's songs that were not war-related but still achieved a great deal of notoriety included "Come Home Father" (1864) and "Grandfather's Clock" (1876). "Come Home Father" was initially regarded as an important temperance ballad. According to Birdseye, it was the "pioneer and pattern for all the many temperance pieces now in the market, not a few of which are very palpable imitations. That it has done a great and good work in the reformation of the drunkard there can be no doubt."[37] The highly sentimental story of a young girl searching in the taverns for her father so that he can come home and tend to a dying son did not stand the test of time. As early as 1937, Spaeth wrote, the song "is generally treated as a joke, serving chiefly as an unintentional boomerang . . . [It] is hard to take seriously and a burlesque performance is the usual result."[38] On the other hand, Work's "Grandfather Clock" is remembered fondly. Sentimental in nature, the song was perfect for its time (and for decades afterwards).

In 1879, Birdseye wrote that Work was "a man of fine appearance, good physique . . . while his whole countenance is expressive of intelligence and character."[39] A firm believer in temperance—including not smoking tobacco—to his death, he died in Brooklyn, in 1884.

William Shakespeare Hays (1837-1907)[40]

Hays, who almost always signed his name Will S. Hays, was born in Louisville, Kentucky, in 1837 and spent the majority of his life there. As he wrote over three hundred songs, it would be a mistake to assume that he dedicated the majority of his time to composition. In fact, Hays' primary career was as a journalist for the *Louisville Courier-Journal.* He also worked as a riverman, commanding a river transport on the Mississippi during the war. According to Silber, Hays was a border Unionist who had very mixed feelings about the war. Unlike Work or Root, Hays had trouble writing the type of patriotic songs Americans found so popular.[41]

His first published song, "Evangeline," dates from 1862 and was set to his own poetry (not Tennyson's). Some of his better known works include "The Drummer Boy of Shiloh" (1862, which capitalized on the astounding popularity of drummer boy songs and may have been an inspiration for Winner's "Drummer Boy's March"), "My Southern Sunny Home" (1864), "Write Me a Letter from Home" (1866), "Driven from Home" (1868), "Oh, I Wish This War Were Over" (1863?) and "Mollie Darling" (1871), one of Hays' most enduring songs. Other songs that are sometimes remembered today include "Little Old Log Cabin in the Lane" and the 1864 McClellan campaign song "The Constitution as It Is—The Union as It Was."

Hays also used Negro dialect in some of his music just as Winner and Foster did. In 1877, his "Walk in de Middle of de Road" and "Roll Out! Heave Dat Cotton!" were considerable hits in their time. He died in his Louisville home in 1907.

Charlotte "Claribel" Alington Barnard (1830-1869)[42]

Most Americans know little of Charlotte Alington Barnard, the successful English songwriter who published the majority of her works under the pseudonym Claribel. She was born in 1830 and married a man named C.C. Barnard. Moving to London from her home in Louth, she began her musical education.

Having married into a family of some means, she composed in relative solitude. She studied composition with a man named W.H. Holmes and voice with many of the singers who would introduce her work, including Euphrosyne Parepa-Rosa and Charlotte Sainton-Dolby.

(Continued on next page)

Charlotte "Claribel" Alington Barnard—Continued

Winner was a keen admirer of her work, publishing many of her songs in the United States.[43] He often imitated her style in his later compositions. Her first success, "Janet's Choice," appeared in 1860 (published in England by Boosey & Sons) but was not published in the United States until 1871. Her work, according to Hamm, reveals the strong influence of not only English song style but also German chromaticism and Italian opera.[44]

Hamm assumes that Barnard's lyrics were autobiographical. Their strongly personal and sentimental nature would have strongly appealed to Winner at this time. Among her most well-known works in the United States were "I Cannot Sing the Old Songs," "Five O'Clock in the Morning" (a significant hit), "Take Back the Heart" (one of her most popular U.S. works) and the children's song "Won't You Tell Me Why, Robin?" According to Root, she undertook further studies to improve her technique, evidencing itself in "Come Back to Erin," still popular today among Irish folk tunes.[45] She died in Brocklesbury, England, near Dover, on January 30, 1869 at the age of thirty-nine.[46]

Notes

1.   George Birdseye, "America's Song Composers, No. VI: Septimus Winner," 435.

2.   Matthias Keller was a Philadelphia bandmaster and violinist who fled his native Germany in 1846. Settling in Philadelphia, he became an enthusiastic American patriot, publishing the song "American Hymn" which was first sung by Patrick S. Gilmore at the National Peace Festival in Boston.

3.   "Songs That Won Fame for Winner," *The Times (Philadelphia),* May 16, 1899.

4.   Silber and Silverman, *Songs of the Civil War,* 304.

5.   "He's Gone to the Arms of Abraham," *Public Domain Music,* http://www.pdmusic.org/winner/sw63hgttaoa.txt [accessed March 8, 2002].

6.   As listed in family records provided to the author by Melissa Claghorn, the composer's great-great-great-granddaughter.

7.   Spaeth, *A History of Popular Music in America,* 128-9. A possible inspiration may have been Foster's "We Are Coming Father Abraham."

8.   Claghorn, *Whispering Hope,* 7-8, and Silber and Silverman, *Songs of the Civil War,* 91.

9.   Silber and Silverman, *Songs of the Civil War,* 91-92.

10.   Silber and Silverman, *Songs of the Civil War,* 54-56.

11.   Garraty, *1001 Things Everyone Should Know about American History,* 164.

12. "George Brinton McClellan (1826-1885)," *The American Civil War Home Page*, http://www.civilwarhome.com/macbio.htm [accessed April 18, 2001].

13. Garraty, *1001 Things Everyone Should Know about American History*, 164.

14. Claghorn, *The Mocking Bird*, 35.

15. Claghorn, *The Mocking Bird*, 35.

16. "Friends Pay Tribute to Septimus Winner," *The North American*, Philadelphia, May 12, 1901.

17. Claghorn, *Whispering Hope*, 25. Among the newspapers that reported these figures were the *New York Herald* (March 13, 1863), the *New York Tribune* (March 11, April 2, April 8, April 9, May 18, and May 23 of 1863), the *Baltimore Sun* (April 1, 1863) and the *Washington Sunday Morning Chronicle* (April 5, 1863).

18. "Ambrose Everett Burnside (1824-1881)," *The American Civil War Home Page*, http://www.civilwarhome.com/burnbio.htm [accessed April 18, 2001].

19. Claghorn, *The Mocking Bird*, 35 and "Mocking Bird Composer Dies After a Long Life," *The Philadelphia Press*, [accessed November 23, 1902].

20. Accounts that give Winner's business address as Ninth Street above Spring Garden are incorrect.

21. Claghorn, *The Mocking Bird*, 35.

22. "Edwin Stanton," *Teaching History Online*, http://www.spartacus.schoolnet.co.uk/USASstanton.htm [accessed March 28, 2002].

23. Septimus Winner, advertisement for the "Ruby Scottische" (Philadelphia: Wm. R. Smith, 1862), back cover.

24. Septimus Winner, advertisement for "He's Gone to the Arms of Abraham" (Philadelphia: Sep. Winner, 1863), back cover. It is also interesting to note that Stephen Foster penned a similar song entitled :When This Dreadful War Is Ended." It is possible that they may have inspired one another in some way.

25. Birdseye, "America's Song Composers, No. VI: Septimus Winner," 435.

26. Winner, "He's Gone to the Arms of Abraham," back cover.

27. Spaeth, *A History of Popular Music in America*, 128.

28. Silber and Silverman, *Songs of the Civil War*, 307.

29. Harry Dichter and Elliott Shapiro, *Early American Sheet Music* (New York: R.R. Bowker, 1941), 246. As quoted in Myers, *The Music of Septimus Winner*, 5.

30. Septimus Winner, advertisement for *New and Popular Melodies Arranged for the Piano Forte* (Philadelphia, Sep. Winner, no year), back cover.

31. Silber and Silverman, *Songs of the Civil War*, 119-20.

32. Silber and Silverman, *Songs of the Civil War*, 117.

33. George Birdseye, "America's Song Composers, No. II: George F. Root," *Potter's American Monthly* (February 1879), 146. "The Music of George Frederick Work (a.k.a. G. Friedrich Wurzel)," http://pdmusic.org/root-gf.html, [accessed April 18, 2001]. Spaeth, *A History of Popular Music in America*, 126-7.

34. Silber and Silverman, *Songs of the Civil War*, 270.

35. Silber and Silverman, *Songs of the Civil War.* 13-14. "Tramp! Tramp! Tramp!" retained its popularity well into the twentieth century but in different forms. According to Silber, Joe Hill, the songwriter for the International Workers of the World, used the song to create a new story about a hobo who couldn't get a job. Additionally, the song was transported to Ireland as early as 1867 and used as the basis for a ballad commemorating the Manchester Martyrs. The resulting ballad, "God Save Ireland," became something of an unofficial Irish anthem in the years to follow.

36. George Birdseye, "America's Song Composers, No. IV: Henry C. Work," *Potter's American Monthly* (April 1879), 284-88. Spaeth, *A History of Popular Music in America,* 155-57.

37. Birdseye, "America's Song Composers, Henry C. Work," 285.

38. Spaeth, *A History of Popular Music in America,* 157.

39. Birdseye, "America's Song Composers, Henry C. Work," 288.

40. Spaeth, *A History of Popular Music in America,* 158-59.

41. Silber and Silverman, *Songs of the Civil* War, 120.

42. Hamm, *Yesterdays,* 184-86. Spaeth, *A History of Popular Music in America,* 143.

43. Among the songs that Winner published were "We Sat by the River (You and I)," "I Cannot Sing the Old Songs," "We'd Better Bide a Wee," and "Take Back the Heart."

44. Hamm, *Yesterdays,* 185.

45. Deane L. Root, "Charlotte Alington Barnard" in *The New Grove Dictionary of Music and Musicians,* edited by Stanley Sadie (London: MacMillan, 1980), vol. 2, 165.

46. One source on Claribel's life that is frequently cited (but difficult to obtain) is Phyllis Mary Smith, *The Story of Claribel (Charlotte Alington Barnard)* (Lincoln, England: J. W. Ruddock & Sons, 1965).

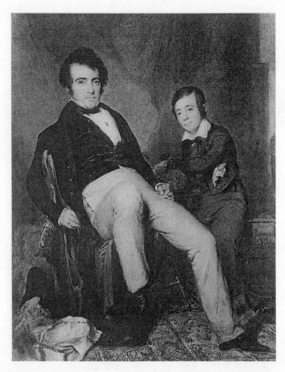

The earliest known image of Septimus Winner appears in this undated portrait of Septimus and his father, Joseph Winner, painted by William E. Winner, the composer's uncle. Septimus would appear to be a youth or teenager at best. (*Courtesy Melissa Claghorn*)

Edgar Allan Poe as depicted in the famous Whitman daguerrotype. For a time, Poe lived in Philadelphia and edited the monthly *Graham's Magazine*. As Poe and Septimus' uncle, William Winner, were friends, it is very likely that this friendship was responsible for Septimus' first public acknowledgment as a creative artist. This engraving by Robert Anderson was used as the frontispiece of John H. Ingram's edition of *The Works of Edgar Allan Poe*, Edinburgh, 1874-75.

119

A photograph of Septimus Winner taken by his friend Gutekunst in either 1847 or 1850. Winner was just beginning his career as a composer and professional musician. (*Courtesy Charles Eugene Claghorn*)

Musical Fund Hall as it appears today on the 800 Block of Locust Street, Philadelphia. For decades, the building was home to the Musical Fund Society Orchestra. Septimus would perform there for many years and the society would be critical to his success as a businessman in Philadelphia musical circles. The building currently houses condominiums. (*Photo by the author*)

Sheet music covers from among the earliest Hawthorne publications, "What Is Home without a Mother?" and "How Sweet Are the Roses?"—including the classic cover shown below by George Swain, Winner's regular lithographer. (*From the collection of the author*)

121

Alice Hawthorne as depicted on the cover of Winner's "Our Good Old Friends" (1855). It is the only depiction of her uncovered to date. The original sheet music cover bears Alice's signature in Winner's unmistakable hand. To create the lithograph, Winner chose not to hire his usual lithographer, George Swain, but instead hired the New York firm of Sarony & Company. (*From the collection of the author*)

The first edition of Winner's "Listen to the Mocking Bird" (1856). After the first edition of the song, Winner no longer credited Whistling Dick a.k.a. Richard Milburn in any published edition of the song. The numerous different stories surrounding the origin of the song have led to speculation as to whether or not Milburn ever existed. (*From the collection of the author*)

An early violin owned by Winner and made, according to family lore, by his father. Family apocrypha indicates that Winner composed on the violin first and then transferred the melodies to the piano. (*From the collection of the author*)

The original lyrics of "Listen to the Mocking Bird," written in Winner's unmistakable hand. (*From the collection of the author*)

A Matter of Influence

Winner was by no means an anomaly in his own time but was, in fact, influenced by some of the most successful composers of his day. Because of prevailing tastes in music, the styles of all of their songs are remarkably similar yet they influenced one another both in terms of musical style and lyric content.

Stephen Foster (1826-1864). His tragic and bizarre death ended several years of songwriting slumps and alcohol abuse. Despite this, he would pen some of the nineteenth century's most beloved songs including, "Old Folks at Home" and "Jeanie with the Light Brown Hair." His songwriting style would influence countless composers well into the twentieth century and, with his contemporaries, hbe would pave the way towards Tin Pan Alley. (*Courtesy PDMusic.org*, http://www.pdmusic. org/foster.html, accessed September 1, 2001)

George Frederick Root (1820-1895). A native of Massachusetts and the composer of more than five hundred songs, his "Battle Cry for Freedom" ("Rally Round the Flag Boys") and "Tramp! Tramp! Tramp!" were some of the most popular songs of the Civil War years. His "Grandfather Clock" stands as one of the most significant and musically influential post-Civil War ballads of the nineteenth century. (*Courtesy Users.erols.com*, (http://users.erols.com/kfraser/authors/ root.htm, accessed August 23, 2002)

The Hutchinson Family as depicted in their most popular and enduring lineup. Their folksy, direct style, combined with a strong sense of moral righteousness, merged the worlds of popular music and politics in a way that had largely been unprecedented. (http://www.geocities. com/unclesamsfarm/hutchinsons, accessed February 10, 2002)

To Our Brave Volunteers

Give us back our old Commander

Give us back our old Commander
Let him manage, let him plan
With M! McClellan as our leader
We can master better man.

WORDS & MUSIC BY

SEP. WINNER.

Philadelphia
Published by WINNER & Co. 933 Spring Garden St.

"Give Us Back Our Old Commander" was the Winner-penned song that caused all the trouble. For his wartime ballads, Winner rarely used the Hawthorne moniker. Alice's resurgence after the war may have been partially spurred by Winner's regrets over using his own name in this case. (*From the collection of the author*)

General George Brinton McClellan, the commander in question. While he almost certainly enjoyed the acclaim the song brought him, he probably never knew the trouble the song caused for Winner. (*Courtesy civilwarhome.com*)

Ambrose Everett Burnside, the general who would unsuccessfully replace McClellan. His distinctive coiffure would spawn the term "sideburns." (*Courtesy civilwarhome.com*)

126

Secretary of State Edwin McMasters Stanton was anti-McClellan from the start. Given the pro-McClellan sentiment Winner caused, it's not surprising that Stanton supposedly threatened Winner with imprisonment at Fort McHenry if he didn't withdraw "Little Mac" from publication and destroy any remaining copies. (*Courtesy spartacus.schoolnet. co.uk*)

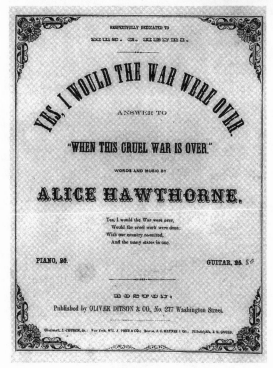

The cover of the sheet music of Alice Hawthorne's popular answer song, "Yes, I Would the War Were Over." Written in response to "Weeping Sad and Lonely" (a.k.a. "When This Cruel War Is Over") by Charles Carroll Sawyer and Henry Tucker, it was one of Alice's few contributions to the war effort. (*From the collection of the author*)

Joseph Winner, photographed in 1863. If the William Winner portrait shown at the beginning of this photospread is to be taken as even reasonably accurate, it is clear that years of alcohol abuse had taken their toll on Septimus' father. (*Courtesy Charles Eugene Claghorn and Melissa Claghorn*)

Septimus Winner photographed in roughly 1870. (*Courtesy Charles Eugene Claghorn*)

Joseph Eastburn Winner

Joseph Eastburn Winner (1837-1918), the composer's brother and a songwriter in his own right, as photographed in roughly 1862 (*left*) and again in 1897 (*right*). The relationship between the brothers appears to have been more competitive than collaborative. (*Both photographs courtesy Melissa Claghorn*)

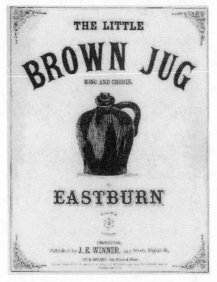

And his most famous song, "Little Brown Jug."
(*From the collection of the author*)

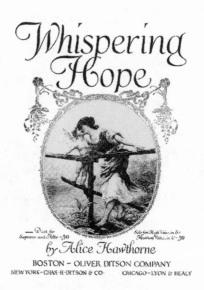

Two of Winner's most popular and enduring songs of the 1870s, the sentimental ballad "Whispering Hope" (*above*) and the children's song "Ten Little Injuns" (*below*). (*From the collection of the author*)

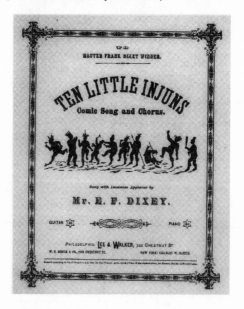

Margaret Ferguson Winner (1866-1937) in an undated photograph (*above*). She was Septimus' youngest daughter and an accomplished artist in her own right. This is the only known photograph of any of Winner's children. A detail from an undated pencil sketch of Septimus drawn by Margaret (*below*). Winner would appear to be in his early- to mid-fifties in this sketch—Margaret would have only been a teenager at the time. (*Both courtesy Melissa Claghorn*)

Hannah Winner, photographed at age 88. (*Courtesy Melissa Claghorn*)

Septimus Winner photographed in the early 1890s . . . (*Courtesy Charles Eugene Claghorn*)

. . . and shortly before his death. (*From the collection of the author*)

Chapter Four (1866-1880)
Reconstruction

Philadelphia during Reconstruction

We have seen that during the Civil War, many of America's composers reflected the political causes and events of the day in the songs they wrote. Hamm summarizes this picture nicely:

> Songs written just before and during the Civil War mirrored events and emotions of the time with such precision and passion that if all other records of the war had been lost, it would be possible to reconstruct from these songs an accurate and vivid picture of the period—the military and political events, the heroes and villains, the civilian folk heroes, the patriotic fervor and pride of both sides, the tragedies and heartbreaks of civilians and soldiers alike.[1]

With the end of the war, one might assume a significant cultural shift in American culture in general and in popular songs in particular. However, according to Hamm, where one might have expected a stylistic shift, none occurred in the Reconstruction era:

> Culturally—with a few important exceptions—it was a quiet period in America . . . But even though songs continued to be written in profusion after the war . . . They offer no insight into political scandals, the difficult emotional adjustments of widowed women, orphaned children, and crippled ex-soldiers, the tragic plight of the millions of black freedmen in the South, [and] the extraordinary bitterness of so many whites in that region.

The South was effectively out of the mainstream of American life for the rest of that century and well into the twentieth. Almost all of America's songs in the last third of the nineteenth century were written by men and women living in the North, East, and West, who quite understandably had little interest in the problems and struggles of either blacks or whites in the South, and who chose not to write songs dealing with post-war problems in the rest of the country, either. It may have been largely a matter of emotional overload; passions had been at such a fever pitch for so long that there seemed to be little force left. Poets and songwriters were quite content to turn out songs of romantic love and nostalgia, many of them reminiscent of the sentiments so popular in American songs of the 1820s and 30s.[2]

Postwar poets and songwriters seemed, whether knowingly or subconsciously, happy to confine themselves to the songs of sentiment that typified their prewar counterparts. In many ways, American popular song was a form of escapism, a means to forget the horrors of the war and return to the perceived simplicity of antebellum life.

In Philadelphia specifically, the situation was similar to the rest of the country. The songs of Philadelphia's Reconstruction composers bear a strong resemblance to their prewar counterparts. In addition, where one might have expected a new generation of songwriters to emerge in the years after the year, only a few young composers would emerge during the postwar period to assume the mantle of their antebellum counterparts. The majority of the active and successful composers after the war had been so before it. While there were only a few significant new names on the horizon between 1866 and 1885, it would be wrong to think that this situation resulted in a diminished amount of musical activity. Philadelphia was as active a musical center following the war as it had been in the first half of the century.

Philadelphia's Academy of Music had already emerged as a strong rival to the Musical Fund Society before the war and it would arguably eclipse that organization in the postwar years.[3] Starting in the late 1860s, the venue hosted such musical luminaries as Anton Rubinstein, Mahler, Tchaikovsky, Strauss and Victor Herbert. Opera would become an important part of Philadelphia musical life from 1865 to 1880. The Academy of Music hosted the American premieres of *La Traviata*, *Faust*, *Aida* and *Lohengrin*. Operetta, too, rose to prominence as a result of such works as Balfe's *Bohemian Girl* and Gilbert and Sullivan's *H.M.S. Pinafore*.

Women, spurred by somewhat more relaxed mores about professional musicianship, emerged as composers in increasing numbers, notably under their own names. Little known today, composers such as Marion Dix Sullivan, Susan Parkhurst, Augusta Browne and Faustina

Hodges would pave the way for the next generation of women composers that included Ethel Smyth and Amy Beach.[4] Changing societal notions away from the notion that women in music were the "personifica-
tion of sensual intoxication"[5] would support these women as they made
new strides to be heard.

A significant musical and nonmusical event of Philadelphia's postwar years was the national centennial, which was celebrated throughout
the country but which was centered in Philadelphia. The great Centennial Exhibition featured exhibitions from almost every state in the Union and many countries from around the world. Beyond the telephone
(of which there were only three thousand in the country at the time) and
the elevator, the list of exhibits and innovations displayed was impressive:

> Spread through 450 acres of exhibition grounds, all accessible
> for a modest admission fee of 50 cents. There were displays
> from 25 foreign countries: jewelry from India, a new contrap-
> tion called a bicycle from England, porcelain from Germany
> and 6,000 live Chinese silkworms obligingly spinning silk.
> Most conspicuous of all were the marvels of American tech-
> nology. In Machinery Hall there was the Corliss 1500-
> horsepower steam engine, the biggest and most powerful in all
> the world. Near it was a machine called a typewriter, on which
> an attendant would write a letter home for any visitor willing
> to fork up 50 cents. In Agriculture Hall, farmers were im-
> pressed by a steam-powered thresher-separator that could
> thresh and clean from 800 to 1000 bushels of what per day. At
> the Main Building, housewives marveled at a new floor cov-
> ering, a waterproof, washable surface that could last a dozen
> years or more; it was called linoleum.[6]

One of the more notable musical events from the exhibition was
the premiere of Richard Wagner's *Centennial Inauguration March*.[7]
The piece, commissioned for the occasion, was performed on the arrival of President Ulysses S. Grant to Centennial Hall. After the performance, James Gibbons Huneker, one of Philadelphia's leading musical
critics, asked "how so much money [reportedly five thousand dollars]
could have been wasted on such commonplace music."[8]

Another musical event of note to coincide with the centennial was
the arrival of John Philip Sousa (1854-1932) in Philadelphia who came
to play as part of Offenbach's orchestra. Sousa would remain in Philadelphia for the next four years. By 1878, at the age of twenty-four, he
was directing Philadelphia's Church Choir Company, a local operetta
troupe. At the same time, he would begin composing what were to become many of his most famous marches and songs. When he rejoined
the United States Marines as the director of its band in 1880 and well

after his permanent residence in the city had ended, Sousa made frequent trips and tours to Philadelphia. Willow Grove, a northern suburb,
was the home of Mrs. Sousa's family and what Gerson calls "as nearly
a home as the writer of *Marching Along* ever knew."[9]

The Rise of the Woman Professional

From the Civil War onward, there are numerous examples of
women who were composing operas, symphonies and chamber music,
as well as leading more active and visible professional lives than their
predecessors. This is best viewed as the result of a number of different
factors. First, the increasing presence of women composers in the
United States may have been spurred by the success and popularity of
their English counterparts including Lady Carew, Lady Dufferin,
Claribel and so forth.

Second, there was a growing societal acceptance of non-
anonymous publication both on the part of publishers and on the part of
women composers themselves. During the period from Reconstruction
to the Jazz Era, society began to accept the notion that women composers were artists and not the "loose moraled" women who abandoned
their "womanly duties." The more society accepted this notion, the
more women composers accepted themselves.[10]

In addition, the spectacular growth of the piano as a medium for
domestic music making,[11] and the concomitant growth of women's
magazines as an outlet for not only the dissemination but also the publication of music by women, would provide a strong foundation for
those who wished to pursue professional careers.[12] These careers would
often include teaching, which was both an outgrowth of and a positive
influence on the increasing levels of compositional activity among
women.

Despite the fact that what Tick calls the musical sphere for women
would remain largely a domestic one, these new changes were a powerful new force for nineteenth-century women composers.[13] Septimus
Winner was aware of these developments and he would respond to
them both in Alice's career and in his own in order to ensure the ongoing success of his business.

Postwar Philadelphia was, in many ways, representative of the
musical scene in much of the country. While there were great strides in
America's musical institutions, it would not be until the turn of the
century, with few exceptions, that America's quest for a distinct musical identity would resume. For the majority of the Reconstruction era,
one might look at cultural advances as being somewhat stifled as the
country struggled to redefine itself politically, economically and so-

cially. It was during this period, what some might call an awkward adolescence in American music, that Septimus Winner would live out the remainder of his life.

Family Matters and a Comfortable Business

1866 to 1880 brought an emotional mixture of happiness and sadness for the Septimus and his family. In 1866, Septimus and Hannah welcomed the final addition to their family, Margaret Ferguson Winner (known as Maggie and named for his business partner James F. Ferguson). The family would be forced to share that joy with an equally compelling tragedy only three years later. Winner's diaries of the time record the events:

> *March 3, 1869*
> A fine day, home in the afternoon. Frank quite sick, went in at seven o'clock to Dr. Stiles for medicine for his cold. Returned at eight and found him much worse, was up with him all night, went out with Gibson at one o'clock for the doctor, could not get him. Frank grew worse and worse all night.

> *March 4, 1869*
> Commenced snowing . . . in the morning. Frank rose at quarter to six. Took a drink of water and said he felt better. Gibson and I went for the doctor at six o'clock and returned at twenty minutes after where we found Frank dying. Poor child breathed his last about half past six. Oh, what a terrible blow. The doctor came in just as he died.

Winner's treasured younger son, Francis Dixey, passed away just sixteen days after his twelfth birthday. The blow was considerable for Septimus. Frank had, in many ways, been Septimus' favorite. Numerous diary entries recount the times he shared with his youngest son. Given the death of an infant daughter ten years earlier, Frank's death must have been a significant blow.

Accounts indicate that Septimus sank into a deep depression and was unable to work for many months. Publication records from this time indicate few published songs in 1869, many of them likely dating from before Frank's death. Winner's diary indicates that his son's death haunted him for many months to come:

> *August 4, 1869*
> A dull dark gloomy morning. Had a terrible storm last night. Felt very sad. Five months to the day since Frank died, and I never forget him. Every day I think of how much enjoyment

he could have had this summer past. I cannot bear to go out
without him and am extremely sad.

This tragedy was compounded three months later with the death of
Hannah's father, Benjamin Guyer, on November 15 of the same year.
No doubt the impact of two deaths was significant on Hannah. Known
for keeping something of a tight rein on Septimus and the children, it is
very likely that she drew her family even closer together in these difficult times. Septimus, already a devoted father, would become even
more attentive to and concerned for his children. In one instance, when
Maggie, the youngest, was ill with dysentery, her day-by-day progress
is recorded meticulously in Septimus' diaries.

Maggie would, in fact, figure prominently in Winner's late life.
With four children over age fifteen at this point and the older children
showing increasing independence and lives of their own, Septimus'
attention turned strongly to Maggie in these later years. She became her
father's constant companion. Given the diary entries, one might even
think that he spent more time with Maggie than with Hannah. Never
marrying herself, Maggie would live with her parents for the rest of her
life. Winner may also have wanted to keep his oldest and only remaining son closer to home. From 1873 to as late as 1897, they joined together in a variety of business partnerships, almost always under the
name Sep. Winner & Son.

These tragedies for the family were likely brightened by the marriage of Septimus and Hannah's first daughter Emily, to Eugene Claghorn, on February 6, 1871. By the end of the decade, several other mar-
riages had occurred in the family, resulting in the birth of Septimus'
first grandchildren. Winner's second daughter, Ella Guyer, married
John M. McCurdy in October 1873. Winner's son, James Gibson, married Florence E. Heiner in August 1874.[14] Later, Mary Ann Winner
would marry Henry T. Claghorn, Eugene's brother, on October 12,
1881. By the end of the decade, Emily and Eugene had one child, William Grumby Claghorn (born November 13, 1875) and Ella and John
had two, Frank Allen McCurdy (born April 10, 1876) and John Kirk
McCurdy (born June 25, 1878). Birdseye's 1879 interview with the
composer notes that, at least on paper, the entire family lived together
under one roof (a highly unlikely occurrence):

He has five children still living, all of whom but one are married, and three of them have children of their own. As they all
live together in one large establishment, it can be imagined
that his family circle is quite an extensive one. They have all
inherited a love for music and some talent, and he remarked
the other day that they performed *Pinafore* at his house the
night previous, and that he had the whole company in his own
household. He didn't say whether they were obliged to double

any of the parts or not. At all events, he is a happy old grandfather.[15]

From a business perspective, it is unclear exactly when Winner's
partnership with James F. Ferguson ended, as Winner continued to use
the name Winner & Co. (a name that applied to several ventures) until
1868. However, it must have ended by 1869, when Septimus was back
in business for himself under the name Sep. Winner at 926 Spring Garden Street. With only one exception (the short-lived partnership of
Winner & Guyer, 1887-88) and for the rest of his life, Winner would
have only one partner, his son Gibson. It very likely that Winner had
tired of partnerships by then and was much happier working with a
member of his family. They ran a business together as Sep. Winner &
Son at 1003 Spring Garden Street beginning in 1869. In 1874, according to Myers, Winner sold his share in the partnership to his son but
less than one year later was back in business as the Hawthorne Publishing Company (not far away at 914 Spring Garden Street). This endeavor was equally short lived as he was back in business with Gib in
1875.
Winner opened a second store, located at 4742 Main Street in the
part of Philadelphia known as Germantown. Indications are that Winner moved his family there, as family records indicate that Francis
Dixey Winner's death occurred in Germantown (which would mean
that Winner had a home there as early as 1869). The Germantown store
was closed in 1876 when Septimus and Gibson consolidated their efforts on the Spring Garden Street store and stayed there through 1882
(moving once from 1003 Spring Garden to 1007). A good sense of
what one might see on a visit to Sep. Winner & Son can be gained from
the following advertisement, featured on the back of an 1870 publication:

Sep. Winner & Son, dealers in sheet music and instruments,
1003 Spring Garden Street, Philadelphia. Violin, guitar and
banjo strings. All kinds of instruments repaired or exchanged.
Music published for authors. Violins from $1 to $80. Violin
bows from 25 cents to $15. Tail boards, rosin, bridges, etc.
Violin bows re-haired, guitars from $3 to $60. Pegs, screws,
strings, &c, &c.[16]

Winner had begun to publish the works of other composers before
the Civil War. By and large, these publications made little money and
few, if any, of the songs achieved any notoriety. It is likely that the fees
Winner charged to budding amateur songwriters offset any later expenses. Winner published several works for others and was not always
thrilled with the projects he accepted. In a letter to Hannah and in reference to a song he accepted called "The Grave of My Mother"[17] (an at-

tempt no doubt to capitalize on the continuing popularity of mother songs), Winner wrote, "It is as wretched a piece as ever I hope to see. I felt called on to praise it somewhat to keep friends and 'get a job.'"[18] A contract with another composer gives an idea of the terms of this business arrangement:

> We the undersigned, *Sep. Winner & Son*, hereby agree to print and publish for Henry Crofts, a new song or ballad entitled "The Grape Vine Giving" for which as composer of the music we hereby promise to pay him four cents per copy on the sale thereof after the first two hundred copies have been disposed of; 50 copies of which we agree to provide him without charge for distribution, the balance, 150 copies, to be used on the same conditions by ourselves. The plates and copyrights to be our exclusive property hereforth. We will agree to give him free access to our printers book in settling our accounts.[19]

These arrangements were very likely a means to support Septimus' songwriting and publishing career and little more.

The Musical Journal(ist)

Following the "civil war" between Septimus and Alice during the war years, Winner seems to have become more comfortable with the simultaneous promotion of both his and Alice's careers. Having been able to dismiss some of the negative criticism leveled at works he published under his own name, Winner likely grew comfortable reinvigorating Alice's career. Perhaps the strongest manifestation of the "peace" between then came in nonmusical forms. It's difficult to pinpoint the exact turnaround but it seems to have occurred at the close of the Civil War. Winner had achieved a level of fame for himself that allowed him to refocus on Alice in a productive way. While "Little Mac" may not have brought the type of fame he sought, Winner had experienced success with other songs, "Der Deutscher's Dog" among the more significant. More importantly, as Winner's career expanded from arranger and songster to pedagogue and composer, Septimus was emotionally able to support Alice in doing the same.

The first significant step Winner took in his newfound ability to promote Alice was with the publication of the *Musical Journal*, a monthly magazine edited by a woman (Alice) and targeted to women for amateur use in the home. No doubt Winner was inspired by the plethora of music magazines already on the market, but the decision to make Alice the editor would distinguish his publication in an already oversaturated market. Winner's self-penned advertisement follows:

A new monthly magazine, edited by Alice Hawthorne. The magazine, besides editorials and communications on musical matters, with various items of interest, will contain thirteen pages of engraved music each month, printed on the finest music paper suitable for binding with any other sheet music and which would cost in any other form $15 a year or $1.25 a month, will be furnished for subscribers for five dollars a year. Besides the above, it will contain a course of instruction in singing or vocal music for the cultivation of the voice which will be continued in each number and form a useful and instructive feature.[20]

Winner hadn't lost the pulse of his local consumers and, with the magazine, would predict their needs on some level. While several magazines already existed that targeted the women's market (see Judith Tick's excellent work in this area for examples), Winner published a journal specifically devoted to musical matters (as opposed to many of the others which featured fashion, poetry, columns on domestic matters, etc.). Not only that, but he used Alice to foster a sense of sisterhood between his alter ego and his customers. A professional and socially acceptable woman like Alice Hawthorne would be the ideal arbiter of taste where musical matters in the home were concerned.

What makes this publication so interesting in terms of Septimus' and Alice's increasingly overlapping careers is that he surrenders an aspect of his own career, pedagogy, to Alice. In addition to her career as a composer and lyricist as well as her foray into children's books, Alice now becomes an authority on vocal pedagogy. Additionally relevant is the notion that Alice is only a pedagogue where it comes to the singing voice, a more "feminine" pursuit, as opposed to on any instruments (even piano) which might be viewed with a certain amount of Victorian disdain.

Winner set forth some aspects of the magazine's highly Victorian tone (and by extension that part of his own personality that was distinctly Alice) in the very first issue:

Another waif is set afloat upon the wide sea of literature. It comes to you with no great pretensions to literary merit. It comes modestly expressing the hope that its mission will not be without success. It comes in the hope that among its readers it will be the means of advancing every thing that is good and true and beautiful and elevating. Whatever tends to draw more closely the links that bind man to his fellows should be assiduously cultivated. Music does this by its touching, tender, sweet expressions, drawing out the sympathies of our nature for every thing that is lovely. To the musician, the world is beautiful. The wind, as it sighs among the foliage of the trees,

is a low, sweet song of love . . . Our hope and mission is to
teach all who may receive our monthly visits, something of the
sweet harmonies of music, to elevate them by urging them to
love every thing that draws man nearer to his fellow, and
nearer to his Supreme Author, who has created everything in
perfect harmony.[21]

Alice or Septimus' religious reference here is also worth mentioning. Even in the sacred ballads, Winner tends to avoid any direct reference to his own religious inclinations. Certainly, he is making Alice's
position on the subject abundantly clear—a position that no doubt
would have made Alice even more appealing to potential readers.

Interestingly, Winner never gave any indication that he felt that
Alice's position as editor of the *Musical Journal* was in any way distinct or unusual. In fact, he may have deliberately worked against
making it appear such by ensuring that Alice would appear as the
height of Victorian feminine propriety. Sensing the needs and social
position of his primary audience, Winner explicitly targeted his niche
(again in the premiere issue) not only as a means to sell the magazine
but also to connect his readers to its editor. Could this, in fact, be seen
as Alice's career "mantra"?

Every woman who has an appetite for music or for singing
should bless God for the gift, and cultivate it with diligence—not that she may dazzle strangers, or win applause
from a crowd, but that she may bring gladness to her own fireside. The influence of music in strengthening the affections is
far from being perceived by many of its admirers. A sweet
melody binds all hearts together, as it were, with a golden
cord. It makes the pulses beat in unison, and the heart thrill
with sympathy. But the music of the fireside must be simple
and unpretending. It does not require a brilliancy of execution,
but tenderness of feeling—a merry tune for the young, a more
subdued strain for the aged, but none of your noisy clap trap
which is so popular in public. It is a mistake to suppose that to
enjoy music requires great cultivation. The degree of enjoy-
ment will, of course, vary with out power of appreciation, but,
like all other great influences, it is able to attack even the ignorant. And this is what the poets taught when they made Orpheus and his brethren the civilizers of earth.[22]

Each month, the magazine set out to meet this goal by featuring
articles on various aspects of music (most often focused on the musical
aspects of nature), news of performances, original poetry, and the
aforementioned course of instruction in vocal pedagogy. In a touch that
was pure Septimus (and perhaps not at all Alice), Winner included a

humor column. These humorous anecdotes were often musically based and feature good-natured parlor-room humor.

Musically, Winner the businessman was very much in charge of the magazine's content. The magazine was, after all, an ideal vehicle for self-promotion whether it was for Alice or Septimus (or potentially others). Each issue would prominently feature at least one Hawthorne ballad (almost always recycled from previous publications) accompanied by several other songs, often by other composers. Occasionally, an arrangement or instrumental by Septimus would also appear.

These other composers featured in the magazine may, in fact, have been Winner under a new guise. In one intriguing example, a composer named A.H. Rosewig might be seen as a derivation of Alice, due to the initials matching the Hawthorne moniker. However, it would appear on the surface that Rosewig was a composer distinct from Winner and Hawthorne.[23] In an even more intriguing, and barely concealed, example, a few works appeared composed by S.W. New. In this instance, the works must have been by Winner.[24]

From a musical perspective, probably the most interesting example featured in the magazine is a Winner-authored arrangement. Using the popular tunes "Yankee Doodle" and "The Fisher's Hornpipe" (Example 4.1), Winner created a clever arrangement that juxtaposes the two melodies on top of one another as shown below ("Yankee Doodle" appears in the left hand part while "The Fisher's Hornpipe" appears in the right hand). While it would be a stretch to think that this work is a precursor to Charles Ives, it does reveal a composer who was fond of experimenting with his arrangements:

Example 4.1

The magazine's articles themselves reveal little of Septimus the man, or of Alice the woman. However, we do get some sense of how

Winner the musician may have felt about the musical matters of the day. After a column savaging the preponderance of "mother songs" (ironically popularized by Winner himself), Alice wrote the following:

> It is not our desire to deprecate any particular style of composi-tion, or mention such as it might be well to introduce or rec-ommend; but is it not strange that Christian families will re-hearse, day after day, in their parlors, such common-place songs as are nightly performed in public bar-rooms and "con-cert saloons," for the edification and amusement of the most illiterate and vulgar crowds that infest these places, introduc-ing low wit, double entendre, Negro absurdities, and the like?[25]

Winner was, once again, pandering to his audience with the strongest of Victorian sensibilities. As savvy a businessman as Winner could be, what clearly started with high hopes and a great deal of promise for the future appears to have been less successful than Winner had imagined. By the seventh or eighth issues, the magazine was suf-fering. Winner was recycling articles and lost interest in even trying to make it appear as if he was creating or finding new music. It ceased publication after the twelfth issue, very likely to meet the contractual obligation to his subscribers.

Perhaps as a result of the *Journal*'s design, Winner began what would ultimately result in at least twelve years as musical editor of *Pe-terson's Magazine,* yet another entry in an increasingly saturated maga-zine market. Winner's title with *Peterson's* overstated his role. Winner did little more than provide one work per month to be printed in the magazine. There were no columns relating to musical matters as there had been in the *Journal* nor was there any commentary. Largely, Win-ner used the opportunity to promote his own music or that of his later pseudonyms (Hawthorne being the most prominently featured).

Formally known as *Peterson's Magazine, the Ladies National Magazine*, it was yet another competitor in, for the 1860s, an astound-ingly crowded magazine market. Initially begun in 1842 as the *Lady's World of Fashion* and then going through a series of name changes including *Lady's World, Artist and Lady's World* and *Ladies' National Magazine,* Peterson's continued as the *New Peterson Magazine* before returning to the name *Peterson Magazine* prior to ceasing publication in 1897.

Winner's involvement seems to have begun as early as 1867, the same year as the first publication of the *Musical Journal*. Clearly, he saw this as a vehicle for self-promotion despite the lack of any real editorial duties. It would almost certainly have impacted his publishing revenues and potentially increased the traffic in his store.

In addition to his "literary" pursuits, the Reconstruction period saw Winner maintaining consistent activity as a pedagogue. From 1866 to 1880, Winner developed at least a dozen new pedagogical books for such instruments as German accordeon [sic], German concertina, clarionet [sic], flute, fife and flageolet. While it may be easy to dismiss these publications, it was these works that, in many ways, would provide a comfortable income for the rest of his life.

New Identities, New Works

Winner's "reconciliation" with Alice would lead to a much more even output of both Winner and Hawthorne works during the Reconstruction era. Having achieved even a modest level of success in his own right, Winner was able to focus his efforts on both careers simultaneously and reconstruct the relationship that existed between them on a more equal level. Moreover, he began to introduce a series of new pseudonyms. If one would characterize Winner's total output as prolific in the years up to and including the Civil War, he thereafter issued new works at an almost frenetic pace.

New works were issued at a fairly steady pace under the Hawthorne and Winner names as well as new pseudonyms. The charts (Figure 4.1) show this increased activity in the pieces that can be certainly dated. While Alice was Winner's cash cow for at least the early years after the war, the relative evenness with which he approached each of his "careers" in the following years is apparent, even as Winner's overall output decreased.

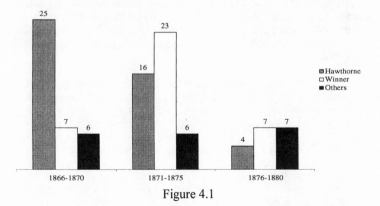

Figure 4.1

Initially Winner may have been looking to broaden his horizons with new pseudonyms but the emphasis was still clearly on Alice. As

Hamm has noted, the style of music changed little in the postwar years. This can be seen in an advertisement written in late 1865, where Winner clearly geared his writing to appeal to his target audience, potentially reactivate Alice's career and promote works that were highly similar to his prewar efforts:

> A selection of beautiful ballads, arranged for the piano, by Alice Hawthorne. These beautiful songs, so universally popular, and so well adapted to the taste of the family circle are recommended as ballads of the highest order; the sentiment being of the most moral and refined character – free from all Negro absurdities and love-sick sentiment. To every admirer of the ballad we would call attention to these charming melodies and affecting words.[26]

Winner continued this emphasis on Alice's work in his advertisement for an 1870 Hawthorne effort, "Love Once Gone, Is Gone Forever":

> Here is certainly a ballad of more than ordinary merit. It is universally admired and we conscientiously recommend it in all who wish a truly beautiful melody set to chaste and pleasing words.[27]

During the Reconstruction years, Winner initially began to stray from, although not altogether abandon, the Alice Hawthorne pseudonym and introduce new pseudonyms. The choice of pseudonyms, or his own name for that matter, largely seems to stem from the type of song he composed. While some level of overlap had already begun between Septimus and Alice, Winner would, for the most part, keep each identity distinct. Before proceeding any further, it's worth exploring each of these names, their origins, and the types of works Winner published under each:

> Alice Hawthorne continued to be used for the sentimental ballads. Winner had, in fact, begun to catalog the Hawthorne ballads with opus numbers, although this numbering system seems to have been haphazard at best.[28] There was a brief upturn in the number of Hawthorne ballads in the years immediately following the war—probably due to the need to earn a living in the lean postwar years—but there was a marked decline beginning around 1870.
>
> Septimus Winner, on the other hand, used his own name for a variety of works. Clearly, he intended not only to continue to further his own name but also to begin to demonstrate his depth as a composer. It was probably the only published name in which so much overlap of song styles occurred. While

he continued to publish instrumental pieces, arrangements and pedagogical books under his own name, he also added comic songs, children's songs and, most importantly, sentimental ballads to his personal repertoire. These sentimental ballads represent the true reconciliation of his career versus Alice's.

Percy Guyer was a new pseudonym derived from his wife's maiden name, although the origin of the first name is unclear. The name Percy may have been chosen in a humorous vein. Winner used this pseudonym sporadically for at least half a dozen publications from 1868 through 1887. The Guyer name was used both for comic songs and, in later years, for sentimental ballads.

Mark Mason, a name of unclear origin, may have also been, as has been speculated, chosen for its alliterative and potentially humorous quality. Winner used the name somewhat more regularly than the Guyer name, for sixteen titles between 1869 and 1892 (including some of the last of Winner's original songs). With the exception of one (highly unusual) temperance ballad, this name was reserved exclusively for comical songs.

Apsley Street was actually the location of Winner's Germantown store. Translated from a location into a name, Winner used it only three times, in 1869, 1870 and 1888. Two of these songs were comical children's songs, while the remaining one was used to publish one of Winner's more successful postwar compositions, "Gone Where the Woodbine Twineth."

Paul Stenton, a name taken from Stenton Avenue, one of the main arteries of the Germantown area, was a pseudonym used only twice, in 1878 and 1880. Both of these works were sentimental ballads.

Leon Dore (given in some sources as Dyer) was only used once, in 1878, for a sentimental ballad.

The earlier pseudonyms, M.A.I., A Lady of Kentucky (assuming this ascription is accurate), and Marion Florence had been either retired or forgotten.[29]

From 1866 through 1870, Winner published at least thirty-seven new original compositions as well as several new arrangements. Hawthorne ballads from these years include "Home Ever Dear," "I Was Thinking, Idly Thinking," "Link'd with Many Bitter Tears," "What Care I?" and "Over My Heart" (all in 1866), as well as "Echoes from Afar" (1867). Other new Hawthorne works include "Faded Leaves," "The Friends We Love," "The Lazaroni Maid," "Make Yourself at Home" and "Our Own" (all from 1868), as well as "Be Happy with Me," "Cruel Words Unwisely Spoken," "Hearth and Home," the instrumental "Dance of the Sprites (Mazurka)," "Love's Offering," "Song of the Winter Wind" (a.k.a. "Pity the Poor") and "My Love to All at Home" (all 1869). In 1870, further Hawthorne works include "Love Once Gone, Is Gone Forever," "No One to Weep When I Am Gone," "Over the Stars is Rest," "When the Corn Is Gathered In" and "Where Mother Is We Call It Home."

At the same time, Winner was equally active as a composer under his own name. Winner continued to publish instrumental works including the "Mountain Rose Schottische" (1866), the "Race Horse Galop" (1869), the "Aberdeen Schottische," the "Congress Schottische" and the "Silver Wedding March" (all from 1870). But he also composed at least one new sentimental ballad, "Lady Art Thou Sleeping" (1868), representing more overlap between Alice and himself.

The first of the new pseudonyms to emerge, Percy Guyer, is credited for the composition of the comic song "When Mother Married Pap" (1868). The second, Apsley Street, is credited with "The Birdie's Ball" (from 1869, and the only work from this period not originally published through Winner's own company) and the very popular "Gone Where the Woodbine Twineth" (1870). "Woodbine" capitalized on at least some post-war sentiment as shown in Example 4.2.

The third pseudonym from the Reconstruction era was somewhat more prolific. Mark Mason is credited with the composition of comical songs "The Lady All Skin and Bone" (1869) and "Rear Back Bob" (also 1869) as well as "Queer People There Be" (1870). Mason would be the only pseudonym used again until 1877.

In the 1870s, Winner continued a frantic pace, issuing new songs, arrangements and pedagogical books with a seemingly effortless pace. Hawthorne ballads continued to be issued but at a lesser pace as the decade proceeds. New Hawthorne ballads included "After Sundown," "Drifting From Home" (a possible reference to the increasing independence of his own children), "God Bless the Little Feet" (a possible tribute to his own grandchildren), "Take Me Mother in Thy Lap" (another in the seemingly unending stream of mother songs) and "We Met No More" (1871) as well as "Only Friends and Nothing More" (1872).

The decade continued with "Bird and Mate," "Lord, Thou Knowest That I Love Thee" (dedicated to Mrs. William Henry Harrison after the death of her husband) and "Some Happier Day" (all from 1873), "The Bow in the Cloud," "The Gates are Ever Open" and "Home By and By" (1874) as well as "If My Wishes Could Come True" (one of two works issued by the short-lived Hawthorne Publishing Company) and "Side By Side" (1875). At least two of these works represent a return to the sacred-oriented songs that occur with greater frequency in Winner's later life.

In the last half of the 1870s, Hawthorne begins to drop from sight as a composer. In both 1876 and 1878, Winner issued no new

Example 4.2

Hawthorne ballads. Toward the end of the decade, the remaining Hawthorne ballads included "Don't Forget to Say Your Prayers" and "One Fond Heart" (both from 1879 and the only original songs issued that year) and "Yours Truly (Bessie Jane)" (1880). In the year between

Hawthorne's periods of least activity, Winner would issue only one
new Hawthorne ballad. "Out of Work" (1877, Example 4.3) capitalized
on the difficult financial times facing many Americans and, in true
Hawthorne style, urged listeners to treat those facing difficulties in the
same manner they would want to be treated themselves.

Example 4.3

New works by Winner the composer dramatically increase in comparison to the Hawthorne works of these years. What is especially relevant is that there is a clear shift from publishing instrumentals to publishing sentimental ballads thereby putting him in direct competition with Alice. While many of these weren't hits in the traditional sense, successes probably occurred at roughly the same rate as for Hawthorne ballads from the earlier years. Winner publications (instrumentals are noted) from this decade include "Blow the Horn for Supper, Kate," "The Coolie Chinee," "Resurgam," "Never a Care I Know" (arrangement?) and "These Are Friends That We Never Forget" (1871) as well as "Dolly Varden" (1872 and one of the few topical songs Winner ever wrote beyond the Civil War ballads—capitalizing on a popular women's outfit from Dickens' *Barnaby Rudge*), "Bury Not Thy Neighbor," "Good Words," "Old Boston Bay," "Patchwork (Medley)," "Sour Krout" and "Down the Quiet Valley" (1873).

The decade continued with the "Anna Polka," the "Ball and Pin Galop" (both instrumentals), "Dear Mollie Magee" (an attempt to capitalize on the new vogue for Irish songs), "Lover's Quarrel," "Tom Collins Is My Name " and "Under the Eaves" (1874) as well as "Archiduc Polka" (instrumental), the "Pavilion Model Polka" (another instrumental written for the upcoming centennial celebration), "The Spelling Bee," the "Swallow-Tail Coat" and "Wherefore?" (1875).

"Wherefore?" represents only one of the many 'concert songs' that Winner wrote during the 1860s and 1870s. Requiring a greater degree of skill from the performers (both voice and piano) and stylistically closer to German lieder than anything Winner had written earlier, these songs represent Winner's increasing maturity as a composer (see Example 4.4).

Remaining works from the 1870s include at least one additional concert song, "Gay as a Lark (Canzonetta)" (1876), as well as the "French Polka," "Royal March" (both instrumentals) and "Let Us Cross over the River" (all from 1876) as well as "Baby's Dance," "Dado Waltz" (both instrumentals) and "Creeds of the Bells" (all from 1880). The years from 1877 to 1879 saw no new Winner-authored works.

From a pseudonymous standpoint, Winner continued to use Mark Mason for publishing comic and humorous songs in the 1870s including "On the Board Walk at Cape May" (1871), "And Yet I Am Not Happy" (1873), "Envy Not Your Neighbor" (1873), "I Don't Got Him Now?" (1873), "The Sister's Prayer" (1874, a temperance ballad), "The Weeping Family" (1875) and "Ellen's Babies" (1877). Winner also continued to use Percy Guyer but the apparent decrease may have been a result of the death of Hannah's father, Benjamin Guyer. The name was used only a few times in the late 1870s to publish "The Meeting House Gate" (1877), "I'll Plant a Rose beside Thy Grave" and "Maid and Sparrow" (both in 1878).

Example 4.4

The last two pseudonyms appeared in the late 1870s. Using the name Leon Dore (sometimes given as Dyer), Winner published the "Early Dawn March," an instrumental, in 1878. The other pseudonym from this time was only slightly more active. Under the name Paul Stenton, Winner published two sentimental ballads, "I Would Not Die Away from Home" (1978) and "A Good Send Off to Thee" (1880).

Given the use of so many new pseudonyms, it once again raises the question of his reasons for selecting them. If we are to believe that Winner was as savvy a businessman as he appeared to be, his decision to employ pseudonyms may have been yet another in a series of calculated business decisions. He may, in fact, have thought that the Hawthorne pseudonym was overexposed. As prolific as he was, one might also consider the fact that, for the most part, patriotic, comical or children's songs may have been inconsistent with the style of songs that were, to this time, so closely associated with the Hawthorne name. It may also have been that given the success of the Hawthorne ballads, Winner made a deliberate choice to continue his "rebellion" against the success of Alice Hawthorne and publish at least some of his music under his own name. This would allow him to continue to capture even more of the limelight away from his fictional counterpart.

Given that there are no diary entries or family apocrypha about Winner's choice of pseudonyms, any thoughts about Winner's motives are speculative at best. The most logical reason would seem to arise from sheer numbers. Even if Winner had only used his own and the Hawthorne names for all of the published songs, this would have been a considerable amount—perhaps too much to stay within the limits of Victorian propriety. Prior to the move to Williamsport, Winner had already written in his diary about the somewhat hostile reactions he had received after achieving some level of personal success. This may have weighed on his mind as he entered one of his most prolific creative periods.

A secondary reason would have almost certainly stemmed from his savvy as a businessman. Alice Hawthorne had a reputation and name worth protecting. Winner now did too in his own right. The songs issued under new names were almost always what we might think of as experiments. Winner was working with new ideas: comic songs, children's songs, even the occasional postwar ballad, sacred song, temperance song or topical song. Were these, in fact, reserved for his new pseudonyms as a means to test the waters? Given the preponderance of the evidence (i.e., the published records), this theory might have been true on a case-by-case basis but was certainly not an overriding concern.

Yet another factor may have been a matter of creative choice. Winner may have used these new names for musical efforts he was unsure about. Of the works Winner published under pseudonyms, only a few achieved even moderate success. Were the pseudonyms an attempt to earn additional monies with potentially lackluster efforts while at the same time protecting the Winner and Hawthorne reputations? This situation may very well be the case. Winner's best-known (and often most skillfully composed) works from this period were, in fact, published under either the Winner or Hawthorne name. The concert songs mentioned earlier were exclusively under the well-known names.

From Winner's perspective, these new works may have been throw-away efforts and nothing more.

Two works from this era illustrate the extent to which Winner was branching out creatively. Working in a variety of genres and speak in a variety of musical languages, Winner penned these mature works and reveal a composer approaching the height of his powers.

"Ten Little Injuns"

One of Winner's two key hits of the post-Civil War era include the children's song, "Ten Little Injuns." Equally, if not as well-known as "Der Deutscher's Dog," "Ten Little Injuns" would bring Winner a great deal of fame (he had published the song under his own name). Two stories concerning the creation of the song exist. While not in direct contradiction of one another, together they provide an excellent picture of the composer at work:

> One afternoon, during the hard days of the Civil War, in 1864 to be exact, Sep. Winner had a party at his home for the chil-dren of the neighborhood and it was at this party that the youngsters prevailed upon Mr. Winner to write a humorous song for them. This he consented to do, and in a very short time composed the piece he entitled, *Ten Little Injuns*. It brought much merriment and broad smiles to the children pre-sent, which made Mr. Winner and everybody happy. His wife, and some of the parents of the children present at the party, asked Winner to read it to them, which he did. They became rather enthusiastic about it and suggested that he publish it. This at first he refused to do as he considered it too childish.[30]

The other story, recounted by Mrs. Winner after her husband's death reads similarly:

> *Ten Little Injuns* was written in 1864. Mrs. Winner said of it: "I was in the sitting room with the children and Mr. Winner was in the parlor, drumming on the piano softly. It was 9 o'clock in the evening, and he had been away from us about two hours. Suddenly, we heard a loud laugh and he came in with a page of manuscript in his hand, and read the Ten Little Injuns that he had just composed aloud to us. He chuckled as he read over the foolishness of the words."[31]

One might forgive Winner for resisting any attempts to publish the work at first. Even by Victorian comedy standards, the words are frivolous at best. Winner almost certainly had no idea how well these lyrics would resonate with audiences yearning for lighthearted diversions. In some ways, Winner was almost prescient—anticipating the later vogue (no matter how superficial) for American Indian culture that was part of the Edwardian era.

> Ten little Injuns going out to dine,
> One choked his little self, and then there were nine.
> Nine little Injuns, crying at his fate,
> One cried himself away, and then there were eight.
> Eight little Injuns slept until eleven,
> One overslept himself and then there were seven.
> Seven little Injuns, cutting up sticks,
> One chopped himself in half, and then there were six.
> Six little Injuns, playing with a hive,
> The bumble bees killed one, and then there were five.
> Five little Injuns, going in for law,
> One got in chancery, and then there were four.
> Four little Injuns, going out to sea,
> A red herring swallowed one, and then there were three.
> Three little Injuns, walking in the zoo,
> A big bear cuddled one, and then there were two.
> Two little Injuns, sitting in the sun,
> One got frizzled up and then there was one.

Winner added this postscript in later editions of the piece:

> Happy Injun couple, living by the shore,
> Raised a little family of ten Injuns more.

Perhaps best-known was the chorus of the song:

> One little, two little, three little Injuns,
> Four little, five little, six little Injuns,
> Seven little, eight little, nine little Injuns,
> Ten little Injun boys.

The tune, once Winner overcame his reluctance as to its frivolity, was instantly popular. Its refrain is still sung by children of all ages today (see Example 4.5).

The song was dedicated to his son in its first publication and the cover noted its introduction by Mr. E.F. Dixey (his son's namesake). The song was popular enough to spur at least two derivatives that both credited Winner with the music but not the lyrics. Lee & Walker published the first, "Ten Little Niggers" (or "Ten Little Nigger Boys") in 1869. In the same year, Lee & Walker also published "Ten Undergraduates," a school rivalry song.[32]

Example 4.5

As early as 1879, Birdseye wrote that the song had become a "de-cided hit" in its own time.[33] That the song later became an inspiration for an Agatha Christie play and was used as the theme music for film shorts by the Three Stooges is a testament to its endurance and popularity.

"Whispering Hope" and a Matter of Religion

Throughout Winner's career, we have seen that he would occasionally issue songs with religious themes. While the sudden appearance of such songs might indicate a turn in Winner's life toward religion, no such trend exists. There also seems to be very little direct correlation between significant events in Winner's life, notably the tragedies, and the appearance of these songs. Numbering less than a dozen in total, the sacred songs appear as early as 1854 with "Mercy's Dream" and as late as 1873 with "Lord, Though Knowest That I Love Thee." Virtually all of the sacred songs were published under the Hawthorne name. It may reveal a side of his own personality that he wished to manifest exclusively through Hawthorne. But for Winner, it appears that the decision or motivation to write a sacred song or one with sacred overtones was sporadic at best.

Little is known about Winner's relationship with religion throughout his life. While he was Episcopalian by birth and attended church as a child, in later years he appears to have largely abandoned this practice. However, comments made by family members regarding Winner's religious feelings and activities give an indication that Winner's religion was of a more spiritual nature. Winner was a Mason but if his membership in this group had a direct influence on his actions, we will never know. There is not, surprisingly, any mention of it in his diaries. We only know of his membership through a membership pin passed down through the family.

Beyond that, two quotes from family members reveal a man who held, at the very least, what one might consider unusual spiritual beliefs. In an interview with his granddaughter, Florence Claghorn described how Winner "invented" his own religion. Winner's fondness for nature was a strong feature of his songs and Septimus' granddaughter provides a link between this fondness and his spiritual beliefs, mentioning frequent trips to the woods and fields in which Winner "received" his religion directly from God.[34] While we know that Hannah regularly took her daughters to attend Sunday services, Septimus would rarely go. His attendance would be predicated on whether he was involved in the music in some capacity or, perhaps, if Hannah had badgered him into it.

Whatever form his spirituality took, Septimus' writings (notably in the *Musical Journal*) and his poetry indicates a belief in God. This excerpt from his published poetry would seem to bear out that belief. But it is poetry of a "higher order"—not recounting any particular religious story or theme but more the belief that a higher power shapes the destiny of man:

> How great is God, how grand His perfect work!
> Far in the firmament bright worlds attest

The grandeur of His deeds made manifest.
We call them stars, which unto naked eyes
Present the same unalterable show;
Yet men have learned through study long and deep
To know their forms and journey through the skies.
But ah! How vain, how fruitless is the search
Of human minds, that seek to comprehend
The ways of Him who rules their destinies.
There is no spiritual instinct born
In mortal flesh to understand our life;
There is no lens through which the soul can search,
Or e'er discover aught that lies beyond;
Our short existence ends as vapors lift
And melt to nothing in the atmosphere;
We die untutored as we long have lived,
In this respect no wiser that we were.[35]

None of Winner's sacred songs are still known today. What is often remembered, however, is a sentimental ballad that was interpreted as being religious both for the solace provided by the words and for the melancholy beauty of its melody. "Whispering Hope" was written and first published in 1868 under the Hawthorne moniker. Its music is indicative of Septimus' maturation as a composer. The words themselves show a poet more confident in his idiom than in the past and certainly impacted by the works of his German and English counterparts. The lyrics follow:

Soft as the voice of an angel,
Breathing a lesson unheard,
Hope with a gentle persuasion
Whispers her comforting word.
Wait, till the darkness is over,
Wait, till the tempest is done,
Hope for a sunshine tomorrow
After the shower is gone.

Whispering Hope, Oh how welcome thy voice,
Making my heart in its sorrow rejoice.

If in the dusk of the twilight,
Dim be the region afar,
Will not the deepening darkness
Brighten the glimmering star?
Then when the night is upon us,
Why should the heart sink away?
When the dark midnight is over,

Watch for the breaking of day.

[*Repeat refrain*]

While there is nothing explicitly religious in the work, it became, according to Claghorn, a favorite around the piano on Sunday nights. It isn't surprising that it was so popular given the Victorian sensibilities of the time. Its tone of comfort and, to some extent, redemption through that which we cannot control is one that is echoed in numerous spirituals and hymns but there are other overtones to consider. Writing about the work in 1977, Winner's great-grandson made the following observation:

> To me . . . it carries the message of the Holy Spirit or Holy Ghost as a woman. When I was a young man, I always thought of "the father, the son and the Holy Ghost" as men. But Sep Winner was an unusual man, and wrote most of his music under the pseudonym Alice Hawthorne. So in *Whispering Hope*, Winner speaks of an angel, and her comforting voice. A novel thought![36]

What Claghorn seems to be saying here is that Winner was a man who confronted religion in unusual ways. His perception that angels were represented, in part, by women may be a reflection not only of his relationship with Alice but also of his own upbringing and his relationship with his parents. It may also have been that by speaking in a woman's voice through this song (with Alice as the author), Winner chose to have a woman identify herself with a woman angel as opposed to the convention of a man. Neither Claghorn nor this author have been able to find any particular event or inspiration for the song, but it clearly arose from some highly personal feelings on the part of its author. Winner may have been at least partly inspired by the lyrics of Charlotte Alington Barnard (a.k.a. Claribel), whose lyrics also featured strong personal overtones.

The song was a great success in its original release and stayed in print for a number of years. While not explicitly religious, it has found its way into at least one hymnal, the Southern Baptist's *Broadman Hymnals*.[37] As late as 1961, the song still retained its popularity in religious circles: a poll of favorite hymns conducted by the *Nashville Tennessean* placed "Whispering Hope" fourth (behind "Amazing Grace," "How Great Thou Art" and "Old Rugged Cross") coming in only one vote ahead of "Rock of Ages."[38]

The musical material is of a nature more closely aligned with German lieder than with his antebellum songs. While not as expansive as his concert songs, the song does require a level of musicianship

stronger than that required of many of the Hawthorne ballads, as shown
in the refrain from "Whispering Hope" (Example 4.6):

Example 4.6

In addition to its popularity in the sacred realm, the song enjoyed a
healthy popularity among mainstream audiences. An early RCA Victor
recording by Alma Gluck and Louise Homer extended the song's
popularity to radio. Fifty years after Winner's death, recordings by Jo
Stafford and Gordon MacRae (1948) and the Andrews Sisters (1949),

among numerous others, brought Winner back in to the public eye. According to a midcentury article on the song in *Newsweek*, the Stafford and MacRae recording sold over one hundred thousand copies in its first month and well over half a million copies before its popularity waned.[39] As late as 1969, there were still eight commercial recordings of the song available. Other contemporary artists to record the song included Pat Boone, Charley Pride, Roy Rogers and Dale Evans, and Tennessee Ernie Ford.

While "Whispering Hope" and "Ten Little Injuns" define Winner's breadth and scope as a composer in this period, he faced creative competition very close to home. While Winner was used to the competition from other songwriters both in Philadelphia and around the country, for the first time he faced competition from within his own family.

Sibling Rivalry and "Little Brown Jug"

Winner's brothers would both follow him into the music industry. His youngest brother, Sivori, appears to have spent at least some of his time working as a music publisher and may, from time to time, have lived at his brother's house. He is mentioned in diaries only briefly and little direct details of his life has been found to date. The diary entries that do exist indicate that their relationship was a warm one although they did not see each other frequently. It never appears that there was either collaboration or partnership or a rivalry between them despite the fact that they shared offices briefly in 1872. Where Sivori may have followed his brother into the publishing business, no records exist to indicate that C. Sivori Winner attempted to forge a creative career as a composer at any point.

Quite the opposite can be said of Septimus' immediate younger brother and his father's namesake, Joseph Eastburn Winner. This Joseph was not only a composer of at least moderate repute but what little evidence exists suggests that Joseph and Septimus were partners in business and songwriting rivals at various points in their lives.

Little direct information exists about the life of Joseph Eastburn Winner (1837-1918). As the younger brother of a successful composer, it is not surprising that Joseph would enter the music business. Some sources indicate that Joseph was in the publishing business at various points between 1854 and 1907. One source indicates that from 1845 to 1854 he was in partnership with his brother.[40] This can't possibly be correct given his age at the time, but it is certainly possible that young Joseph may have assisted his brother in the very early years. In addition, at an early age Joseph made some sort of journey, but its purpose and length are unclear. It is certain that Joseph was involved in the store at one point, very likely as an apprentice to his brother. The relationship may not have always been smooth. Septimus recounted at least some of the events in his diary:

June 10, 1852
Made new arrangements with Joseph, concluded to take him
back again in the store.

It appears that the relationship between Septimus and his brother
Joe was an on-and-off one. Joe is mentioned in Septimus' diaries but
only sporadically. Winner would dedicate his 1863 composition, the
"Comet Waltz," to his brother, but the relationship appears to have
been an alternation of episodes of contention and reconciliation. Beyond these entries, there are precious few entries in Winner's diaries
concerning Joseph for the rest of his life. Probably the only other recorded story concerning their relationship is related by Claghorn:

> Septimus had a younger brother named Joseph, who went
> about his work very much like any of the rest of us. Though
> musically inclined, like the other members of the Winner
> family, Joseph had never tried his hand at composing. One day
> he became rather jealous of his brother's fame and popularity
> as a songwriter and announced to the family that he was going
> to write a piece which would sweep the entire country and be
> better known than anything Septimus could write. All of the
> family laughed as Joseph had never written a piece of music in
> all his life. But full of determination and with the zeal of gen-
> ius that may come once in a lifetime to man, Joseph went
> ahead and wrote [a] simple little ditty.[41]

The story may have happened as Claghorn reports it but the time-
line in unclear. Joseph began publishing in 1862.[42] Two earlier publications exist, both under the pseudonym Eastburn, but it is more likely
that these songs were by Septimus.[43] Given the publication years (1852
and 1853), these songs, both published by Septimus, were either his
own works or, perhaps, the result of an older brother giving a supportive leg up. From the style, it would seem that the "Night Spirit Polka"
(1852) and the "Surprise Schottische" (1853) were almost certainly by
Septimus.

When Joseph did begin to issue his works, he followed his
brother's lead, publishing under pseudonyms but, unlike his brother,
primarily using only one. Whether Septimus gave him the idea or if, in
fact, the works from the early 1850s were his, the Eastburn pseudonym
would remain in use until 1897.

By 1869, Joseph had already published at least twenty-five songs,
none of them outright hits. They must have been significant enough to
encourage him to continue. But it was also in this year that Joseph
would achieve his stated goal. He wrote what was destined to become a
nineteenth-century standard, rivaling his brother's songs in popularity

and arguably even eclipsing them on this one occasion. That song, the "Little Brown Jug," (Examples 4.7 and 4.8) has been immortalized in a variety of venues:

My wife and I lived all alone,
In a little log hut we called our own;
She loved gin and I loved rum,
I tell you what, we'd lots of fun.

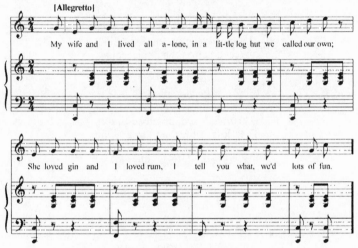

Example 4.7

[*Chorus*]
Ha, ha, ha, you and me,
Little Brown Jug don't I love thee;
Ha, ha, ha, you and me,
Little Brown Jug don't I love thee.

'Tis you who makes my friends my foes,
'Tis you who makes me wear old clothes;
Here you are, so near my nose,
So tip her up, and down she goes.

[*Repeat chorus*]

When I go toiling to my farm,
I take Little Brown Jug under my arm;
I place it under a shady tree,

Little Brown Jug, 'tis you and me.

[*Repeat chorus*]

If all the folks in Adam's race,
Were gathered together in one place;
Then I'd prepare to shed a tear,
Before I'd part from you, my dear.

[*Repeat chorus*]

If I'd a cow that gave such milk,
I'd clothe her in the finest silk;
I'd feed her on the choicest hay,
And milk her forty times a day.

[*Repeat chorus*]

The rose is red, my nose is, too,
The violet's blue, and so are you;
And yet I guess before I stop
We'd better take another drop.

[*Repeat chorus*]

Example 4.8

Joseph's ultimate success may not have had the poetic or musical sophistication of at least some of his brother's work, but it was also no more simplistic in its appeal than "Der Deutscher's Dog" or "Ten Little Injuns." Barring any comparisons, the song was a bona fide sensation and certainly would have given Joseph at least some bragging rights at family events. Interestingly, Joseph would follow in his brother's footsteps yet again, issuing the song under the pseudonym Betta at least once after its initial publication.[44]

Joseph would remain in the music business until his retirement in 1895 despite the fact that he was never as successful as his brother at any other point in his life. Records indicate that he had a shop located at 545 North Eighth Street for the majority of his publishing career. Joseph's on-again, off-again relationship with his brother may, in many ways, have culminated when the two shared this location. At some point in 1885, Septimus and his son Gibson relocated to this same address and remained there through 1886.

While there is no mention of any of this in his diaries, the arrangement must have initially been amicable (as it may have been the first time Joseph was part of Septimus' store). But by 1887, Septimus and Gibson would relocate again, this time to 1736 Columbia Avenue. The move itself might not even be worth mentioning if it weren't for how Septimus and Gibson described their new situation:

> We have everything in the music line no matter where published, anything you want order from us and get it at cut rates. The various music stores (no. 545 N. 8th Street, 2018 Columbia Avenue, &c, &c) formerly occupied by us have been consolidated and we are now established at one stand. No. 1736 Columbia Avenue. We have no connection with any other music store in Philadelphia bearing the name of Winner.[45]

Although no record of any conflict exists and there is no mention of any strife in Septimus' diaries, there must have been some type of conflict that would result in the harshness of language, even by Victorian standards. If what little we know of their earlier relationship is an indication, it is very likely that this business arrangement resulted in at least a partial estrangement—one that, it would seem, would never be fully resolved. Septimus' diaries make little mention of Joseph other than those provided here and while he often spoke warmly of at least some of his other brothers and sisters, he rarely mentions Joseph in such a context. Even later in life, it would seem, the conflicts between them would not be resolved. In many of Septimus' obituaries, there is no mention of Joseph or of his accomplishments.

The brothers would, at least indirectly, come into conflict at least one more time during the course of their careers. Inspired by the same event in Philadelphia, both brothers wrote songs commemorating the occasion. While this wasn't necessarily an unusual situation for matters of national import or to commemorate the many new trends and inventions that were popularized in these years, this event is more unusual in its specificity and relevance to such a specific audience.

Example 4.9

Example 4.9 (*Continued*)

The situation at hand concerned a Philadelphia actor of some repute, Joseph Jefferson, who had been selected to eulogize a fellow actor, one Mr. Holland. When the priest learned that Mr. Holland had also
been an actor, he withdrew his permission to have the services at his
church (an indication, to some extent, as to how actors were still perceived in the nineteenth century). The priest advised Jefferson to make
an application for services at another church nearby where actors were
known to have had funerals in the past. As he left, Jefferson made the
remark "all honor to that little church around the corner!"

The event must have been reported in newspapers at the time or at
least have been the subject of some gossip in Philadelphia, as both
brothers immediately seized upon the occasion to issue new songs. A
comparison of these two songs is revealing in that it shows why Joseph,
on some levels, may have had trouble replicating the success his
brother had enjoyed for more than twenty years.

Stylistically, both versions of "That Little Church around the Corner" are quite similar and are, oddly enough, in the same key. The refrain of Joseph's (Example 4.9) reveals the less-experienced hand compositionally. He maintains a consistent texture throughout and is
completely homophonic in the treatment of Grace Tarleton's text. Septimus' version (Example 4.10), published under the Hawthorne name,
reveals the larger musical palette: less homophonic treatment of the
voices, changing piano textures, some light chromatic alterations and

expressive devices all result in a work, that from a compositional
standpoint, is much more advanced than his brother's (even within the
fairly narrow constraints of American popular song).

Example 4.10

Example 4.10 (*Continued*)

For the remainder of his life, Joseph would never be able to repro-
duce the success of "Little Brown Jug." While he published over fifty
songs in his lifetime, Joseph would never achieve a level of fame that
would place him beside his brother in the annals of music history.

A Matter of Maturity

The Reconstruction era ushered in what might best be thought of as
Winner's most mature period as a composer and songwriter. However,
the notion of maturity cannot be thought of in the same way that the
musicology field looks at the works of Schumann or Brahms. Because
Septimus limited himself to popular songwriting, the constraints of
popular taste would still be paramount in his mind as he issued new
works. Where one might look to the mature works of Schumann or
Brahms in terms of rich harmonic expressiveness, more distant or unusual modulations and innovative uses of form, Winner must be considered in a different light.

As Hamm has noted, there were few advances in the musical characteristics of American popular song in the years following the war.
Because a distinct format had evolved over time and had gained acceptance by the public, the general characteristics discussed in earlier
chapters are still very much the same.

At the same time, Winner and other composers did introduce some
new changes into American popular song, largely as a result of the in-

creasing influence of European music and the growing influence of African American culture. The combination of these elements, combined with the existing popular song model would ultimately yield striking new musical genres such as ragtime, blues and jazz. As this evolution to new styles occurred, Winner and other composers were redefining themselves.

Among the key changes to popular music include the rising popularity of songs in waltz time. With the growing popularity of waltzes in Europe, America could not help but respond. Where a smaller percentage of popular songs in 3/4 time existed before the war, there was a steady increase throughout the 1870s and 1880s.

Composers were also strongly influenced by the increasing popularity of minstrel shows and "Ethiopian ballads," as well as the increasing visibility of professional African American performers such as the Fisk University Jubilee Singers. As a result, many white composers of the former Union states began to adapt and arrange music of African Americans for white audiences. For example, Winner published an arrangement of Daniel Decatur Emmett's "Dixie" with the new words "I'm Captain of a Darkie Band"[46] as well as an arrangement of "Heaven's a Great Way Off."

Far more influential from Winner's perspective was the increasing popularity of the German art song repertory. English composers of the time were also strongly influential. Winner in particular seems to have been strongly influenced by the works of Charlotte Alington Barnard (a.k.a. Claribel). Her use of a more through-composed style and increasing chromaticism (Claribel herself was also influenced by the Germans) would impact Winner's later works, especially those featured in this section. Other aspects of the growing influence of the art song repertory include greater experimentation with song form (within certain constraints) and increasingly independent accompaniments in the piano part. Texts in American songs would also begin to increasingly emulate those of the poets who exemplified the German tradition.

Hamm notes that Winner was among the first composers to create arrangements of African American melodies[47] but given his past statements against "Negro absurdities" in popular songs, it's not surprising that Winner would have done more arrangements from the European repertory as opposed to the African American tradition. Late in life, one of Winner's crowning achievements was a set of piano arrangements of more than one hundred arias and ariettas from the operatic repertory.

Stylistically, Winner's maturity as a songwriter is best revealed through the concert songs that appeared with increasing frequency after the Civil War. There appears to have been no direct correlation with the appearance of these songs and new performance opportunities through professional singers. Instead, it is more likely that they were written as a direct result of the increasing visibility of the German art song repertory as well as a steady increase in the abilities of amateur performers.

Given almost three decades since the explosive popularity of the pianoforte and the concomitant growth of amateur performance in the home,
it's not surprising to see a new generation of amateurs who were better
trained then their predecessors.

Winner's "Gay As a Lark" (1876) provides only one in a number
of excellent examples of concert songs in the mature style. The growing influence of the art song repertory is already evident in this work.
Written in a quick-paced waltz time, the song includes a jaunty introduction that begins to break away from simply introducing the primary
melodic material. The inclusion of a postlude that changes to a lively
tarantella reveals the growing influence of Schumann.

While the piano accompaniment in and of itself maintains the
"oom-pah" texture so prevalent in Winner's music, he also takes significant steps away from it in other sections (notably in the fourth system). Harmonically, the work is slightly more advanced with its inclusion of secondary dominant chords, especially in the fifth system. In
addition, the song is unique in Winner's repertory in that it is in minor.

Despite the introduction of new structural ideas, the song maintains
a more traditional verse and refrain structure that was at least somewhat
more consistent with the style of popular songs of its time (see Example 4.11). The lyrics follow:

Gay as a lark in the sunshine of spring,
Floating and singing upon the wing,
Sporting in pleasure beneath a fair sky
Happy for ever just so am I
So, so, so am I
So, so, so am I
Bright as the sunshine lighting my way
Fair as the moonlight as cheerful as day.

[*Refrain*]
Joyful and happy oh there let me live
Sharing the pleasures that life can give
Free as a birdling let loose on the ark,
Cheerful and merry, "gay as a lark."

Idly I squander the moments away,
Floating and singing upon the wing;
Never, oh never, to murmur and sigh,
Pining and whining? Oh no, not I,
No, no, no not I
No, no, no not I
Let me be merry, let me be gay
Life is too precious to fritter away.

The text is largely consistent with Winner's earlier work with its themes of nature and, at least in this example, does not reveal much European influence. At the same time, however, it is unusually cheerful in its manner. Many Winner texts feature an undertone of sadness or of sad events even in the liveliest and most upbeat of contexts ("Mocking Bird" being one excellent example). Here, no such undertones exist—the text is almost uncharacteristic for its author.

Example 4.11

Example 4.11 (*Continued*)

Example 4.11 (*Continued*)

Perhaps Winner's most mature work, or at least his most ambitious work, is the lengthy epic "Resurgam" which predates "Gay as a Lark" by five years (1871). In this particular case, Winner seems to have been strongly influenced by the German art song repertory and, according to Myers, the character of Christian in John Bunyan's *Pilgrim's Progress*.[48] The text, epic in and of itself, is an eight-stanza poem on a topic typical of the repertory: a young man with no friends or wealth resolves to live a better life. Faced with disappointment at every turn, he resolves to keep trying and does so to his dying day, never fully realizing his goal. The moral, told in the last stanza, urges the listener to live a virtuous life, as he or she will ultimately reap the rewards in heaven. *Resurgam*, or I will rise again, refers to the spirit of the song's subject, a never-give-up attitude that in many ways is characteristic of Winner's own life. Both the text and the music (Example 4.12) can be found on the following pages.

Example 4.12

Example 4.12 (*Continued*)

Example 4.12 (*Continued*)

Example 4.12 (*Continued*)

I
The setting sun, thro' wind-torn clouds,
That closed a dark and stormy day,
Sent to the twilight gloom, that shrouds
The distant east, its feeble ray.
One who had waited long indeed
For sunshine, ere the gloom of night,
Seemed in the purple mist to read
"Resurgam," as it sank from sight.

II
A wayward youth, in feeble health
Thro' sin and dissipation lost;
Bereft of friends, devoid of wealth,

Reviewed his life with tearful cost.
With frenzied brain and knitted brow
Yet with a proud resolve, swore he
An earnest vow, deep, muttered low,
    "Resurgam" shall my motto be.

III

I've learned, said he, how frail is man;
    How dissolute in all his ways.
Now with reform I'll strive and plan
For woman's love, and win her praise.
    But after many days he learned
That none were faultless whom he met:
With spirit crushed, again he turned,
    "Resurgam" was his motto yet.

IV

And though the world dealt harshly, still
    When nearly ev'ry hope had died,
He fought with strong persistent will
'Gainst all the ills that could betide.
    He scorned to murmur at his fate,
    Or, like a coward, sign and fret;
But cried with passion deep and great
    "Resurgam" is my motto yet.

V

But life brought crosses for the man,
And troubles o'er his pathway crept,
    Destroying every hopeful plan,
Till nature, almost conquered, wept.
    Yet like a hero still he fought
The world's reverses with a will:
Whate'er the lesson time had taught,
    "Resurgam" was his motto still.

VI

Whate'er he set in worthy ground
Seemed sown and wasted all in vain;
    A fruitless harvest came around,
For want of Heaven's refreshing rain.
    And when at last the Reaper came
To separate the grain and chaff,
Was placed above a noble name,
    "Resurgam" as an epitaph!

VII

The step of time, with steady pace,
Without a halt goes marching on;
Yet man must find a resting place
When life is o'er – his mission done.
And oh, how blest our final day,
When death comes as a last relief,
If, filled with faith, we then can say,
"Resurgam" is my firm belief!

VIII

We all must strive and work with might,
Till our existence wears away;
Tho' earth may be a long, long night,
Yet Heav'n is one eternal day.
We may endure a world like this,
Awaiting comfort in the next,
If we but take – nor go amiss –
"Resurgam" as our guiding text.

Harmonically, it is probably among the most advanced of the Winner compositions, featuring a series of tonicizations and secondary dominants. At the same time, however, it reveals his inexperience with advanced harmonic idioms, as several of the usages fail to live up to their harmonic expectations. Winner also placed difficult demands on his performer, requiring an extended range of two octaves starting on a low E-flat, awkward melodic leaps (including an augmented octave), and somewhat more complex rhythms created through the frequent use of ties. Winner also makes greater use of the pianistic possibilities of his accompaniment, switching textures frequently and dramatically to underscore the nature of the text. Beyond that, the frequency of expressive marks is indicative of the care Winner took to ensure an accurate and fully realized performance. There is no indication that the song was a success when issued, but the song must have brought Winner a great deal of pride and satisfaction in completing an art song of such epic scale (when seen in light of his more mainstream efforts).

An aspect of Winner's music that is worth noting at this point is that he generally chose to avoid the vogue for topical songs that exploited the events of the day whether they were political, scientific or aspects of popular culture. Many of the new generation of composers turned to these songs to achieve quick sales and temporary fame. Such songs included "The Flying Trapeze" (1868), "Girl on Roller Skates" (1882) and "The Bicycle Girl" (1895). Each in their own way was a commentary on the changing times. Winner wrote few such songs, the most notable being "Dolly Varden" (1872) which capitalized on the popular dress style from Dickens' *Barnaby Rudge*. While topical songs may have had some level of appeal to Winner in terms of quick sales, it may have also been that he wished not to have works of such a nature associated with his ultimate legacy.

Notes

1. Hamm, *Yesterdays*, 253-54.
2. Hamm, *Yesterdays*, 253-54.
3. The hall was also an important part of Philadelphia's political life. Every president of the United States from 1856 to the turn of the century spoke there as part of campaign tours or speaking engagements.
4. Other important predecessors to Amy Beach and Ethyl Smyth include Mary Knight Wood, Mary Turner Salter and Carrie Jacobs Bond.
5. Jane Bowers, "Feminist Scholarship and the Field of Musicology I", *College Music Symposium*, vol. 20, no. 1, 1989, 89.
6. Jerry Korn (*ed.*), *This Fabulous Century 1870-1900* (New York: Time-Life Books, 1970), 28.
7. Henry T. Finck, *Wagner and His Works; The Story of His Life* (New York: Greenwood Press, 1968) vol. 2, 509. In a rare moment of levity, Wagner later said that the "best thing about that composition was the money I got for it."
8. Gerson, *Music in Philadelphia,* 135.
9. Gerson, *Music in Philadelphia,* 124.
10. Prior to many of the women cited earlier, numerous examples of women publishing songs under the pseudonym A Lady, A Lady from state or city or simply a first name can be found among the literature. For additional information on this topic see Tick, *American Women Composers before 1870,* ch. 4 and 6.
11. Arthur Loesser, *Men, Women and Pianos; A Social History* (New York: Simon and Schuster, 1954). For more information, Loesser provides a highly detailed account.
12. Tick, *American Women Composers before 1870.* Tick's detailed account of the rise of music magazines for women is chronicled in chapter 6.
13. Tick, *American Women Composers before 1870,* 92.
14. The details of family weddings and the births of Winner's grandchildren appear in family archival records, copies of which were kindly provided by Melissa Claghorn, the composer's great-great-great-granddaughter.
15. Birdseye, "America's Song Composers, No. VI: Septimus Winner," 436.
16. Septimus Winner, *Penny Music* (Philadelphia: Sep. Winner & Son, 1870). Advertisement on the back of published sheet music edition.
17. This song appears to be lost to history. No records of the song exist in the online catalogs of either the Library of Congress, the Duke archives of American sheet music or the Lester S. Levy collection.
18. Myers, *The Music of Septimus Winner,* 31.
19. From a private letter in the Septimus Winner collection at the Historical Society of Pennsylvania, Philadelphia, donated by Charles Eugene Claghorn.

20. Septimus Winner, *Farewell Song of Enoch Arden (or I'll Sail the Seas Over)* (Philadelphia: Sep. Winner & Co., 1865). Advertisement on the back of published sheet music edition.

21. Septimus Winner, "Salutation," The Musical Journal, January, 1867, vol. 1, no. 1, 2.

22. Septimus Winner, "Music at Home," *The Musical Journal*, Philadelphia, January, 1867, vol. 1, no. 1, 1.

23. It would appear that A.H. Rosewig published several songs in his lifetime, many by publishers with whom Winner already had a relationship. It is unlikely that even Septimus would have created a Rosewig Publishing Company only to issue a few songs under this pseudonym, especially since he had never done it for any other pseudonym (Hawthorne Publishing Company excepted).

24. Each S.W. New song was, in fact, previously published under either the Winner or Hawthorne names.

25. Septimus Winner, "Fashionable Music," The Musical Journal, February, 1867, vol. 1, no. 2, 2.

26. Septimus Winner, *Oil on the Brain* (Philadelphia: Lee & Walker, 1865). Septimus either penned or approved of this advertisement that was featured on the back page of this song, written by his brother Joseph and published under the Eastburn moniker.

27. Winner, *Penny Music,* advertisement on the back of published sheet music edition.

28. See Appendix D for a listing of this short-lived numbering system.

29. Other pseudonyms that cannot be independently confirmed include Tony Emmett and John Holdsworth. Because they have yet to be verified, these names have been excluded from this discussion.

30. Claghorn, *The Mocking Bird,* 38. Essentially the same story is told in Claghorn, *Whispering Hope,* 10. While the 1864 composition date for the piece may be accurate as recounted by Claghorn, "Ten Little Injuns" would not be published until 1868.

31. "Septimus Winner Dead," *The New York Tribune,* December 14, 1902, n.p. Interview with Hannah Winner.

32. Myers, *The Music of Septimus Winner*, 134.

33. Birdseye, "America's Song Composers, No. VI: Septimus Winner," 435.

34. Myers, *The Music of Septimus Winner*, 14.

35. Septimus Winner, *Cogitations of a Crank at Three Score and Ten* (Philadelphia: Drexel Biddle, 1903), 21.

36. Claghorn, *Whispering Hope,* 16.

37. This author's 1940 edition of the *Broadman Hymnal* includes the song (no. 466, no page number) and gives Hawthorne the composing credit.

38. Untitled article, *The Nashville Tennessean*, October 6, 1961, n.p. As quoted in Claghorn, *Whispering Hope,* 2.

39. "Renewed Hope," *Newsweek,* October 3, 1949, vol. 34, no. 14, n.p. as quoted in Claghorn, *Whispering Hope,* 18.

40. "Philadelphia Composers and Music Publishers: Joseph Eastburn Winner (1837-1918)", *Department of Special Collections, University of Pennsylvania Libraries, Keffer Collection of Sheet Music ca. 1790-1895,* http://www.library.upenn.edu/special/keffer/winnerj.html (accessed September

20, 2001). The biography of Joseph Winner listed on this website quotes both of these facts.

41. Claghorn, *The Mocking Bird*, vii.

42. See Appendix I in this volume for a complete listing of Joseph Eastburn Winner's compositions.

43. Claghorn (*The Mocking Bird*, 63) mistakenly identifies other Eastburn compositions as being by Septimus. Equally mistaken, Myers determined that none of the Eastburn compositions was by Septimus.

44. Tick, *American Women Composers before 1870*, 255.

45. Septimus Winner, *Winner's Octavo Music* (Philadelphia, Sep. Winner & Son, 1887), back cover.

46. Spaeth, *A History of Popular Music in America*, 128. This publication cannot be corroborated through other sources and is not mentioned in any of the bibliographical information currently available.

47. Hamm, *Yesterdays*, 261.

48. Myers, *The Music of Septimus Winner*, 50.

Chapter Five (1881-1902)
Legacy

Alice Revealed

Where Septimus appears to have spent much of the Reconstruction era reconciling his relationship with Alice, he would only enjoy the private nature of that reconciliation for a few remaining years. From the information available, Winner gave the first interview publicly acknowledging his dual identity in 1879. Following an interview with George Birdseye, the article appeared in the June 1879 issue of *Potter's American Monthly*.

For Septimus, the article must have felt like quite an honor. Few, if any, articles had appeared about him previously. In addition, the article, part of a series, placed him in excellent company. In the article, titled "America's Song Composers," Winner found himself featured alongside Stephen Foster, George Root, Will Shakespeare Hays, H.P. Danks, Henry Work and, in a stroke of irony, Matthias Keller, his former critic.

Septimus' disclosure of his dual identity in the article is treated with an almost casual nature:

> The name of "Alice Hawthorne," the nom de plume of Sep. Winner, has become a household word; and the *Hawthorne Ballads*, as they are generally called, have for more than a quarter of a century been well known and well loved both in England and in our own country. The many who are familiar with the songs . . . would no doubt be pleased to know something of the author of those and many another good song.[1]

This casual nature may have been a product of the Edwardian times. Given that pseudonyms were still a prominent practice, Birdseye may not have felt that the revelation was worth making anything of. At the same time, it might also indicate that Septimus had become more public about his pseudonyms throughout the 1870s. Given the absence of any evidence to the contrary, it would seem that this article was the first very public acknowledgment of not only his dual identity with Alice but also of the pseudonyms Mark Mason, Percy Guyer and Paul Stenton.

For Septimus, the decision was probably nowhere near as momentous as it might be perceived to be from a modern perspective. The preponderance of pseudonyms among so many writers and musicians and the ultimate revelation of these pseudonyms to the public were very likely treated with more interest than shock or surprise. For most, one might conclude, the fact that Alice and Septimus were one and the same would very likely have been met with a response similar to the casual nature with which it was reported. After all, it would not have changed anyone's opinion about the creations themselves. The songs were the songs, regardless of who may have written them.

One might wonder if the gender issue would have brought about somewhat more of a response. However, one must view the circumstances with Edwardian sensibilities rather than contemporary ones. There would have been no speculation whatsoever that the nature of Septimus' disguise would indicate anything deviant of a sexual nature. Beyond that, the general public had seen other artists who took nom de plume of the opposite gender (although admittedly not many). Frankly, if Winner had felt in any way that taking a woman's name as a pseudonym would or could have even hinted at any such thought, he most certainly would have never done so. As there is no indication that Alice represented anything even remotely associated with cross-dressing, gender confusion or any other gender disassociation, Septimus' ultimate decision to reveal himself must have stemmed from other motives.

These motives very likely stemmed from his complex relationship with Alice. Initially, Alice's astounding success, especially after "Mocking Bird," would have thwarted any notions of revealing his dual identity. Winner had, to put it mildly, a "meal ticket" and needed to, at least initially, let Alice's fame run its course before he could acknowledge his identity without hurting Alice.

Perhaps unfortunately for Winner, Alice's career saw no signs of slowing down. Winner, faced with the growing popularity of Alice's career and the relative nonexistence of his own, in many ways had no choice but to attempt to equal her success, but on his own merits and by his own name. It is here that he begins to publish more than just arrangements and instrumentals under his own name.

At the point when Winner was criticized for his own work and especially when he was compared unfavorably to Alice, the jealousy that arose between Septimus and his alter ego would never have permitted Winner to admit the duality. Winner, whether consciously or not, must have been driven to achieve the same success that he gave to

Alice. Having sacrificed his own success, Septimus acted in a way that reveals he was determined to win that same success on his own merits.

As Winner achieved at least some level of success, especially after "Give Us Back Our Old Commander," "Ten Little Injuns" and "Der Deutscher's Dog," Septimus almost certainly softened in his attitude toward Alice. Having spent much of the Civil War era on two parallel career tracks and having achieved success with both of them (and in different genres), Winner very likely achieved a comfort level with the reconciliation. That comfort level with both careers was very likely behind the decision to launch still more pseudonyms. Winner, his ego healed, and Alice, still popular after fifteen years, could *both* proceed forward. Septimus, now managing two careers, may have seen his next career as trying to replicate this success with a new identity. As a result, Winner launched Paul Stenton, Mark Mason and Percy Guyer in the hope of achieving success in new arenas.

Winner would then spend much of the late 1860s and early 1870s managing his multiple careers, not only as a songwriter under so many different names, but also as a publisher, pedagogue, poet and magazine publisher. Despite the fact that Winner had fewer successes in these years than he had had before the war, it *was* Winner's most productive period.

As the 1870s progressed, Winner was very likely beginning to rest on his multiple laurels. He had achieved the success he wanted, on every front. His careers as composer, teacher and pedagogue were all well-established and earning him an income. Septimus may have seen this as a new opportunity to relax and enjoy his declining years. Not only must have Septimus been reasonably comfortable financially but, as it is critical to remember, each of his careers was a means to a financial end. Winner never gave any indication that composition was a means to ensure some kind of immortality. Much to the contrary, it was a way to support his family and provide for them in a manner consistent with middle-class American ideals. As the 1870s drew to a close, Winner had reached two different kinds of comfort level where these notions are concerned: that of at least a comfortable financial status, as well as a parity that took him over twenty years to achieve with Alice. It was these comfort levels that almost assuredly led him to acknowledge not only Alice but the remaining pseudonyms as well.

At the time of the interview, Winner gave every indication that his multiple careers would remain as active as they had been previously:

> Mr. Winner is still writing his ballads under his own name, or the pleasant nom de plume of Alice Hawthorne, and words and music seem just as new and fresh and full of sentiment and feeling as in the first years of his career as a popular songwriter, more than a quarter of a century ago.[2]

While this was true on pedagogical and entrepreneurial levels, Winner's career as a songwriter was beginning to wind down. Alice, meanwhile, would only appear before her musical public three more times. Where Winner may have had the best of intentions (or at least created the best of impressions for his interviewer), Alice's career was, for all intents and purposes, ending if not over.

Family Matters

At the dawn of the 1880s, Winner found himself beginning to slow down a little. Never one to seek out crowds and public events, he began to retreat more and more into the comfort of family and friends. Much of this would take the form of spending time with his son Gibson, still his business partner, and his daughter Margaret. The family, living on Fishers Lane in the Philadelphia suburb of Germantown, would move in August 1881 to Septimus' final home located at 1706 North Sixteenth Street, still in Germantown. Winner, who, as time wore on, would become meticulous in the recording of his financial status, carefully calculated the cost of the move in his diary:

Cost of house at 1706 N. 16th street	$5500
Carpentering	126
Plumbing	62
Painting	72
Insurance policy	72
Sundry expenses, repairs, &c.	10
Paper hanging	35
5% at interest on 5500	275
Taxes	87
Water rent	16
Gas	32
Coal	32

The article (one extract appearing on pages 138-39) makes some cautious exaggerations here in that Winner's daughters Emily, Ella and Mary Ann (Chick) and his son Gibson were all happily married and living on their own by this time (Margaret still lived at home). While they were frequent visitors to their father's home, Birdseye's portrait idealizes his subject in this case.

While Birdseye paints an image of an ideal family for his readers, both Septimus and Hannah would experience a series of personal losses that no doubt cast a shadow on the dawn of the Edwardian era.

The first of these losses had occurred prior to the beginning of the 1880s. In 1878 (the exact date is unknown), Septimus' father, Joseph Winner, would pass away.[3] No diary from 1878 has survived that might give us an indication of his feelings at the time. However, Joseph's passing must have been a bittersweet occasion. After years and years of Joseph's intolerable behavior, Septimus must have been, on some levels, relieved to be able to finally put his father behind him. At the same time, Winner must have also been extremely saddened.

As the 1880s dawned, Septimus' losses would be compounded over and over again. Although not noted in his diary of 1883, Winner's treasured uncle William E. Winner passed away at the age of sixty-eight. Uncle William's passing was very likely much more traumatic for Septimus that his father's. In many ways a father figure, William Winner was instrumental in helping Septimus to get his first start as a creative artist. It is very likely that it was William's support and encouragement that propelled Septimus into music and the career that would sustain him throughout his life.

Later in 1883, Septimus would experience more tragedy in his life. His diary of the time relates the circumstances:

August 3, 1883
Mom [Hannah] and Maggie went to Elm Station to see Emily and Willie [her husband], all were very well and happy.

August 6, 1883
Emily died yesterday at Elm. Went up to New Britain this morning for mom, May Keiner and Maggie, brought them home in the afternoon, a terrible scene to witness. Everything happened so suddenly, an awful day at home. Gibson and Florie [his wife] came up from Atlantic City and many friends called on us . . . Emily was taken sick on Saturday night and died on Sunday evening, perfectly conscious and willing to face death without fear. A noble girl, always.

Winner's oldest daughter, Emily Hawthorne Winner Claghorn, died at her home from what, at the time, was described as a case of cholera morbus, a severe form of gastroenteritis. There is some speculation that her death was caused by digesting watermelon seeds, which the family had for dessert after lunch on Saturday. The cause notwithstanding, the effects were considerable not only on Winner but on Emily's family:

August 7, 1883
Poor Eugene [Emily's husband], I pity him sadly, he seems heartbroken and quite overcome. Hannah takes the loss terribly, God be with us.

Septimus and Hannah, having already lost two children, would face the unimaginable prospect of losing a third. While it had been more than twelve years since the death of Francis Dixey Winner, the impact must have been considerable. This tragedy would then be compounded further almost exactly a year later:

August 11, 1884
A very fine morning, had an earthquake yesterday, felt it moving sensibly at the house. Ella sick, all the rest are well, a dark gloomy afternoon.

August 15, 1884
Ella died at Doylestown this morning at 3 o'clock. All the folks home again at noon, dreadful sad time at the house.

August 19, 1884
Ella was buried this morning at North Laurel Hill, a sad time. Gibson returned to Atlantic City after the funeral.

Winner's second-oldest child, Ella Guyer Winner McCurdy, died of typhoid fever. No doubt both Septimus and Hannah would have drawn their remaining children even closer. Gibson, as a result of his ongoing partnerships with his father, would have already been close to home. Margaret, still living at home, would remain devoted to her parents and would ultimately never marry. The only question mark among the remaining children was Mary Ann (Chick). While there is no indication of any strain in their relationship, Chick seems to have had a more elusive relationship with her parents. She is mentioned the least frequently in the diaries and only for family occasions after her marriage.

Other losses would follow: the mother of Emily and Mary Ann's husbands in August 1895; Emma Gibson (the wife of his son's namesake) in February 1896; and others. No doubt Septimus was beginning to feel his age as he and Hannah watched so many around them pass away. Both Septimus and Hannah stayed as active as they could, but they were not immune to their advancing years.

Business Matters

Septimus and his son Gibson maintained an active business partnership together for much of these remaining years. As Septimus grew older, he was probably less and less interested in the day-to-day operations of the business and let much of the management of the concern fall to his son. Initially located on Spring Garden Street in 1880, they would move far less than Septimus had in previous years.

Septimus and Gib made one move in 1885, apparently joining forces with Septimus' brother, Joseph Eastburn Winner, at his location on North Eighth Street. As discussed earlier, the mechanics behind this arrangement are unknown. Septimus and Gib may have been unable to sustain the store on Spring Garden, or perhaps this was some way toward achieving another reconciliation between brothers. Whatever the motives behind it, the arrangement was short-lived. In 1887, Gib left this new business and opened a new store at 1736 Columbia Avenue. At the same time, Septimus appears to have begun one last partnership. The firm Winner & Guyer published a few works from the Eighth Street address but would last less than one year. Septimus' partner in this endeavor, almost certainly a family member, is unknown. It may have been that a family member gave him some seed money to begin publishing again and that Septimus chose to honor that favor by using the Guyer name in the firm.

By 1888, Septimus would abandon Winner & Guyer and rejoin his son at their new Columbia Avenue location. As shown in the advertisement for Septimus' and Gib's new venture on page 165, the parting between Septimus and his brother Joe was not an amicable one—given the extent to which he and Gib made it very clear that they were not affiliated with any other publishers and store owners in town.

Septimus and Gibson would stay at the Columbia Avenue location for the next seven years. It would seem, however, that for a brief period they withdrew from the publishing business and focused more on selling instruments and sheet music, as there were no new songs issued from 1889 to 1891. In 1892, Winner issued two new songs but, for reasons that remain unclear, used his brother's Eighth Street location as business location despite the fact that the Columbia Avenue store was still active.

The Sep. Winner & Son business would ultimately remain active until 1895, when Septimus evidently decided that he was done with the music business. His diary makes what almost looks like a passing reference to the event:

June 13, 1895
James Gibson and myself settled up our partnership and passed receipts, destroying our original agreement. A final close.

After forty years as an entrepreneur, Winner was finally out of the business. However, it seems as if retirement didn't suit him as well as he might have hoped. Winner would frequently visit his son's store and would often manage the enterprise in his son's absence. As late as 1901, Winner wrote the address in his diary, clearly a reminder of his on-going involvement even in these late years:

January 1, 1901
J. Gibson Winner, Music Store, Orchestra Office, Music Studio, 1736 Columbia Avenue, Philadelphia.

It is difficult to ascertain exactly how comfortable financially Septimus was in these later years. While he continued to earn royalties not only for his original songs but also for his pedagogy books and arrangements, he was also still producing them, completing the massive set of arrangements *Grand Opera Melodies* (fifty works arranged for guitar) and *Light Opera Melodies* (fifty works arranged for mandolin) in 1901 (Septimus was paid $110 each for these books by Oliver Ditson).

Winner was meticulous in recording his income and expenses in his diaries. While this might be indicative of a level of ongoing concern on his part, it might also be seen as simply good record keeping. It might also be the product of the fact that Septimus genuinely loved what he did.

Septimus' meticulous record keeping, however, may not have extended to his keeping watch over the sales of his songs. In an 1879 letter, written apparently to resolve some form of business dispute, he seems almost oblivious to the relative sales of his works:

Dear Sirs,

I really cannot tell how many copies of *Birdie's Ball* have been printed. It was not a success when first issued. Shortly after I printed it I sold the plates with many others to Messrs. Lee & Walker. When they failed in business, Oliver Ditson & Co. came into possession of them.

I am sorry to have unintentionally infringed upon your rights by being imposed upon myself. Suppose you write to Ditson & Co. and see if you can fix it up with them.

I have just written a published a new song entitled *Don't Forget to Say Your Prayers* a copy of which I send you by mail. It is now being ordered 500 copies at a time, and would be just such a song as you could use in a new book. If it would be of any recompense for my mistake, I will allow you to introduce it in any new book you may issue. Yours respectfully.[4]

Winner was still active as a pedagogue, issuing several new series of books including the *Ideal Method* (starting in 1882), the *New American School* (begun in 1883), the *Self-Instructor* series (started in 1886) and ultimately the *Eureka Method* series (beginning in 1891) among many others. He also expanded his repertory of instruments to include mandolin (1884), zither (also in 1884), double bass (1894) and trombone (first publication date unknown).

Beyond that, Winner was still active as a private teacher. The extant diaries from 1880 to 1902 all indicate that he continued to see private students. As late as 1898, Septimus maintained roster of thirty-one students, nine in violin, seven in guitar, thirteen in mandolin and one each in piano and banjo. It is unlikely Septimus would have needed such additional funds. It is far more likely that he taught most of these students for the sheer joy of doing so.

Of particular note was the career of a young violin student Septimus was teaching at the time. Victor Schertzinger, at the time a teenage violinist, would visit Winner frequently for lessons. Later, Schertzinger would become a well-known face in Hollywood, not only as a film composer and songwriter (he wrote the song "Arthur Murray Taught Me Dancing in a Hurry") but also as a film director (he would direct two of the Bing Crosby-Bob Hope "Road" films).

Returning to his financial condition, it would seem as though the earnings from royalties and his partnership in the store was not enough to sustain the Winner family. Septimus and Hannah also appear to have taken in boarders at their Sixteenth Street home. Winner's diaries make frequent mention of a Miss Turner who boarded with the family and, it would seem, became very much a part of the family, keeping company with Septimus and often accompanying Maggie to various concerts and events. Winner noted her departure with at least a hint of sadness if the description of the day's weather can be taken as an indication of his emotions:

December 19, 1901
Dark, dismal morning. Miss Turner left us after a seven years stay.

The Winners also took in a young doctor, Dr. Woldeck, who would be invaluable to Winner as his health began to decline. What is most likely the case was that, where the money was concerned, it didn't hurt to have more of it but taking in boarders may have also been a way to fill an increasingly empty house.

As shown in Figure 5.1, Winner's output of songs began to drop dramatically in the years after 1880. In the years 1883, 1884, 1886 and 1889-1891, no new songs were published, under any pseudonym, and Winner would stop publishing original songs and instrumentals entirely after 1894.[5] While there is no direct reference to it in his diaries, one might surmise that Septimus saw the taste for popular music beginning to change, especially after 1890. Sensing that the sentimental ballads on which he had built his reputation were no longer as popular with the musical public, he may have gradually decided to stop composing in response to this or perhaps through an unwillingness or inability to adapt to the overwhelming changes occurring as a result of African American influences in popular music.

Also significant was the gradual phasing out of Alice Hawthorne. With his dual identity exposed, the cachet that made Alice special in the minds of the musical public was gone. As a result, there would be little reason to perpetuate her career.

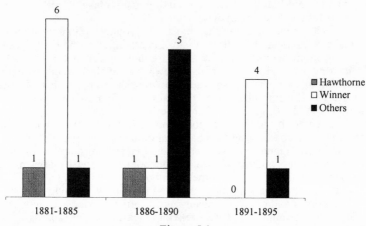

Figure 5.1

The remaining Hawthorne ballads of these years were both sentimental ballads, "Pass Us Not By" (1881) and, following what appears to have been a seven year gap, "Good-Bye Dear Mother" (1888). Neither song was especially successful. Winner's output under his own name was also decreasing, as he published only eleven new songs including three instrumentals between 1881 and 1894. These songs included "The Gypsy's Tent" (1882), the concert song "The Robin's Roundelay" and the patriotic ballad "The Soldiers Are Passing" (both also from 1882). Additional songs included "A Spring Carol" (1892), "A Little Closer Please," "Sue, My Darling Sue" and "Winter Sweets" (all from 1893-94), and the instrumentals "Fritz Lullaby" (1882), "Little Fairy Polka" (1882) and "Winstar Gavotte" (1887).

Winner's other pseudonymous alter egos would also remain active in these closing years, occasionally eclipsing either Hawthorne or Winner in volume. Just as he held Alice aside for the publication of new sentimental ballads, he held the others aside for the publication of comic or children's songs.

The Percy Guyer pseudonym was still reserved for comic or children's songs, making only two more appearances in these final years. The first was the humorous ballad "Don't Blame Your Wife" (featured in Example 5.3) in 1885. Guyer's final appearance (coinciding with the end of the Winner & Guyer publishing concern although not published by it) was "Christmas Comes But Once a Year" (1887), a children's song and one of Winner's personal favorites in later life. Apsley Street also made one appearance in these years with the children's song "The Party at the Zoo" (1888).

Example 5.1

Mark Mason would remain the most active pseudonym in these final years, publishing four songs between 1887 and 1892, all comic ballads. Winner issued "Johnny Get Your Hair Cut" (1887), "Let Her Go Gallagher! Don't Be a Clam" (also in 1887), "Just Gone Out"

(1888) and the "Lilliputian's Beer Song" (1892). As before, the Mason pseudonym would be held aside almost exclusively for comic ballads. While none of the songs appear to have been successful, Winner did use them to help his son launch the sporadically used publishing entity, J. Gibson Winner (still at the Columbia Avenue address) in 1887.

Example 5.2

Winner would also write one more patriotic ballad, "God Save Our President" (Example 5.1 and also called "A Nation's Prayer") after the assassination attempt of President James Garfield. The song, featuring an extended introduction, reveals the extent to which the chromaticism of the German art song repertory that had previously only been found in his concert songs, had now become de rigueur in almost all of his original works. In addition, it demonstrates still more growth on Winner's part as a composer. An increased vocal range and the tonicizations of both the dominant and relative minor keys show a level of musical variety and understanding not regularly seen in the earlier works. As a song expressly written as a popular song, it demonstrates how far the popular genre had come. Winner was by no means alone in his use of these musical devices—most composers of the day employed this musical language in songs intended for "parlor use."

The chorus of this song (shown in Example 5.2) would also reveal Winner's increasing comfort level with contrapuntal activity between voices, as he had already demonstrated in songs as early as "Whispering Hope" but also in later works like "That Little Church around the Corner."

On Being a Poet

As Alice's career drew to a close, Winner may have wanted to provide her with a final legacy to the musical and literary public. He may have also wanted to use her name for a final moneymaking opportunity. The motive behind it may never fully be known but Winner, having now spent almost three decades as not just a composer but as a poet, must have gradually felt that his nonmusical poetry deserved attention not only on its own merit but also beyond the ears of his immediate family.

It is interesting that Winner chose Alice to be the first vehicle for bringing his poetry to publication. Just as he had done with his original songs, Septimus chose to conceal his identity with Alice's poetry, even after the Birdseye article acknowledging their dual identity. As before, if the effort failed, it would likely not reflect badly on him. This might explain one reason behind the title of the work, *Hawthorn Leaves*. Perhaps Septimus left out the final *e* of Alice's name as a means, at least initially, to conceal his identity.

Beyond using Alice's misspelled name for this volume of poetry, Winner also chose to issue the book through a publisher far away from home. Published in 1886 through the Gazette Press in Louisville, Kentucky, the *Hawthorn Leaves* collection contains just over three dozen original poems, none of them used as part of an original song. By now, the prominent features of Winner's song lyrics have been well-covered and the poetry of *Hawthorn Leaves* continues their well-worn tradition. Poems of nature abound as in "Let the Sunshine In," "Under the Willow," "April," "Only a Rose Bud," "Beauty Land," "A Heavy Rainfall" and "The Merciless River" (written after the flood of 1884). Other themes featured in the volume include mother and family ("Kiss Me Mother Dear," "Little Foot-Prints") the importance of home ("A Dream of Home") and lost love ("My Heart is Aching for Thee," "Hopeful Heart," "Broken Heart" and "My Love For You"). However, Winner also used the opportunity to write poetry on topics that many may have chosen to avoid.

In "The Southern Woman," Winner would address, however superficially, the issues facing women in the Southern states which many would not address even twenty years after the war was over:

> In our own dreamy thoughts of countries grand,
> We kindly turn to that sweet, sunny land
> With a verdant sod, and skies of pale blue,
> With brave, gallant men, and their daughters true,
> Whose sunny smiles—how delightful to see—
> Prove solace to man in Southland free.
> Woman's fond heart, in the land of flowers,
> Was treasured by him in his darkest hours;
> When widows were left, and little ones, too,
> Left proud on the world with nothing to do,
> She pressed a Jasmine close to her lip,
> Like the little bee, its honey to sip.
> The dear little bee culls from the flower—
> Hers was a hive, with a "soulful power;"
> And now she can work, and with willing hands
> Will try to compete with all other hands.

In "Our Confederate Dead," Winner takes an even more forgiving and peaceful tone and shares his thinking that, regardless of politics, God loves every man equally.

> Throw open the gate—near the soft velvet sod
> The dead are so near us, and yet so near god;
> Speak in sweet accents, with a whispering voice;
> Among the rude graves you may find your own choice.
> Tread on the grass lightly and lower each breath,
> For here Southern soldiers are sleeping in death
> So far from their homes 'neath the tropical skies—
> From mothers and daughters, their sweethearts and wives.
> O bring the sweet garlands of red, white and blue,
> Sweet roses and flowers of every hue;
> With love we will strew them all over each grave;
> Shed tears at the thoughts of the "Cause" they would save.
> Oh, poor fallen heroes, the noblest of men!
> You fought with ambition, you fought to the end,

And while you thus sleep in a far distant clime
Loved ones endeavor your poor graves to find.
Some have a rude slab, while others have none,
But the sod on their graves has beautiful grown,
God's mercy in this is alike unto all;
He loveth his children, and on them will call
In hovel or palace, on water or land;
In the dear quiet homes and the battle so grand,
He raised his broad hand o'er the ranks of the Blue,
While stronger in number, the great army grew;
He stretched out his broad arm o'er the ranks of the Gray,
Who died with the honors of battle array,
Bring forth the sweet flowers, bedew them with tears;
Poor mothers have grieved and been sighing for years;
Fathers are sad, and while bending with sorrow,
Oft breathe the sweet words "A bright to-morrow!"
While sisters have wept o'er a dead brother's fall,
Poor sweethearts have pined the dearest of all.
O bring the bright flowers! Soldiers are sleeping,
And those who have loved them far away weeping.
O strew them around with a light, gentle tread,
On the graves of our brave "Confederate Dead."

The relative success of the *Hawthorn Leaves* volume is not known.
Winner, however, must have been pleased by the publication, as he
would take this path again towards the end of his life.

As Winner's death drew near, he was busily completing another
volume of poetry, this time to be published under his own name. While
he died before it was completed, his descendants would ultimately see
that the volume was published in 1903, by Philadelphia publisher
Drexel Biddle. Entitled *Cogitations of a Crank at Three Score and Ten*,
this volume of poetry, his last of any kind, represents a man who has
reached an ultimate peace in his own creative identity not only with
himself but with Alice and all the others he had struggled with or
against over the years.

The poetry in *Cogitations* shows Winner at his greatest level of
comfort with himself, unafraid to display who he was and unconcerned
as to what others might think. As a result, it is also most revealing of a
man who, in many ways, had spent four decades living in the shadows
of others, especially Alice. Just as he allowed himself to express difficult emotions through Alice in *Hawthorn Leaves*, he was now able to
stand by his own convictions on his own merits. It is no wonder his
family worked so hard to see the book published. Even the introduction, written by his grandson, emphasizes the many different sides (or
better yet, personalities) of the man in question.

   The book contains some sixty-eight poems, none of them previously published nor used as song lyrics. It is divided into nine large sections, each one clearly designed by Winner to reflect the character of the poetry—emotional, pastoral, cynical, lyrical, satirical, incidental, occasional, ironical and sentimental—characters, it would seem, that are reflective of Winner's own personality.

   In Winner's emotional personality, he returns to his awe of nature and, in many ways, uses his religious beliefs as a vehicle for his emotional expression, as in the following poem, excerpted earlier:

> God is the Master of the universe,
> The great Creator of all living things,
> And man is but a mite exceeding small
> Who cannot deign to change one given law,
> He binds the waters with one mighty wall
> That frail humanity dares not remove,
> He sends the tempest with its awful force
> That none can check nor venture to obstruct.
>
> I gaze upon the earth about my path,
> And smile with pleasure on the varied scene,
> I see the Maker's mighty hand in all
> And lift my heart in earnest thanks to Him.
> The waters and the land spread far and wide,
> Yet not an acre claim I as my own,
> It matters not, no selfish grasping hand
> Can hide His handiwork from human eyes.
>
> The overlooking stars, that hang on high,
> Tell of the great Almighty's perfect power,
> They glisten as the diamonds of His crown
> And none can blot them from the arch of Heaven.
> I hear the songsters soaring overhead,
> Their cheerful music, 'neath the varied skies;
> I see the splendid flowers about my path,
> And breathe their odor sweet, in ecstacy.
> What if the cultured garden be fenced in,
> The roadside and the meadows still must bloom;
> The hills, the valleys and the woodlands yield
> A thousand beauties free to every soul;
> The great Jehovah ever gives to man
> A multitude of blessings to enjoy,
> And he who cannot these appreciate
> Should not complain where others must rejoice.
>
> How great is God, how grand His perfect work!

Far in the firmament bright worlds attest
The grandeur of His deeds made manifest.
We call them stars, which unto naked eyes
Present the same unalterable show;
Yet men have learned through study long and deep
To know their forms and journey through the skies.
But ah! How vain, how fruitless is the search
Of human minds, that seek to comprehend
The ways of Him who rules their destinies.
There is no lens through which the soul can search,
Or e'er discover aught that lies beyond;
Our short existence ends as vapors lift
And melt to nothing in the atmosphere;
We die untutored as we long have lived,
In this respect no wiser than we were.

The follow excerpt reveals Winner's "lyrical" side. It allowed him, once again, to explore some of the painful issues of Reconstruction:

Southern roses brightly bloom,
And spreading vines their shadows throw,
Shedding shade and sweet perfume
O'er the wrecks of long ago.

Pensive mothers kiss their babes,
Sighing still for treasures lost,
Sons and daughters sigh alas!
Dreaming o'er life's tearful cost.

Southern roses still shall bloom
O'er the dust of fallen braves,
Bloom for sons and daughters fair
To decorate their early graves.

In another excerpt, from Winner's "satirical" side, he could have easily been writing about his now fifty-year relationship with Hannah:

King Solomon was wise when he declared
Out of a thousand women well compared
A truly honest female found he none,
And yet among the men but only one!

We have our happy moments with the sex
However much their manner may perplex;
We have our diff'rences at times, although
Our hearts with love for them may overflow;

Misunderstandings, like the clouds above,
Roll on till those estranged return to love.

Lastly, returning to Winner's "lyrical" side, we get a flavor of the
man and his attitude toward his life:

"Which is life's most happy season?"
Asked an aged man one day
Of a group of merry schoolboys,
Gathered 'round his house at play.
Some then, laughing, told him "summer,"
Some the spring did most enjoy,
But not a welcome word for winter
Had each bright, light-hearted boy.
Then the old man answer'd, smiling,
"There is joy our whole life through,
But the eyes of boys see never,
As the eyes of old men do,"
"Three score years ago the spring time
Was a happy time to me,
After that I loved the summer,
With the blossom, bird and bees
Youth and manhood this passed o'er me,
Happy seasons, though they fled,
Now I love the golden autumn,
With its leaves so brown and dead;
And when comes at last the winter
It shall find me happy too,
For when every branch is leafless
I shall see the stars shine through."

A Matter of Closure

In the last few works to be published in his lifetime, Winner's style
shows an evolution that transcends the changes of the 1870s. As already shown in "God Save Our President," Winner's sense of harmony
was changing. No longer confined by, perhaps, his own sense of what
amateur audiences could perform, his use of harmony expands to reveal
even more influence from his European counterparts. Secondary dominants, tonicization of closely related keys and chromatic inflections all
find their way into his vocabulary, even in the comic songs as shown in
the excerpt from "Don't Blame Your Wife" (Example 5.3).

Similarly, Winner employs these devices in one of his last concert
songs, a more through-composed effort that incorporates many of the
harmonic devices mentioned earlier. It also features a wider range (in-

cluding an optional *ossia* for high soprano) as well as the 3/4 meter that would predominate so many songs toward the end of the century.

Example 5.3

"The Robin's Roundelay" (Example 5.4) shows Winner at his most flexible as a composer. After years of evolution, in many ways, he has

Example 5.4

Example 5.4 (*Continued*)

Example 5.4 (*Continued*)

come full flower and is comfortable with the evolution of musical genres not only in American popular song but also of his own style. In both
this piece and in "Don't Blame Your Wife," note how Winner continues to incorporate a variety of different pianistic textures to maintain
compositional interest and create a sense of call and response between
the voice and piano in the middle sections. Beyond that, as he did in
"Resurgam," Winner continues to exploit the expressive possibilities of
both the voice and the instrument, happily coloring his musical ideas
not only with ornaments but also with tempo changes befitting the
character of the song. Winner accomplishes this within the constraints
of what would still be considered consistency with the popular song
repertory but with a flair that is only evident in his latest works. If, as
some might point out, the early successes are indicative of savvy musical instincts, in these later works like "Robin's Roundelay," we have
savvy instincts combined with musical instiinct and elasticity. Here,
Winner embraces everything that is his style and also that which was so
crucial to the shaping of the Hawthorne ballads over the years.

The Public Face

The 1879 interview with Birdseye provided Winner with the first of a
series of publicity pieces that would feature the composer for the remainder of his life. Returning to Birdseye, the article provides a romanticized insight into the now fifty-three-year-old composer:

In his personal appearance, Sep Winner is quite stout, but tall in proportion, weighing some two hundred and twenty-five pounds; a face beaming with intelligence and good nature, gray hair, mustache and short stiff beard; his manner, frank and affable . . . Altogether a hale, hearty, cheerful well-preserved successful man; and to look at him you would scarcely suppose that he had already passed his fifty-third birthday. He is able to boast that he has never been confined to the house by sickness for longer than a day at a time in his life . . . He is a genial companion, a good conversationalist, quick at repartee, fond of a joke, and full of anecdote and pleasant reminiscences.[6]

Much later, Winner would begin to garner the accolades and praise that many felt was due him after a lifetime in music. By and large, the interviews talk of his upbringing and the stories behind the creation of his most famous songs (thereby leading to the multiplicity of stories surrounding their creation).

Beyond the expected material, however, several quotes give insight not only into the man himself (or at least how he chose to present himself to the public) as well as into the songs he wrote. In an interview with the *Philadelphia Press* in May 1901, Winner was asked if he had earned much money from his songs:

"Decidedly, no," was the quick reply. "Of the two hundred or more songs that I have written and set to music, most were written in a single night and sold the next day at a price so absurdly small that I would rather not tell you."[7]

And when asked about the song that he considered his best, Winner replied:

Whispering Hope and that recalls to me what I consider the most delicate compliment ever paid me. It was during a performance of *A Mid-Summer Night's Dream*, which was given at the Walnut Street Theater about twenty years ago, that this song was sung, and while its effect on the audience was very pleasing to me, it was nothing to the emotion I experienced when after the play a friend of mine came to me and said: "Wasn't that a grand song? Who but Mendelssohn could write such music." I am afraid I took him seriously at the time but I have since taken his remark as a reflection on his musical appreciation.

Perhaps most interesting of all, Winner was asked if had every composed anything outside of popular songs. To this question Winner replied:

> "No; absolutely nothing. I had an idea for an opera many years ago, but it died ere it saw the light"—and this with characteristic modesty—"the public and I are so much the better off."

Perhaps this opera was a folly of his youth. In Winner's 1853 diary, a hastily written set of notes appears upside-down in the back of the diary. There is no way to tell when exactly this sketch was written or if it was for the abandoned opera. What it is, however, is a scenario for some kind of dramatic work (the actual structure of which is difficult to determine)—perhaps the very opera Winner once mused about:

> *Scene 1*: railroad station, people waiting the arrival of train, several incidents: as the train is heard in the station approaching; railroad group with chorus of passengers. Hero arrives on the same train—makes observations and falls in love with heroine who is the daughter of one of his tenants.

> *Scene 2*: woods, picnic. Introduces him to company, makes the acquaintance of heroine's cousin—a gay lady of an animated nature. She introduces heroine.

> *Scene 3*: Office—day of business—hero calls on father of heroine—he mistakes him as an application for situation, which he accepts—proving competent. Is introduced to the daughter as forewoman and cousin as assistant. She does not recognize him, finally is accepting of him.

> *Scene 4*: Crisis in the house. Cousin disguises herself in the dress of heroine and discovers his designs, telling how the cousin has intentions on the hero.

Perhaps it was better that Winner abandoned the project. Clearly, the outline in Winner's head must have been more fully realized than these pencil scratches might indicate.

The Private Life

In September 1890, Winner took trips to New York and Boston to attend to business matters. His letters home are revealing in that they demonstrate his childlike awe of the world around him. While it had been some time since Winner had left Philadelphia, his fascination with these cities would appear to be the musings of a man very used to his own surroundings and very unused to others. His letter to Hannah:

> It has been so long since I traveled around that I cannot but observe how different the people are in so short a distance apart. Just think of a big circus, with a dozen different side shows on the outside, well New York is the side show and Boston is the real circus. I must say I admire Yankees, they are quiet but right down to work, and are splendid in manners and fine working. I have been watching for some of those short haired women but have not met any, they are all splendidly dressed but not at all gaudy, tho young ones like Maggie are so plain but high toned, and the old ladies display their gray hair in a most bewitching manner and fly around "wonderful smart." I do not want you to think that I have been flirting around to see all these things, but I think if I could join a Bible class with one of the guests as a school mate I wouldn't mind it, I don't mean anything by this remark, it only occurred to me.

Beyond these trips away, Winner appears to have settled happily in to his retirement. What diaries exist indicate that he spent the majority of his free time attending concerts with his children (Hannah appears to have never wanted to go) and going to local parks to rest among the trees and nature. While society was changing rapidly around him, Winner seems to have made little notice of passing events unless they directly affected him. In one example, Winner noted the virtual hysteria that gripped Philadelphia during the trolley strike of 1895.

Begun as a protest to the "Trolley Grab," a doubling of streetcar fares to eight cents, the city was held at a virtual standstill as Winner recorded in his diaries:

December 17, 1895
A magnificent day, splendid for pedestrians, we all to walk on account of the Great Strike in opposition to the *Trolley Grab* of double fare, 8 cents. A very exciting day all over the city, big rows, cars smashed and lots of fun.

December 18, 1895
The car strike is still on, people going along with cards on their hats saying "We are walking." Maggie rode down town in an extempore conveyance, along with many others. It was an old furniture car in red, white, and blue, fun all around city and fights again today.

December 23, 1895
The car strike worse than ever, riots and bloodshed today tremendous, excitement everywhere. [The strike would be settled the next day.]

Winner was also swept up in the event of Jubilee Week in Philadelphia, celebrating the end of the Spanish-American war. Winner was especially proud that his grandsons Kirk and Allen McCurdy had been part of Roosevelt's Rough Riders:

October 25, 1898
Peace Jubilee opened. Great Naval Review on the Delaware. Went to the Delaware to see the big warships, was on a ferry boat and had a grand view, in the morning took a walk with Maggie to see the illumination.

October 26, 1898
Military parade and review on Broad Street the whole length from Jackson to Cumberland Streets. The Grand Military Parade came off in glorious array. Momma, Maggie and I saw General Miles, Commander Hobson, Allen and Kirk McCurdy with the Rough Riders, and all worth noticing. Could not get down to see the illumination, the cars could not accommodate the people.

And one amusing event of later years:

November 17, 1899
Went with Maggie to Academy of Music in evening, Madam Nevada's concert, had a grand time, heard her sing *The Mocking Bird*, and was introduced to her in the Green Room.

What Winner's diary fails to mention is what happened after the introduction: Madam Nevada, apparently delighted to be meeting the eminent composer, planted a kiss on Septimus. While he claimed to be embarrassed, he would recount the story for the rest of his life.

In November 1897, Septimus and Hannah celebrated their golden wedding anniversary. Winner's reputation was sufficient at this point for the event to attract the attention of the local newspapers:

The celebration last night of the golden wedding of Mr. and Mrs. Septimus Winner was made more of a family reunion than a formal occasion. During nearly half a century, perhaps, no name connected with the musical profession in Philadelphia has been more familiar to students of music in this city, especially youthful ones, than that of Mr. Winner. He has arranged over 100 books of instruction on the violin and piano, and is likewise the author of numerous songs, some of which have achieved international popularity . . . Of his seven children, the three still living are Mrs. Henry Claghorn . . . James G. Winner and Miss Margaret F. Ferguson, all of whom were present last evening.[8]

Winner's final years were spent in much the same way as he had spent the 1880s and 1890s, with the notable difference that his health was beginning to decline. Troubled by episodes of lumbago (back pain), boils, colic and heart trouble, Winner was forced to reduce his work schedule and spend more time at home. While concerts and visits to the park would still take much of his time, Winner was clearly feeling the effects of his advancing age:

May 11, 1900
My birthday, 73 years old today. Felt as well as usual but realize that I am growing old, especially about the legs.

November 27, 1901
A beautiful day, home all the morning . . . after dinner did not feel well. Called on Dr. Ruoff who came to see me, "heart trouble" he said.

November 28, 1901
Fine day, had to stay in doors all day and live on milk diet, did not feel so very bad, but had to take a rest. Dr. Ruoff called again and gave me more drugs to digest.

November 29, 1901
A most beautiful day of mild and spring-like temperatures. I had to stay in doors all day, not even to go downstairs, something of heart troubles. Dr. Ruoff called again today, says my heart is improving, took more pills!

In his final year, Winner would enjoy the fruits of his labor and the entrances it gave him:

May 31, 1902
A beautiful day, nothing of any note transpiring, home all the morning, went out to Willow Grove after noon, met Mr. J.P. Sousa and had a nice greeting.

November 20, 1902
Dr. Wilson's high school reunion of the class of 1846 . . . A
fine, mild, salubrious day, did not get home until 12 o'clock, a
"big feed," fine time.

Apparently, the big feed Septimus mentioned would have lasting effects:

November 21, 1902
Variable day but very warm and mild, all are well, at home all
day and evening, feel the effects of last night! Heavy feeding!

The next day, Winner had been asked, as a local celebrity, to take part
in the ribbon-cutting ceremony at the new high school.

November 22, 1902
A fine beautiful day, a nice parade with President Rosenveldt
[note the improper or "Jewish" spelling of Roosevelt's name]
to open the new High School at Broad and Green.

According to Myers' interview with Florence Claghorn, the composer's granddaughter, Winner was struck by a heart attack after returning from the ceremonies that afternoon. According to Ms. Claghorn, neighbors were called to help the 225 pound man onto the couch
and the doctors were called. Winner was warned not to try and get up
without help but, left alone, he tried to go to the bathroom on his own.
Before he could even cross the room, he had a final, lethal heart attack.[9]
The death certificate listed the death as being caused by fatty deposits
of the heart. As he had been throughout Winner's illness, Dr. Ruoff was
the attending physician.

As is so often the case, it would seem that Septimus would earn his
greatest tributes after his death. Obituary articles abounded, many of
them contributing to the confusion regarding certain stories from his
life. Most focused on "Mocking Bird" and the apocrypha around the
creation of the song, but many others mentioned the other songs that
were already firmly entrenched in popular Americana including "Der
Deutscher's Dog," "Whispering Hope" and "Ten Little Injuns."

Just as his golden anniversary had been, Winner's burial was also
noted in the newspapers:

Septimus Winner was buried this afternoon in West Laurel
Hill Cemetery. The funeral services took place at the Winner
residence, 1706 N. 16th St., beginning at 2 o'clock. The house
was crowded with friends of the family, not all of whom could
find room in the front parlor, where the casket containing the
body was placed. The regular service of the Presbyterian

Church was read by the Rev. Dr. G.A. Latimer, who assisted the Rev. William T. Nelson, of the Oxford Street Presbyterian Church, the officiating clergyman.

The honorary pall-bearers, beside two members of a Masonic Lodge, to which Mr. Winner belonged, were chosen from among his life-long friends. They are Charles Weatherill, Murray Gibson, Charles Turner, Dr. Samuel Cary, Albert Gardiner and George Rouband. Many members of Masonic lodges attended the funeral.

Septimus Winner died Sunday of heart disease. He had been ill but a few hours. Born May 11, 1827, he came into public notice as a composer of famous songs in his twenty-sixth year. Among his productions which will long be remembered are *The Mocking Bird* and *What is Home Without a Mother*. Mr. Winner also wrote *Give Us Back Our Old Commander* and other songs and verses of note. He was the oldest member of the Musical Fund Society in this city.[10]

Another description provides much more information of a more sentimental variety:

His last song uttered, his last note written, the remains of Septimus Winner, song writer and musician, were borne from his late home at No. 1706 North Sixteenth street this afternoon and laid in their last resting place in Laurel Hill. Having lived simply all his life, it was fitting that the well-known Philadelphian's funeral should be marked by extremely simple services. By the wishes of his family, no music was permitted, only his pastor's words of encomium and the solemn words committing the remains to await the Resurrection Day. The interment was private, only the near relatives and friends following the flower-covered casket. But for more than an hour musicians, friends, admirers and members of the Mendelssohn Club, Fortnightly Club, Choral Society, Manuscript Music Society, Junger Maennerchor, the maennerchor, such composers as Dr. W.W. Gilchrist, Dr. A.H. Rosewig, Ellis Clarke Hammann, Philip Goepp, Frank G. Caufmann, Dr. M. Wendell Case, H.G. Staton and others passed by the bier and viewed the quiet features. Many other vocalists, musicians, soldiers and men prominent in all walks of life came for a last look.

Among them were many old Central High School men, attracted by a pathetic incident which occurred during the banquet of the Central High School Alumni in Musical Fund Hall last night. Just before Professor Edwin J. Houston spoke, William H. Stake arose, and indicating two papers framed and placed at the front of the platform, said: "In the midst of our rejoicing we are called upon to remember that one of our number has gone. On Saturday morning Septimus Winner, author of *Listen to the Mocking Bird* attended our dedication exercises. To-night he lied still in death and to-morrow will be carried to the grave. He was an alumnus of our school, graduating when quite young. This frame contains the original manuscript and notes of his famous song."

Many of those present today read the sweet words and many went today to take a last look at their writer to-day. "Sep" Winner certainly had a place in the hearts of the many, rich and poor alike.[11]

As with so many, time has a way of enhancing the reputation of those who have passed. While there were several articles that would follow Winner's death, only a few avoided waxing poetic. Perhaps this one sums up Winner's life as he would have liked to be remembered:

He was not a genius in any sense of the word, but it is doubtful if this country has produced a man of so much talent who has at the same time had such a widespread effect on the country in its attempt at culture . . . He had a capacity for seeing how to make music available for the masses that has never been approached by any man in the world. Is there another instance in the world where a man has written two hundred books on instruction in any art? Yet we venture to say that there is scarcely a hamlet in this country where to-day may not be found one of the Sep Winner's instruction books. It is true that these books brought woe to many. There were books about learning how to play without masters on the violin, piano, trombone, cornet, flute and every other instrument, and much misery was undoubtedly produced; but we say in all sincerity that the man who denies the value of these books has no understanding of the way in which this country has developed. This writer is pleased to put on record that nearly forty years ago he bought "Sep Winner on how to play the flute without a teacher." He worked a long time and failed, but he did manage to discover that it was his brother who could play the flute, while his own ability seemed to be in the nature of a bass horn, where the volume of wind counted for more than on the flute . . . There are much bad music and an awful lot of discord to be laid at the door of Sep Winner, and at the same time we say without hesitation that few men have added more to the sum of human happiness in his own peculiar line than he, and that, therefore, we are glad to honor him . . . He was one who deserves more of his countrymen than he is ever apt to receive.[12]

A Dual Legacy

As history has often had a way of taking different spins on those who have found their way into it, the legacy of Septimus Winner is complex at best. Certainly, as a songwriter, Winner has earned some level of recognition for his ability to tap in to the sentiment and mood of the American public. In his own work, Myers notes that Winner doesn't demonstrate any "real genius" due to the relative calm of his domestic and emotional life.[13] While the link between domestic tranquility and artistic genius seems tenuous, one might agree with Myers based purely on the notion that Septimus wasn't necessarily a compositional innovator nor were his songs shining examples of their genre. What they were, however, were songs that touched the American public whether through sentiment or through humor. Winner, as something of an everyman himself, was able to *consistently* reach his audiences in ways that many other songwriters might only do once, if at all. Winner's brother Joseph is an excellent example of this difference. Where Septimus was able to create a steady stream of successful works, his brother is consigned to history having had only one "moment of genius."

Septimus also clearly demonstrates an evolution as a songwriter—an important factor in his legacy and in his ability to consistently publish successful songs. Beyond that, he was able to do so within the fairly narrow constraints of American popular song, a highly specific genre. Winner was canny enough to recognize that songs that were too difficult to play or sing would not sell. As a result, he created playable, performable works that appealed to his audience while demonstrating the evolution of his craft. Starting with the first three published songs, all simple melodies in the same key, Winner was able to look at other genres and styles and absorb stylistic elements in his work in a context that would be deemed acceptable by his musical constituents.

Winner's role as a pedagogue is also significant. As the earlier quote makes clear, the *Winner Methods* books, in whatever guise, were ubiquitous. Whether, as this author would argue, it was his business savvy or it was just the fortuitousness of being in the right place at the right time, Winner recognized a clear need among his customers and moved aggressively to meet that need. As he watched parlor culture mature around him, he clearly recognized that the ability to play a musical instrument would be an important component of middle- or upper-middle-class aspirations. His response was nothing short of inspired. There is no indication that any other nineteenth century musician was able to respond to the evolving needs of amateur musicians in the same way. With his works ultimately numbering over one hundred separate publications for twenty-seven different instruments, Septimus' impact in this arena cannot be discounted.

Winner's business savvy is an important part of his evolving legacy as well. While he may have had some good luck and reasonable instincts initially, the evolution of his business acumen and marketing ability cannot be discounted. This savvy not only manifested itself as part of his previously discussed work as a pedagogue but also his work as a composer and arranger. His ability to tap into the changing tastes of his musical public would, according to many researchers, put him at the forefront of changing musical tastes. These changes would include the increasing desire for songs in waltz time, the growing influence of African American music and the growing taste for opera and light opera throughout the country (his massive anthology of arrangements completed at the end of his life was only part of his response to this change in public taste—his concert songs, influenced by light opera in their character).

Winner's business savvy also could be seen as extending to how he responded to Alice's phenomenal success. Despite the up-and-down relationship Winner had with his alter ego, Winner would successfully promote and market Alice as a model for nineteenth-century American women. Her image is chaste yet tasteful. Her activities were always within the bounds of acceptable behavior. Her creative efforts pleasant and never showy—the products of the creative artistry of an "amateur woman" whether it was the songs, the poetry and song lyrics, her children's books or the musical magazine. In many ways, Alice ultimately represented Septimus' ideal woman (no matter how misguided we might view that image from a contemporary perspective).

However, it will probably be Septimus' anomalous relationship with Alice for which he will likely be best remembered. Certainly, the situation is a unique one: Winner is the only American composer we know of to date who created a female pseudonym and consistently used that identity for thirty years. While others may still be uncovered, the Winner and Hawthorne partnership is an anomaly in music history. While the nature of that relationship, its nuances and the reasons behind Winner's alternating embracing of and distancing from Alice are far more interesting, history tends to avoid such nuances and take the broader view.

The relationship itself, its origins and evolution raise many questions (and will likely continue to raise them), only some of which can be answered or at least raise a dialogue of conjecture.

Why create Alice? Was Alice a gimmick to sell songs? As we have seen, the pseudonym, as a generic article, was very likely a way for Winner to deflect any potential personal criticism as well as to spare his ego should his public attempts as a composer and a poet meet with disdain or derision. It was also a way for him to cautiously divide his careers as an entrepreneur/shop owner and as a creative artist. Alice as a concept was almost certainly initially motivated by his devotion to his mother. However, once the first successes had been achieved, it is very likely that Septimus viewed Alice as a means to an end—a way to sell sentimental ballads. From that perspective alone, one might very well describe her as a gimmick or at the very least, a clever marketing ploy.

If Alice was a gimmick, then why not abandon her early on? The answer to this is simple. Like any other young businessman, especially one facing uncertain financial times in the 1850s, Winner needed to make money. Alice had already demonstrated her ability to earn an income. Winner would have been foolhardy to abandon her.

Did Alice ultimately become a stranglehold on Septimus? Undoubtedly. Septimus' personal struggle to achieve recognition in his own right was unquestionably an outgrowth of Alice's success. Publication records alone verify Winner's varying attempts to focus more on his own career while Alice would, at times, languish. Clearly, her success came, at least initially, at the cost of his own. From a historical perspective, it is why Winner has remained virtually unknown.

Winner's relationship with Alice raises additional questions about Septimus, his life, his career plan and his compositional technique from both a musicology and feminist standpoint:

Was Winner a cross-dresser or homosexual? There is no indication to suggest anything of the kind. The question is, frankly, more a product of contemporary views than historical ones.[14]

Did Winner write "female" music as Hawthorne? This raises the incredibly thorny question of gender coding in music. From a musicology perspective, it is difficult to say that there are distinct musical concepts that specifically distinguish works written by women as opposed to their male counterparts. This author has yet to see a successful argument that distinguishes the musical characteristics of women as being different from men. This, of course, excludes music that incorporates text (a topic to be dealt with later). Leaving aside the notion that musical styles change from generation to generation, any attempt to distinguish music by men as opposed to music by women must be dealt with in its own specific context. The far more interesting question in this context is:

Is there a musical difference between Winner's songs and Hawthorne's? Here Winner presents us with an unusual opportunity—to compare music written by a man versus that written by a "woman." Purists would, I suspect, argue that this comparison is specious in that Alice was not really a woman, but a man composing under a woman's name. However, from the perspective of the musical public, Alice was a real woman. That perception of Alice as a woman allows us to continue this train of thought. Sadly, for those who might hope to execute such a musical comparison, there seems to be little difference. If Winner intended to distinguish his "male" repertory from his "female" repertory musically, it is not evidenced either by comparing Hawthorne to the others, nor can a distinction be seen in his work under the A Lady of Kentucky pseudonym (assuming the ascription is correct).

Assuming there is no difference, why didn't Winner vary the style more to distinguish his personal work from that of Alice? It would be too simplistic an answer to say that Winner was unable to do this compositionally. The evolution of Winner's broader style as a songwriter (regardless of authorship) is easily seen in the progression from such songs as "Mocking Bird" to later songs such as "Whispering Hope" and "The Robin's Roundelay." If we assume that Winner was as canny a businessman as this volume implies, he surely understood the formula for successful popular songs. Assuming he consciously attempted to differentiate the Hawthorne versus Winner songs musically,[15] by varying that formula too strongly Winner would have known that he ran the risk of marginalizing either the Winner or Hawthorne repertory from a popular perspective. The boundaries of popular taste in music were limited in the nineteenth century—just as they are today. If Winner's primary goal was to be a success from a popular perspective—regardless of the authorship—varying an already successful formula would have seemed a poor business choice.

Assuming that there was a subgenre of women's music that women were more inclined to buy and perform and that amateur musical women felt a sense of sisterhood with Alice, is there an implication that Winner hoodwinked this market? The cultural developments for nineteenth-century women as defined by the woman's musical role in the home and the proliferation of music magazines would indicate that a subgenre did, in fact, exist. Just as we are currently faced with a plethora of musical subgenres from a cultural perspective, one might easily look to this point in American cultural history as a similar subgenre aimed explicitly at women. There is not enough evidence to conclude that women responded to this subgenre. It certainly seems sound from an anthropological standpoint to assume that a particular subculture would be drawn to things created for them. However, to assume that women were drawn to this subgenre out of some form of sisterhood assumes that such feelings of sisterhood were commonplace in their day. While the women's suffrage movement was in its infancy during Winner's lifetime, it would be too strong a statement to say that it influenced the day-to-day activities of the majority of American women at the time—especially those interested in pursuing what were evolving into traditional middle-class values, Winner's primary audience. Given that, it would be incorrect to assume that Winner's motives in publishing as Hawthorne were intentionally deceptive. There is no indication in his diaries of any such motivation nor would it be consistent with artistic values of the time as they relate to pseudonymous publication.

Was Winner's decision to publish under a female pseudonym a way to avoid accusations of being unmanly or an expression of chauvinism? Were Winner's decisions an indication of his desire to flout the conventions of this time? There were virtually no attempts to gender code music and musical genres before the twentieth century and while there were societal conventions of what men and women should do in a musical context, to mix the two blends anthropological and feminist arguments. To believe that Winner used Hawthorne to avoid being called unmanly assumes that nineteenth-century society held the same feminist viewpoints as it does today. Furthermore, the notion that Winner may have wanted to flout the conventions of the day by publishing his songs under a female pseudonym assumes that doing so would have actually been perceived by either Winner or the public as doing such. From the historical accounts, it appears that Winner's activities would have been viewed as much less of a break with societal conventions than they would be today.

What about the poetry and the genres of music? Did Winner make more of a distinction here? As we have seen, Winner almost uniformly split the genres of his various songs between his various personae. The sentimental ballads were almost exclusively reserved for publication under Alice's name. While exceptions exist, the preponderance of the songs indicates that Winner intended to keep the genre separate (especially in the years when he was more focused on Alice's career). Sentimentality, in Winner's mind, may have been more strongly linked to a feminine sensibility although it is unlikely he would have thought of it as being "female." Conversely, the children's songs, the comic songs, "Ethiopian" ballads and war songs were almost exclusively reserved for the remaining pseudonyms (all male) or for publication under Winner's own name. Since Winner made such a clear distinction for the genres it is also fairly safe to conclude that he did the same for his song lyrics. While the notion of nineteenth-century sentimentality is pervasive in almost all of Winner's song lyrics, it is their context that differentiates them. From a poetic perspective, it was not until he neared his death that Winner would reveal his own sentimental or lyrical side with the poems published in *Cogitations of a Crank*.

Is the conclusion that it may have been easier to write poetry "as a woman" than to compose music as one? It may very well have been. Music theorists have struggled for over two decades to define gender coding in music, especially instrumental music. To date, there has been little agreement on how to proceed in that regard. In fact, the majority of feminist writings on music and musicology have focused largely on women's history in music and, where specific works are concerned, those influenced by text. Even so-called program music has presented difficulties for theorists and analysts. Where feminist critics in the literary arts have achieved much greater success in gender coding poetry, novels, etc.—despite a wide variety of opinions on a theory of how to do so—musicology has yet to offer any theories that can account for music in general, much less that of a specific period or composer. The implications of this question in terms of Septimus Winner are, on some levels, negligible.

Might one infer, then, that it was easier for a man to compose music as a woman than it was for a woman to compose music as a woman at this time? While it may not necessarily have been easier for a man to compose as a woman than it was for a woman, it certainly was easier for a man to *publish* his compositions as a woman than it would have been for a woman to do the same. Societal conventions of the time made any kind of public or professional expression for women composers difficult at best (although not altogether impossible). At the same time, Winner was able to decrease the potential difficulties, at least initially, by publishing his works as Alice on his own. Once Alice was successfully established, it became even easier for Septimus to license his works as Alice through other publishers.

From a feminist perspective, isn't Winner already coded as female as a result of his composing only vocal works? This question should be answered from two perspectives. First, any coding of Winner as female must be viewed in the context of its time. In the nineteenth century, composition was still very much a male profession. But to code Winner as female, one would then have to group Winner with the other male composers who would be similarly coded as a result of the type of music they wrote. The Schubert, Schumann and Wolf song repertories as well as the works of Chopin and Liszt would have to be coded as such—not to mention the efforts of such popular composers as Arlen, Berlin, Kern, Loesser, Sondheim and numerous others. This author has yet to hear of such an assertion.

What about the fact that Winner wrote no music that might be coded male—e.g., symphonies, operas, chamber music, etc.? While Winner made one mention of writing an opera and Austin made an unsubstantiated reference to another operatic work, it is true that Winner did not publish works that weren't popular songs.[16] However, the larger question is why Winner chose not to do this regardless of how we might code it from a contemporary perspective. Despite his publication of over two hundred *Method* books for various instruments that featured arrangements of popular songs, Winner never was drawn to write either large-scale or more "classically" oriented compositions. Did the market understanding of an astute businessman fuel this decision? One hypothesis could be that having already achieved success as a songwriter and arranger, Winner may have known a good thing when he saw it. His achievements in this realm would have seemed considerable. He may, as a result, have felt that there was no need to exceed those achievements. A second hypothesis in this context may have been that Winner, the astute businessman, recognized his own limitations as a composer and never aspired beyond them. We know that Winner only studied composition for a limited time. Was Winner's comment late in life about his abandoned opera the modesty of an aging composer or does it reveal a man who recognized his limitations and shrewdly decided not to attempt to exceed them—potentially at the expense of his already successful career? If this is the case, as this author believes, Winner would join the ranks of many composers throughout history who recognized their own technical strengths and weaknesses and rarely ventured beyond them. Perhaps this was the mark of the true artist.

Postscript

Of the over three hundred songs Winner wrote, only a few are recalled today. "Whispering Hope" can be found on old recordings from the 1950s and 1960s and is occasionally heard at church services. "Listen to the Mocking Bird" is often remembered in the south especially by people of a "certain age." "Der Deutscher's Dog" and "Ten Little Injuns" live on in the pantheon of well-established children's literature.

Septimus Winner was buried in North Laurel Hill cemetery in Philadelphia a few days after his death on November 22, 1902.

Hannah Guyer Winner, Septimus' wife of over fifty years, lived until October 12, 1918, partially with support she received from Septimus' lifelong membership in the Musical Fund Society. She was buried next to her husband at North Laurel Hill.

Joseph Eastburn Winner died in 1918. He would never be able to repeat the acclaim he achieved with "Little Brown Jug."

Mary Ann "Chick" Winner Claghorn died on June 10, 1939. Little is known about her life once she reached adulthood.

James Gibson Winner would continue in the music business until his death on November 19, 1931. He was elected a member of the Musical Fund Society (giving his father great pride) and frequently performed in both Philadelphia and Atlantic City.

Margaret "Maggie" Ferguson Winner became an accomplished portrait artist, taking a cue from her great-uncle William E. Winner. She died on December 21, 1937, having never married.

Notes

1.   Birdseye, "America's Song Composers, No. VI: Septimus Winner," 433.

2.   Birdseye, "America's Song Composers, No. VI: Septimus Winner," 436.

3.   Mary Ann Hawthorne Winner, Septimus' mother, must have also died by this time or shortly afterwards. The exact dates are unknown and there is no mention of her in the extant diaries from these years.

4.   Myers, *The Music of Septimus Winner,* 34. Myers quotes this letter in his work but its source is unknown. It is not currently in the collection of Winner's letters housed at the Pennsylvania Historical Society in Philadelphia.

5.   Given the death of his daughters in 1883 and 1884, it is not surprising that there are no new songs. Very much the same situation occurred after the death of his son in 1869.

6.   Birdseye, "America's Song Composers, No. VI: Septimus Winner," 435.

7.   "A Chat with the Author of *The Mocking Bird,*" *The Philadelphia Press,* May 1901, n.p. Copy provided by Charles Eugene Claghorn.

8.   "Their Golden Wedding," *The Times (Philadelphia),* November 26, 1897, n.p. Copy provided by Charles Eugene Claghorn.

9.   Myers, *The Music of Septimus Winner*, 36. Myers had personally interviewed Florence Claghorn and recounts the composer's death based on their
conversation.

10.   "Septimus Winner Buried," *The Times (Philadelphia),* n.d., n.p. Copy
provided by Charles Eugene Claghorn.

11.   "'Sep' Winner at Rest," *The Public Ledger (Philadelphia),* n.d., n.p.
Copy provided by Charles Eugene Claghorn.

12.   Claghorn, *The Mocking Bird,* 58-9. The article quoted the *Philadelphia Inquirer* (date unknown) commenting on the publication of the posthumous volume *Cogitations of a Crank at Three Score and Ten* (presumably
sometime in 1903).

13.   Myers, *The Music of Septimus Winner*, 12.

14.   The reader might be surprised to learn the frequency with which the
author is asked this question, hence its inclusion in this volume.

15.   An assumption that would assume Winner felt this was necessary or,
for that matter, was even conscious that a distinction might be made.

16.   William W. Austin, *Susanna, Jeanie and the Old Folks at Home: The
Songs of Stephen C. Foster from His Time to Ours* (New York: MacMillan,
1975), 159. Austin's reference to a 1901 operetta with guitar accompaniment
mistakenly refers to Winner's set of light opera arrangements completed that
same year.

Appendix A
Nineteenth-Century Popular Song

By no means is this list meant to represent a comprehensive listing of popular songs in the nineteenth century. Instead, it is meant to provide a context for the best known songs of Septimus Winner, Alice Hawthorne and many of the other composers mentioned in this volume. The other songs selected in this list represent those that many may still know today, a purely subjective choice.

1740?	*Mother Goose Melodies for Children* (author unknown)
1767?	"Yankee Doodle"[1] (author unknown)
1789	"Drink To Me Only With Thine Eyes"[2] (author unknown)
1794	"Oh, Dear, What Can the Matter Be?" (author unknown)
1814	"Star-Spangled Banner" (previously "Adams and Liberty"; author unknown)
1820?	"Nearer My God to Thee" (Lowell Mason)
1823	"Home Sweet Home" (author unknown)
1831	"America" (Rev. Samuel Frances Smith/"God Save the King")
1834	"Zip Coon" (a.k.a. "Turkey in the Straw"; author unknown))
1837	"Woodman, Spare That Tree!" (Henry Russell)
1840	"Kathleen Mavourneen" (Mrs. Annie Barry Crawford/Frederick Nicholls William Crouch)
1843	"Old Dan Tucker" (Daniel Decatur Emmett)
1846	"The Blue Fly Tail" (a.k.a. "Jimmy Crack Corn"; Daniel Decatur Emmett)
1848	"Oh! Susannah" (Stephen Foster)
1850	"Jeannie With the Light Brown Hair" (Stephen Foster)
1850	"Camptown Races" (Stephen Foster)

1850   "Skip to My Lou" (author unknown)
1851   "Old Folks at Home" (Stephen Foster)
1852   "Massas in de Cold Cold Ground" (Stephen Foster)
1853   "Pop Goes the Weasel" (author unknown)
1855   "My Old Kentucky Home" (Stephen Foster)
1856   "Listen to the Mocking Bird" (Septimus Winner)
1857   "Jingle Bells" (J.S. Pierpont)
1860   "The Yellow Rose of Texas" (J.K. or anonymous)
1860   "Dixie" (Daniel Decatur Emmett)
1861   "Aura Lee" (W.W. Fosdick/George R. Poulton)
1862   "Battle Hymn of the Republic" (Julia Ward Howe/"Glory
            Hallelujah")
1862   "When Johnny Comes Marching Home" (Patrick Sarsfield
            Gilmore
1863   "The Battle Cry of Freedom" (a.k.a. "Rally Round the
            Flag, Boys"; George Frederick Root)
1864   "Beautiful Dreamer" (Stephen Foster)
1864   "Der Deutscher's Dog" (Septimus Winner)
1868   "The Flying Trapeze" (author unknown)
1868   "Ten Little Injuns" (Septimus Winner)
1868   "Whispering Hope" (Septimus Winner)
1869   "Little Brown Jug" (Joseph Eastburn Winner)
1869   "Shoo Fly, Don't Bother Me" (Billy Reeves/Frank Camp-
            bell)
1872   "Silver Threads among the Gold" (Hart Pease Danks)
1873   "The Mulligan Guard" (Harrigan and Hart)
1876   "Grandfather Clock" (Henry C. Work)
1876   "I'll Take You Home Again Kathleen" (Thomas Paine
            Westendorf)
1878   "Carry Me Back to Old Virginny" (James A. Bland)
1879   "Home on the Range" (Brewster-Bruce-Higley/Dan Kelly
            or Kelley)
1882   "My Bonnie (Lies over the Ocean)" (H.J. Fulmer a.k.a.
            Charles E. Pratt)
1883   "Clementine" (Percy Montross)
1884   "While Strolling through the Park One Day" (a.k.a. "The
            Fountain in the Park"; Ed Hadley or Robert A. Keiser)
1885   "Frankie and Johnnie" (author unknown)
1888   "Semper Fideles" (John Philip Sousa)

1889	"Down Went McGinty" (Joseph Flynn)
1890	"Throw Him down McCloskey" (J.W. Kelly)
1890?	"Stars and Stripes Forever" (John Philip Sousa)
1891	"Ta-ra-ra-boom-der-é" (Henry J. Sayers)
1894	"The Sidewalks of New York" (Charles B. Lawlow/James W. Blake)
1896	"A Hot Time in the Old Town Tonight" (Mama Lou?/Theodore Metz)
1896	"Sweet Rosie O'Grady" (Maude Nugent)
1897?	"Maple Leaf Rag" (Scott Joplin)
1899	"My Wild Irish Rose" (Chancellor John Olcott)
1899	"Hello Ma Baby" (Joseph E. Howard)
1901	"Just a Wearyin for You" (Carrie Jacobs Bond/Frank Stanton)
1902	"Bill Bailey, Won't You Please Come Home?" (Hughie Cannon)
1902	"In the Good Old Summertime" (George Evans)
1903	"Sweet Adeline" (Richard Gerard/Harry Armstrong)
1904	"Meet Me in St. Louis" (Kerry Mills/Andrew B. Sterling)
1905	"I Love You Truly" (Carrie Jacobs Bond)
1906	"You're a Grand Old Flag" (George M. Cohan)
1907	"By the Light of the Silvery Moon" (Gus Edwards/Edward Madden)
1907	"Take Me Out to the Ballgame" (Albert Von Tilzer/Jack Norworth)
1907	"The Merry Widow Waltz" (Franz Lehar)
1908	"Shine On Harvest Moon" (Nora Bayes/Jack Norworth)
1909	"Put on Your Old Gray Bonnet" (Stanley Murphy/Percy Weinrich)
1910	"Mother Machree" (Ernest Ball)
1910	"Ah! Sweet Mystery of Life"[3] (Victor Herbert)

Notes

1.   Unquestionably, "Yankee Doodle" was known before 1767. This date corresponds to the song's first publication in the United States, as part of the *Federal Overture* medley by Benjamin Carr and Company.

2.   1789 was the date of this song's first U.S. publication.

3.   From the opera *Naughty Marietta*.

Appendix B
Chronology of Business Locations

The information in this chronology has been constructed from three sources. The first is Myers (*The Music of Septimus Winner*, 17-18). The second source is the card catalog listing Winner's businesses compiled by the Historical Society of Pennsylvania (author unknown). The third source was compiled by the author based on publications of Winner's music, arrangements and methods books from 1850-1902. Together, these sources represent the most complete listing of Winner's businesses compiled to date. Myers specifically avoided the use of Harry Dichter and Elliott Shapiro, *Early American Sheet Music* (New York: R.R. Bowker Co., 1941) as it often includes references to Winner's uncle Septimus and locations that may have only been teaching studios.

1845-48 Some sources list Winner's first business address as 345 North Third Street, Philadelphia. This ascription is speculative at best; it may have only been a teaching studio.[1]

1849 Winner begins his first publishing venture publishing under the name S. Winner from his 257 Callowhill Street home.

1851-52 Some records indicate that Winner moved his music business down the street to 267 Callowhill Street while still publishing under the name S. Winner. As cited earlier, records are unclear as to whether this was an actual move, a mistaken listing, or a renumbering of Philadelphia's streets. 1853 records indicate some form of business at N.E. Callowhill and Franklin.

1853-56 Septimus forms the partnership of Winner & Shuster and moves his business to 110 North Eighth Street, Philadelphia.

1855-56 There are indications that Winner continued to use the publishing name S. Winner while the Winner & Shuster partnership continued. Both business names continued at 110 North Eighth Street. Locations at Eleven Logan Square and at 379 North Eleventh Street were either teaching studios or offices of some kind.

1856   Winner's partner, William Shuster, also published at the 110 North Eighth Street address under the name Wm. Shuster.

1856-57 While still at the 110 North Eighth Street address, Winner forms a new partnership, Winner & Kerk, with Philadelphia businessman E.M. Kerk. Winner also publishes his first works under the name Sep. Winner in 1857 using the same address.

1858   Winner ends the partnership with Kerk and moves his family and business to Williamsport, Pa., north of Philadelphia. While most works were issued by other publishers, Winner publishes one song this year using a new address at 148 North Eighth Street. This location was only used once and may have been an office or teaching studio.

1859-60 Returning to Philadelphia late in the year, Winner sets up a new publishing business, using the name Sep. Winner, at 716 Spring Garden Street. The 1112 Hunters Row location given in some sources was most likely a teaching studio or office.

1861-62 Maintaining the name Sep. Winner, Septimus moves his business to 531 North Eighth Street.

1863-66 Winner returns to Spring Garden Street, at number 933. He publishes under the name Sep. Winner and the name Winner & Co. as part of a new partnership with M.A. Smith.

1865-67 There are some indications that Winner either moved briefly to 929 Chestnut Street or began to use a second location. Only a few publications from the Chestnut Street location were issued in 1865. This location may have been maintained as late as 1867 or may have been part of a new partnership, Sep. Winner & Co., with James F. Ferguson. Both the Chestnut and Spring Garden Street locations remain in use at the time.

1867   Joseph Eastburn Winner opens what appears to have been his first business, under the name J.E. Winner at 545 North Eighth Street. He remains at this address through 1871 (and possibly through 1895).

1868   Septimus Winner uses the name Sep. Winner at two alternating addresses: 929 Chestnut Street and a new location at 926 Spring Garden Street.

1869-73 Winner goes into business with his son J. Gibson Winner under the name Sep. Winner & Son and opens a new store located at 1003 Spring Garden Street.

1874   Sep. Winner & Son suspends operations. There were no self-published works in this year.

1875   Winner opens the short-lived Hawthorne Publishing Company at 914 Spring Garden Street. Later, Septimus goes back into business with his son and returns to the 1003 Spring Garden Street address and appears to remain there through 1880.

1875-76 Winner opens a second store at 4742 Main Street in Germantown, Pa., a northern suburb of Philadelphia.

1880-82 Sep. Winner & Son moves down the street to 1007 Spring Garden Street. It remains in this location through at least 1882 and possibly through 1885.

1885-86 Sep. Winner & Son moves to 545 North Eighth Street. This may have been some form of partnership with his brother Joseph Eastburn Winner.

1887   Winner's son, J. Gibson Winner opens a new store at 1736 Columbia Avenue.

1887-88 Winner appears to have begun and ended another brief partnership. The firm of Winner & Guyer issues few publications from the 545 North Eighth Street address. The identity of Winner's partner in this venture is unknown but must have been a member of his wife's family.

1887-88 Winner joins his son under the revitalized name Sep. Winner & Son at the 1736 Columbia Avenue location. It appears that there may have been a dispute with either Guyer or his brother as advertisements read as quoted on page 165. The origin or subsequent fate of the 2018 Columbia Avenue address is unknown. It was never used as a publishing base.

1889-91 No publishing activities exist from this period. Most sources theorize that the Columbia Avenue location remained in business during these years but did not publish any new music.

1892-93 Sep. Winner & Son publishes music using the 545 North Eighth Street address. It is unclear whether this represents a move or was used for other reasons.

1893   J. Gibson Winner is actively publishing at the Columbia Avenue address.

1894-96 Sep. Winner & Son publishes new works from the Columbia Avenue address.

1896   Winner moves his family and remaining business to his final home located at 1706 North Sixteenth Street. He remains at this location through his death in 1902.

Notes

1. Myers cites William Arms Fisher, *One Hundred and Fifty Years of Music Publishing in the United States* (Boston: Oliver Ditson, 1933), 89, as a source. The 1845 date may have been too early for Winner to have been engaged in business (especially as Myers notes with his younger brother Joe). The Historical Society of Pennsylvania also lists this address but with an 1849 date. While it is possible that Winner taught at this address, it is not corroborated in his diaries or in any family records nor is there any published music using this address.

Appendix C
Alphabetical Listing of Songs

The format of this bibliography is as follows: song name, pseudonym song was published under and lyricist where applicable (publication city: publisher, publisher address (provided only if the song was self-published), year of publication), dedication. Where a second paragraph appears following the citation, it will contain notes and information related to this song that are relevant to its composition. As appropriate, sources are cited in parentheses and include the following:

KEF　University of Pennsylvania Special Collections, Keffer Collection of Sheet Music, Philadelphia PA.

Levy　Levy, Lester S. Picture the Songs: Lithographs from the Sheet Music of Nineteenth-Century America. Baltimore: Johns Hopkins University Press, 1976.

LOC　Library of Congress catalogs, Washington, DC.

Myers　Meyers, Howard L. *The Music of Septimus Winner*. Chapel Hill, NC: University of North Carolina, 1950, MM Thesis.

NUC　*The National Union Catalog*, Catalog of the Library of Congress (Washington: United States Government Printing Office, 1869).

PDM　Public Domain Music (http://www.pdmusic.org).

Spaeth　Spaeth, Sigmund. *History of Popular Music in America*. New York: Random House, 1948.

"Aberdeen Scottische," Septimus Winner (unknown city: unknown publisher, unknown address, 1870), instrumental.

This work, cited by other biographers, has yet to be located in any of the archives currently available on Winner's music. It was originally advertised on the back of "No One to Weep When I Am Gone" (Myers).

"Abraham's Daughter," Tony Emmett (Philadelphia: Sep. Winner, 531 North Eighth Street, 1861), *Respectfully Dedicated To Wm. Munyan Esq.*

> The song is also listed as "Raw Recruits" (PDM). Tony Emmett may have been an actual poet or another pseudonym. No other records of Emmett have been found to date.

"Acceptance," Septimus Winner (unknown city: unknown publisher, unknown address, unknown year).

"After Sundown," Alice Hawthorne (Philadelphia: Sep. Winner & Son, 1003 Spring Garden Street, 1871), *To Maggie F. Winner.*

"Alice Vane," Septimus Winner, (Philadelphia: Chas. W.A. Trumpler, unknown year).

"Am I Not True to Thee?," Alice Hawthorn (Philadelphia: Winner & Shuster, 110 North Eighth Street, 1856), *To Mrs. Hannah J. Winner.*

"And Yet I Am Not Happy," Mark Mason (unknown city: unknown publisher, unknown address, 1873).

> Publication date provided by PDM.

"Anna Polka," Septimus Winner (unknown city: unknown publisher, unknown address, 1874), instrumental.

"Arbor Day Waltz," Septimus Winner (unknown city: unknown publisher, unknown address, unknown year).

"Archiduc Polka," Septimus Winner (unknown city: unknown publisher, unknown address, 1875).

"As Dear Today as Ever," Alice Hawthorne (Philadelphia: Lee & Walker, 1862), *To Mrs. Sophia E. Wray.*

"As We Gathered in the Hay," Alice Hawthorne (New York: Firth Pond & Co., 1857), *To William N. Toy, Esq.*

"Aunt Jemima's Plaster," M.A.I. (Philadelphia: Winner & Shuster, 110 North 8th Street, 1855).

> Levy lists the song as having been "written for and sung by Samuel S. Sanford," a well-known minstrel show performer.

"Away, Away the Morn Is Brightly Breaking," Septimus Winner (Philadelphia: Lee & Walker, 1862).

> The cover examined (KEF) lists this song as being part of a collection of "Ethiopian Songs." It is unclear whether this song was an arrangement or an original. Winner apparently abandoned this collection.

"Away From Home," Alice Hawthorne (Baltimore: Henry McCaffrey, 1858).

"Baby's Dance," Septimus Winner (unknown city: unknown publisher, unknown address, 1880), instrumental.

Listed as "No. 2 from the Pet Set of Easy Airs for the piano or organ" (PDM).

"Ball and Pin Galop," Septimus Winner (unknown city: unknown publisher, unknown address, 1874), instrumental.

"Banner March," Septimus Winner (Philadelphia: Sep. Winner, 531 North Eighth Street, unknown year), *To Miss M. Therese Patten,* instrumental.

"Be Happy with Me," Alice Hawthorne (Philadelphia: Sep. Winner & Son, 1003 Spring Garden Street, 1869), *To Miss Mame D. Brusstar.*

"Because Thou Art So Far Away," Alice Hawthorne (unknown city: unknown publisher, unknown address, unknown year).

Copy unavailable. Advertised on "No One to Weep."

"Bid Me Goodbye (The Soldier's Song *or* The Soldier's Farewell)," Alice Hawthorne (unknown city: unknown publisher, unknown address, unknown year).

Copy unavailable. Advertised on "Away, Away the Morn is Brightly Breaking."

"Bird and Mate," Alice Hawthorne (unknown city: unknown publisher, unknown address, 1873).

"Bird Note Galop," Septimus Winner (unknown city: unknown publisher, unknown address, unknown year), instrumental.

"Birdie's Ball, The," Apsley Street (Boston: Oliver Ditson, 1869).

"Blow the Horn for Supper, Kate," Septimus Winner (Philadelphia: Sep. Winner & Son, 1003 Spring Garden Street, 1871).

Listed as part of a new series *Farm Ballads No. 1* and apparently including a horn duet for any of flute, violin or trumpet (Myers).

"Blue Note Galop," Septimus Winner (unknown city: unknown publisher, unknown address, unknown year), instrumental.

Also listed as "Bird Note Galop" (Myers).

"Bound Brook Polka," Septimus Winner (Philadelphia: Sep. Winner & Son, 545 North Eighth Street, unknown year), instrumental.

"Bow in the Cloud, The," Alice Hawthorne (Philadelphia: F.A. North & Co., 1874), *To Mrs. H.J. Winner.*

"Bower Scottische, The," Septimus Winner (Philadelphia: Sep. Winner & Son, 1003 Spring Garden Street, unknown year), *To Prof. John Bower,* instrumental.

"Boy and the Sparrow, The," Mark Mason (unknown city: unknown publisher, unknown address, unknown year).

"Bully for You (Oh, I'm a Single Man)," Septimus Winner (Philadelphia: Lee & Walker, 1861).

"Bury Not Thy Neighbor," Septimus Winner (unknown city: unknown publisher, unknown address, 1873).

"Cast Thy Bread upon the Waters," Alice Hawthorne (Philadelphia: Winner & Shuster, 110 North Eighth Street, 1855), *To Miss Minnie Banks.*

"Chickey Polka," Septimus Winner (unknown city: unknown publisher, unknown address, unknown year), instrumental.

"Chimes of the Monastery, The," music by Wely, lyrics by Alice Hawthorne (Philadelphia: Winner & Shuster, 110 North Eighth Street, 1854), *To Miss Caroline Richings.*
    Adapted to Wely's air "Les Cloches du Monastere" and arranged by Leopold Meignen (Myers).

"Christmas Comes But Once a Year," Percy Guyer (Philadelphia: Sep. Winner & Son, 1736 Columbia Avenue, 1887?).

"Colonel Ellsworth's Funeral March," Septimus Winner (Philadelphia: Lee & Walker, 1861), *Composed And Respectfully Dedicated To Francis E. Brownell, Esq.*, instrumental.
    Written in memorial to the first man killed in the Civil War identified in NUC as Ephraim Elmer Ellsworth (1837-1961).

"Come, Gather 'round the Hearth," Alice Hawthorne (Philadelphia: Winner & Shuster, 110 North Eighth Street, 1854), *To Messrs. Huntington, Franklin, Frisbie And Smith Of The Continental Vocalists, As Sung By Them Throughout The United States".*

"Come to Our Hearts and Abide," Septimus Winner (Boston: Oliver Ditson, 1922).
    Earlier publication records for this song have not been found. NUC lists it as having new words to the tune of "Whispering Hope" and having been published after Winner's death. Apparently, there was an attempt to make the song "more sacred." Author of lyrics unknown.

"Comet Waltz," Septimus Winner (Philadelphia: Sep. Winner, 933 Spring Garden Street, 1863), *To My Brother, Joe.*
    Levy lists this song as being by one J.X.A. Wimmer.

"Commonwealth March," Septimus Winner (unknown city: unknown publisher, unknown address, unknown year), instrumental.

Copy unavailable. Eight bars are listed on an advertisement for "Bound Brook Polka."

"Companions of Old," music by Septimus Winner, lyrics by Alice Hawthorne (Boston: Orpheus Music Co., 908 Walnut Street, 1906).

Earlier publication records for this song have not been found. Myers lists it as having been arranged by W.L. Rosenburg (perhaps from an unfinished sketch). The original publication features a picture of Septimus as an old man on the cover.

"Congress Scottische," Septimus Winner (unknown city: unknown publisher, unknown address, 1870), instrumental.

"Contraband Scottische, The," Septimus Winner (Philadelphia: Lee & Walker, 1861), *To General B.F. Butler,* instrumental.

"Coolie Chinee, The," Septimus Winner (Philadelphia: Lee & Walker, 1871).

The original score includes a separate stave indicating a variety of percussion instruments to be used during the refrain.

"Cozy Nook, The," Alice Hawthorne (Philadelphia: Sep. Winner, 531 North Eighth Street, 1861), *To Miss Emma Farrington*

"Creeds of the Bells," music by Septimus Winner, lyrics by George W. Bungay (Philadelphia: Sep. Winner & Son, 1007 Spring Garden Street, 1880).

Both Myers and PDM list this song as a solo, duet and quartet "as sung by the Hayes Quartet."

"Cruel Words Unwisely Spoken," Alice Hawthorne (Philadelphia: Sep. Winner & Son, 1003 Spring Garden Street, 1869)*, To Miss Cordelia Bates.*

"Dado Waltz," Septimus Winner (Philadelphia: Sep. Winner & Son, 1007 Spring Garden Street, 1880), *To Edwin S. Johnson Esq., Decorative Artist,* instrumental.

Myers recounts that Johnson had a store at 1033 Spring Garden Street when the song was written.

"Dance of the Sprites (Mazurka)," Alice Hawthorne, (New York: S.T. Gordon, 1869), instrumental.

"Danish Dance, The," Septimus Winner (Philadelphia: Sep. Winner, 933 Spring Garden Street, unknown year), instrumental.

"Days Gone By, The," Alice Hawthorne (Boston: Oliver Ditson, 1855).

A revised edition of the song was also published in 1891 (Myers).

"Dead Leaves Fall, The," music by Septimus Winner, lyrics by Alice Hawthorne (unknown city: unknown publisher, unknown address, unknown year).

"Dear Mollie Magee," words by Septimus Winner, lyrics by Alice Hawthorne (Philadelphia: J.M. Stoddart & Co., 1874).

"Der Deutscher's Dog," Septimus Winner (Philadelphia: Sep. Winner, 933 Spring Garden Street, 1864), *To E.F. Dixey, Esq.*
A later publication, "Little Wee Dog," was issued by other publishers with new words by Barton Hill (Levy). The 1854 date of original publication (KFR) is an error. An English edition called the song "The Dutchman's Lee-tle Dog" (Myers).

"Did You Think of Me Today," Alice Hawthorne (Baltimore: Henry McCaffrey, 1864), *To Miss Emma Douglass, Newark, NJ.*

"Dolly Varden," Septimus Winner (Philadelphia: Sep. Winner & Son, 1003 Spring Garden Street, 1872), *To Mr. Robert Helm.*

"Don't Blame Your Wife," Percy Guyer (Philadelphia: Sep. Winner & Son, 545 North Eighth Street, 1885), *To Frank A Conly Esq. as Sung by Him with Greatest Success.*

"Don't Forget to Say Your Prayers," Alice Hawthorne (Philadelphia: Sep. Winner & Son, 1003 Spring Garden Street, 1879), *To My Friend Henry T. Claghorn Esq.*

"Down Below," Septimus Winner (unknown city: unknown publisher, unknown address, unknown year).
Advertised on the back cover of "The Lazaroni Maid."

"Down the Quiet Valley," Septimus Winner (Philadelphia: Sep. Winner & Son, 1003 Spring Garden Street, 1873 (1870?)), *To Miss Nettie G. Rogers.*

"Down Upon the Rappahannock," Alice Hawthorne (Philadelphia: Winner & Co., 933 Spring Garden Street, 1863), *To J. Lamont.*

"Drama March," Septimus Winner (Philadelphia: Sep. Winner, 110 North Eighth Street, 1857), *To Edwin Forrest Esq.,* instrumental.

"Dreams That Charmed Me When a Child," Alice Hawthorne (Philadelphia: Winner & Shuster, 110 North Eighth Street, 1855).

"Drifting from Home," Alice Hawthorne (Philadelphia: Lee & Walker, 1871), *To Mrs. A.K. Gregory.*

"Drummer Boy's March," Septimus Winner (Boston: Oliver Ditson, 1864), instrumental.
Listed as introducing the song "The Captain" (Myers).

"Early Dawn March," Leon Dore (Philadelphia?: W.F. Shaw, 1878), instrumental.

"Easter Lilies Waltzes," Septimus Winner (unknown city: unknown publisher, unknown address, unknown year), instrumental.

"Echoes from Afar," music by Alice Hawthorne, lyrics by Dr. Gillet F. Watson (Philadelphia: Sep. Winner and Co., 929 Chestnut Street, 1867), *To Miss Sallie J. Watson of Virginia.*

"Edwin Forrest Quickstep," Septimus Winner (Philadelphia: Winner & Kerk, 110 North Eighth Street, 1857), *Col. Wm. H. Maurice*, instrumental.

"Ellen's Babies," Mark Mason (Philadelphia: Sep. Winner & Son, 1003 Spring Garden Street, 1877).

The song is also listed by the alternate name "I'm Kept on Pins and Needles" (PDM).

"Envy Not Your Neighbor," Mark Mason (Philadelphia: Sep. Winner & Son, 1003 Spring Garden Street, 1873).

The name Richard Arthur is also associated with the song but PDM does not provide a context (PDM).

"Eyes Will Watch for Thee," Septimus Winner (unknown city: unknown publisher, 1865?).

"Faded Leaves," music by Alice Hawthorne, lyrics by W.T. Dodson (Philadelphia: Sep. Winner, 926 Spring Garden Street, 1868), *To Misses Fannie Dodson and Virgil Van Horn.*

"Farewell Song of Enoch Garden (I'll Sail the Seas Over)," Septimus Winner (Philadelphia: Sep. Winner and Co., 929 Chestnut Street, 1865), *To L. De Brookes (of New York).*

A note about the song featured in the *Musical Journal* (1867) lists it as being "sung with great success by Jas. LaMont." A version of the song in theme and variations form also appears in the magazine.

"Fireside Scottisch, The," Septimus Winner (Philadelphia: Winner & Shuster, 110 North Eighth Street, 1854), *To Miss Mary M'Clain by S.H.W.*, instrumental.

"Flash Scottische," Septimus Winner (Philadelphia: Sep. Winner, 933 Spring Garden Street, 1864), *To My Friend, Harry Coleman*, instrumental.

"Flower Fadeth, The," Alice Hawthorne (Philadelphia: Winner & Kerk, 110 North Eighth Street, 1857), *To Miss Sallie Lynch.*

"Fond Moments of My Childhood," Alice Hawthorne (Philadelphia: Lee & Walker, 1855?), *To Miss Emma L. Gibson.*

"Four-in-Hand Scottische," Septimus Winner (unknown city: unknown publisher, unknown address, unknown year), instrumental.

"French Polka," Septimus Winner (Philadelphia: F.A. North & Co., 1876), instrumental.

"Friend of My Heart," Alice Hawthorne (Philadelphia: Sep. Winner, 531 North Eighth Street, 1862), *To Miss Etta M. Hicks of Maryland.*

"Friends We Love, The," Alice Hawthorne (Philadelphia: Sep. Winner and Co., 929 Chestnut Street, 1868), *To Miss Evelyn and Kate Baird Of Cardenes, Cuba.*

"Fritz Lullaby," Septimus Winner (unknown city: W.A. Evans?: 1882), instrumental.

"Gates Are Ever Open, The," Alice Hawthorne (Philadelphia: Lee & Walker, 1874).

An advertisement for the song lists it as being "adapted to an original melody by Alice Hawthorne" and as a companion song to the song "The Gate's Ajar."

"Gay As a Lark (Canzonetta)," Septimus Winner (Germantown, Pa.: Sep. Winner, 4742 Main Street, 1876), *To Mrs. Alfred Smith, Germantown.*

"General Halleck's Grand March," Septimus Winner (Philadelphia: Lee & Walker, 1862), *Respectfully Dedicated To Major General Halleck,* instrumental.

A strange note on the cover of the sheet music provides the opus number 931. It is one of only two examples in all of the Winner music examined that features such an indication. Myers notes that the music also contains excerpts from "Glory Glory Hallelujah."

"General Hancock's Grand March," Septimus Winner (Philadelphia: Lee & Walker, 722 Chestnut Street, 1864, *To Major General Hancock,* instrumental.

"Gentle Maggie (I'm Coming Home from Sea)," Alice Hawthorne (Philadelphia: Lee & Walker, 1858), *To Miss Maggie Shallcross.* Listed as a companion piece to the popular song "Maggie By My Side" (Myers).

"Give Us Back Our Old Commander, Little Mac, the People's Pride," Septimus Winner (Philadelphia: Winner & Co., 933 Spring Garden Street, 1863), *To Our Brave Volunteers.*

"God Bless the Little Feet," Alice Hawthorne (Philadelphia: Lee & Walker, 922 Chestnut Street, 1871).

"God Save Our President," Septimus Winner (Philadelphia: Sep. Winner & Son, 1007 Spring Garden Street, 1881).

Written during the illness of President James Garfield after a failed assassination attempt by Charles Guiteau. The song is alternatively listed under the title "A Nation's Prayer" (NUC/PDM).

"Golden Moon, The," Alice Hawthorne (Philadelphia: Winner & Shuster, 110 North Eighth Street, 1855), *To Miss Mary Roesche.*

"Gone Where the Woodbine Twineth," Apsley Street (Philadelphia: Sep. Winner & Son, 1003 Spring Garden Street, 1870), *To the Children of the Soldier's Home.*

"Good Send Off to Thee, A," Paul Stenton (Philadelphia: Sep. Winner & Son, 1007 Spring Garden Street, 1880), *To Capt. E. Robertson, Steamship Ontario.*

Advertised as a "Baritone solo as sung by Mr. Alfred Holland." Two verses and refrain.

"Good Words," Septimus Winner (Philadelphia: Sep. Winner & Son, 1003 Spring Garden Street, 1873), *To Mrs. John Stapf.*

"Good-Bye Dear Mother," Alice Hawthorne (Philadelphia: Winner & Guyer, 545 North Eighth Street, 1888).

"Good-Night But Not Good-Bye," music by Alice Hawthorne, lyrics by A. Fleetwood (Cincinnati: W.C. Peters & Sons, 1858).

"Grandmother's Chair," Percy Guyer (unknown city: unknown publisher, unknown address, unknown year).

The origin of this song is unclear and may have been some kind of arrangement. A version of the song Winner published as part of his editorial duties in *Peterson's Magazine* lists it as having been "written, composed and sung by John Read." Whether Winner made an arrangement or created a new pseudonym to promote the song is unknown.

"Greenback Quickstep," Septimus Winner (Philadelphia: Lee & Walker, 722 Chestnut Street, 1863), *To Secretary of the Treasury Chase,* instrumental.

"Gypsy's Tent, The," Septimus Winner (Philadelphia: Sep. Winner & Son, 1007 Spring Garden Street, 1882), *To Miss Zulema.*

One source lists an affiliation with the "melo-drama" *Loriena* but no independent verification for this fact has been found to date (PDM).

"Happiness of Home, The," Alice Hawthorne (Philadelphia: Winner & Shuster, 110 North Eighth Street, 1855), *To Miss Susan Hunt of Wyoming.*

"Hawthorne Polka, The," John Holdsworth (Philadelphia: Sep. Winner, 110 North Eighth Street, 1856), *Composed and Respectfully Dedicated to Miss Mary Ball*, instrumental.

It is unclear whether this represents a Winner work under a new pseudonym or if it was by an actual composer, written as a tribute to Alice Hawthorne. It is listed by some sources but not by others.

"He's Gone to the Arms of Abraham," Septimus Winner (Philadelphia: Sep. Winner, 933 Spring Garden Street, 1863), *To E.F. Dixey, Esq.*

The "secesh" (sland for secessionist) melody of this song is actually "Bonnie Blue Flag" (PDM). Another source lists the publication date as 1862 by the publisher J.H. Johnson but this cannot be independently verified (NUC).

"Heart's Mission, The," Alice Hawthorne (Philadelphia: Lee & Walker, 1857), *To Miss Lizzie Hetzell of Philadelphia.*

"Hearth and Home," Alice Hawthorne (Philadelphia: Sep. Winner & Son, 1003 Spring Garden Street, 1869), *To Mrs. Mary A. Quirk.*

"Hiawatha Polka," Alice Hawthorne (Philadelphia: Winner & Shuster, 110 North Eighth Street, 1856), *Wayne Olwine Esq.,* instrumental.

"Home and Friends (When the Sun Goes Down)," Alice Hawthorne (New York: Firth Pond & Co., 1857).

"Home By and By," Alice Hawthorne (Philadelphia?: W.F. Shaw, 1874).

"Home Ever Dear," Alice Hawthorne (Philadelphia: Sep. Winner & Co., 933 Spring Garden Street, 1866), *To Miss Sallie D. Cook.*

"Hop De Dood'n Doo ("Ethiopian" ballad)," M.A.I. (Philadelphia: Winner & Shuster, 110 North Eighth Street, 1854).

Only Levy lists this song as being by Winner but given the use of the pseudonym elsewhere and the publication record, it must be a Winner tune. Levy also lists it as being "sung by Luke West of Murphy, West and Peel's Original Campbell Minstrels."

"How Sweet Are the Roses?," Alice Hawthorne (Philadelphia: Winner & Shuster, 110 North Eighth Street, 1853).

Written in 1850 but not published until 1853.

"I Am Dreaming of the Loved Ones," Alice Hawthorne (Philadelphia: Sep. Winner, 933 Spring Garden Street, 1865), *To Miss Katie Hassell.*

"I Don't Got Him Now?," Mark Mason (Philadelphia: Sep. Winner & Son, 1003 Spring Garden Street, 1873).

"I Have Tidings," Alice Hawthorne (Baltimore: Miller & Beacham, 1858), *To Miss Virginia Lewis.*

"I Set My Heart upon a Flower," Alice Hawthorne (Philadelphia: Winner & Shuster, 110 North Eighth Street, 1854), *To Misses Clemens.*
Also mistakenly listed as "I Set My Hearth upon a Flower."

"I Was Thinking, Idly Thinking," Alice Hawthorne (Baltimore: Henry McCaffrey, 1866), *To Miss Mary E. Johnson (Patterson N.J.).*

"I Would Not Die Away from Home," Paul Stenton (unknown city: unknown publisher, unknown address, 1878?).

"I'll Kiss You Quick and Stay," Septimus Winner (Philadelphia: Lee & Walker, 1858), *To Sallie J. Winner.*
Advertised as an answer song to "Kiss Me Quick and Go."

"I'll Plant a Rose Beside Thy Grave," Percy Guyer (unknown city: unknown publisher, unknown address, 1878).

"I'm Here, I'm There, I'm Everywhere," Septimus Winner (unknown city: unknown publisher, unknown address, unknown date). (See "Tom Collins Is My Name").

"If My Wishes Could Come True," music by Septimus Winner, lyrics by Alice Hawthorne (Philadelphia: Hawthorne Publishing Company, 914 Spring Garden Street, 1875), *To Julius Lee Jr.*

"Jenny, Darling Jenny," Alice Hawthorne (Philadelphia: Sep. Winner, 716 Spring Garden Street, 1859), *To Miss Maggie R. Toy.*

"Johnny Get Your Hair Cut," Mark Mason (Philadelphia: J. Gibson Winner, 1736 Columbia Avenue, 1887), *To "Who Is Grose."*

"Jovial Scottische," Alice Hawthorne (Philadelphia: Lee & Walker, 1862?), instrumental.

"Juana, Cuba's Fair Isle," Septimus Winner (Philadelphia: Lee & Walker, 1858), *Dedicated to the Ladies of the United States and Cuba.*

"Just as of Old," Alice Hawthorne (Philadelphia: Lee & Walker, 1865), *To Miss Emily L. Graham.*

"Just Gone Out," Mark Mason (Philadelphia: Sep. Winner & Son, 1736 Columbia Avenue, 1888).

"Kettle and the Clock, The," Percy Guyer (unknown city: unknown publisher, unknown address, unknown date).
This song is also sometimes listed as being by Eastburn (Joseph Eastburn Winner).

"Kissing in Fun," Music by F. Harris, lyrics by Septimus Winner (Philadelphia: Louis Meyer, 1864).
The identity of Mr. or Ms. Harris is unknown.

"Kissing thro' the Bars," Septimus Winner, (Philadelphia: Winner & Kerk, 110 North Eighth Street, 1857).

As with many others, the origin of this song is unclear. It is advertised as being by Winner in an advertisement on the back of "Listen to the Mocking Bird" and is confirmed by Myers. However, it is also listed as being composed by Joseph Wood Jr. with lyrics by General William F. Small and published by Lee & Walker (Levy). It is unclear as to whether Winner appropriated the song or if there were, in fact, two versions.

"Kitty Tyrell," Septimus Winner (unknown city: unknown publisher, unknown address, unknown date).

"L'amour Trois Temps," George W. Allen (Philadelphia: The Musical Journal, 1867), *To L. De G. Brookes,* instrumental.

An instrumental work that strongly resembles the Winner style. In addition, this is the same dedicatee to whom Winner dedicated "Farewell Song of Enoch Arden." It may indicate that this was, in fact, another Winner pseudonym.

"Lady All Skin and Bone, The," Mark Mason (Philadelphia: Sep. Winner & Son, 1003 Spring Garden Street, 1869).

Myers indicates that this comic ballad was sung "with great success by Robert H. Craig," the popular comedian.

"Lady Art Thou Sleeping," Septimus Winner (Philadelphia: Sep. Winner, 926 Spring Garden Street, 1868).

"Lazaroni Maid, The," Alice Hawthorne (Philadelphia: Sep. Winner, 926 Spring Garden Street, 1868), *To Mrs. S.M. Kelly.*

"Le Solitaire Schottische," Alice Hawthorne (Philadelphia: Sep. Winner, 531 North Eighth Street, 1862), *To Fanny G. Linton,* instrumental.

"Let Her Go Gallagher! Don't Be a Clam," Mark Mason (Philadelphia: J. Gibson Winner, 1736 Columbia Avenue, 1887), *To Master Edgar Wilkinson.*

"Let the Light of Days Depart,*"* Septimus Winner (unknown city: unknown publisher, unknown address, unknown date).

The publication date of 1851, provided by the Library of Congress, is incorrect. The actual publication date is unknown.

"Let Us Cross over the River," music by Septimus Winner, words by Alice Hawthorne (Germantown, Pa.: Sep. Winner, 4742 Main Street, 1876), *To J.M. Dredger, Esq.*

Advertised as containing the "last words of Stonewall Jackson" (Myers).

"Let Us Hope for the Best," Alice Hawthorne (unknown city: unknown publisher, unknown address, unknown date).

"Let Us Live with a Hope," Alice Hawthorne (Philadelphia: Winner & Shuster, 110 North Eighth Street, 1855), *To J.P. Ordway, Esq.*

"Lilliputian's Beer Song," Mark Mason (Philadelphia: Sep. Winner & Son, 545 North Eighth Street, 1892), *To the Misses Lillie and Gussie D'Alve.*

"Link'd with Many Bitter Tears," Alice Hawthorne (Philadelphia: Sep. Winner & Co., 933 Spring Garden Street, 1866), *To Mrs. Lizzie N. Martin, Stowe VT.*

"Listen to the Mocking Bird," tune by Richard Milburn "Whistling Dick", music and lyrics by Alice Hawthorne (Philadelphia: Winner & Shuster, 110 North Eighth Street; 1856), *To Aaron R. Dutcher, Esq.*

Later editions of the song removed the credit to Richard Milburn and advertised the words and music as being by Hawthorne. The song was later advertised with the phrase "as sung by Rose Merrifield" (Myers). As discussed in this volume, the origins of Mr. Milburn remain unclear. Later variations of the song abounded including a quickstep, waltz, fantasia, galop, quickstep for four hands, polka, polonaise, quadrille, redowa, barcarolle, variations, schottische, easy quickstep, easy air, march, quickstep, mazurka, nocturne, minuet, rondo, and varsovienne (NUC). Claghorn[1] frequently mentions that the song "With A Little Bit of Luck" from *My Fair Lady* by Frederick Loewe and Alan Jay Lerner was based on "Mocking Bird." While there is some similarity between the close of Loewe's refrain and Winner's refrain, the similarity is probably more coincidence than tribute or parody.

"Little Closer Please, A," Septimus Winner (Philadelphia, J. Gibson Winner, 1736 Columbia Avenue, 1887/1893?).

It is possible that this work was published as early as 1887 having been advertised as a "humorous ditty" on *Winner's Octavo Music.* However, the earliest publication record that has been found is from 1893.

"Little Fairy Polka," Septimus Winner (Boston: Oliver Ditson, 1882), instrumental.

"Look with Thy Fond Eyes Upon Me," Alice Hawthorne (Philadelphia: Sep. Winner, 933 Spring Garden Street, 1860?), *Respectfully Dedicated to Lizzie A. Walker of Brooklyn, N.Y.*

Myers notes the song was popularized by Miss Caroline Richings. Some sources use the word "fond" in the title (Levy) while others use the word "fine" instead.

"Lord, Thou Knowest That I Love Thee," Alice Hawthorne (Philadelphia: Sep. Winner & Son, 1003 Spring Garden Street, 1873), *To Mrs. W.H. Harrison (New York)*.

Written after the death of President William Henry Harrison.

"Lost Isabel (Isabel, Lost Isabel)," Alice Hawthorne (Boston: Oliver Ditson, 1863, *To C. Campbell, Esq.*

The title is variously listed as above, as "Isabel Lost Isabel" and as the "new" "Remember Me." Myers also lists the song as published under the Winner name (unverified). The song was written to capitalize on the popularity of the play *East Lynne* and may, at times, have been sung as part of its performances.

"Love of One Fond Heart, The," Alice Hawthorne (Philadelphia: Sep. Winner, 110 North Eighth Street, 1855).

"Love Once Gone, Is Gone Forever," Alice Hawthorne (Philadelphia: Sep. Winner & Son, 1003 Spring Garden Street, 1870), *To Stiles Huber, Esq.*

"Love's Chiding's Waltz," Septimus Winner (Baltimore: Henry McCaffrey, 1864), instrumental.

"Love's Offering," Alice Hawthorne (New York: S.T. Gordon, 1869).

"Lover's Quarrel," Septimus Winner (unknown city: unknown publisher, unknown address, 1874).

"Maid and Sparrow," Percy Guyer (unknown city: unknown publisher, unknown address, 1878).

"Make Yourself at Home," Alice Hawthorne (Philadelphia: Sep. Winner, 926 Spring Garden Street, 1868), *The Composer and Publisher Beg to Leave Offer Their Thanks to Mr. E.S. Rosenthal, the Popular Vocalist for Kindly Introducing this Ballad to the Public.*

A different edition is dedicated to H.J. Murdoch, Esq. (LOC).

"Meeting-House Gate, The," Percy Guyer (Philadelphia: Sep. Winner & Son, 1003 Spring Garden Street, 1877), *To Walter D. Styer.*

"Mercy's Dream," Alice Hawthorne (Philadelphia: Winner & Shuster, 110 North Eighth Street, 1854), *To the Misses Gibson.*

Myers notes that the subject comes from John Bunyan's *Pilgrim's Progress*. Given his theory that "Resurgam" (1871) is based on the same book, Winner's fascination with it would have lasted for almost twenty years. (See "Resurgam," "Shepherd Boy," "Vanity Fair" and "Wicket Gate").

"Morn and Eventide," Alice Hawthorne (unknown city: unknown publisher, unknown address, unknown date).

According to Myers this song was advertised as follows: "A charming piece for two voices. This duet can be sung in character, with interesting effect, one person representing day with a white spangled dress. The other, night, with dark blue dress and silver stars with head dress to match the make up. It is also a dialogue song." This is probably the closest to opera Winner ever came.

"Motherless Kate," Alice Hawthorne (Boston: Oliver Ditson, 1858), *To Maggie P. Mayer.*

"Mountain Rose Scottische," Septimus Winner (Philadelphia: Lee & Walker, 1866), *To Mrs. M.A. French,* instrumental.

"My Cottage Home," Alice Hawthorne (Philadelphia: Winner & Shuster, 1853).

"My Early Fireside," Alice Hawthorne (Philadelphia: Winner & Shuster, 110 North Eighth Street, 1855), *To Miss Louisa Carr.*

"My Love to All at Home," Alice Hawthorne (Philadelphia: J.E. Winner, 545 North Eighth Street, 1869), *To Miss E.B. Dickson.*

"My Mother's Kiss," music by Alice Hawthorne, lyrics by J.C.A. Jr. (Philadelphia: Lee & Walker, 1861), *To Miss Annie M. Cross (Gross?).*

"Nation Mourns Her Martyr'd Son (An Honest Man's the Noblest Work of God), A" music by Septimus Winner, lyrics by Alice Hawthorne (Philadelphia: Sep. Winner, 933 Spring Garden Street, 1865), *In Memory Of Abraham Lincoln, Sixteenth President Of The United States.*

Written following the assassination of Lincoln, Winner used the same music for this song as he did in "Our Nation Calls for Peace Again" (Myers).

"Netty Moore," Alice Hawthorne (Philadelphia: Lee & Walker, 1858), *To Miss Jenny Cassell, Mariondale, Mo.*

"New Friends True Friends," Alice Hawthorne (Philadelphia: Sep. Winner, 716 Spring Garden Street, 1860), *To John S. Fisher.*

A later version is dedicated to John L. Feikes (LOC).

"New Hearts and Faces," Alice Hawthorne (unknown city: unknown publisher, unknown address, unknown date).

While the original publication date is unknown, the song did appear in an issue of the *Musical Journal* in 1867.

"Night Spirit Polka, The," Eastburn (Septimus Winner?) (Philadelphia: S. Winner, 267 Callowhill Street, 1852).

Speculation that this was composed by a young Joseph Eastburn Winner makes authenticating this title virtually impossible.

"No One to Kiss!," Septimus Winner (Philadelphia: Lee & Walker, 1857), *To William N. Toy, Esq.*

"No One To Weep When I Am Gone," Alice Hawthorne (Philadelphia: Sep. Winner & Son, 1003 Spring Garden Street, 1870), *To Miss Emma P. Markley.*

"Nothing to Wear," Septimus Winner (Philadelphia: Lee & Walker, 1857), *William S. Hassall, Esq.*

This song was later arranged as the "Nothing to Wear Polka," Septimus Winner (Philadelphia: Lee & Walker, 1857).

"Old Boston Bay," Septimus Winner (unknown city: unknown publisher, unknown address, 1873), instrumental?

"Old Maid," Septimus Winner (unknown city: unknown publisher, unknown address, unknown date).

"Old Red Cent, The," Alice Hawthorne (Boston: Oliver Ditson, 1858), *To Miss Sallie J. Winner.*

"On the Board-Walk at Cape May," Mark Mason (Philadelphia: Sep. Winner & Son, 1003 Spring Garden Street, 1871), *To Gus Williams, The American Star Comique.*

"One Fond Heart," Alice Hawthorne (Philadelphia: Sep. Winner & Son, 1003 Spring Garden Street, 1878), *To Misses Lillie and Gussie D'Alve.*

Listed as also having been published under the Paul Stenton pseudonym (LOC). Myers notes that the song was popularized by the D'Alve Sisters "throughout the United States."

"Only a Child," Alice Hawthorne (unknown city: unknown publisher, unknown address, unknown date).

"Only Friends and Nothing More," music by Septimus Winner, lyrics by Alice Hawthorne (Philadelphia: Sep. Winner & Son, 1003 Spring Garden Street, 1872).

"Only One," Alice Hawthorne (unknown city: unknown publisher, unknown address, unknown date).

"Our Flag o'er Georgia Floats Again," Septimus Winner (Philadelphia: Sep. Winner, 933 Spring Garden Street, 1864), *To Geo. F. Swain, Esq.*

"Our Good Old Friends," Alice Hawthorne (Philadelphia: Winner & Shuster, 110 North Eighth Street, 1855), *To Francis E. Harding Esq.*

This song is the only published song to feature an image of Alice Hawthorne. Placed on the back of the music, Winner hired the New York firm of Sarony & Company to create the image rather than using his regular lithographer, George Swain. The image is signed Alice Hawthorne but it is unmistakably Winner's handwriting.

"Our Nation Calls for Peace Again," Septimus Winner, (Philadelphia: Sep. Winner, 933 Spring Garden Street, 1864).

Myers notes that the song features the same music as "A Nation Mourns Her Martyr'd Son."

"Our Own," Alice Hawthorne, (Philadelphia: Sep. Winner, 926 Spring Garden Street, 1868).

"Our Sweethearts at Home," Septimus Winner, (Philadelphia: Sep. Winner, 933 Spring Garden Street, 1863), *To Miss Mary Burrouch, Haddonfield, N.J.*

"Out of Work," Alice Hawthorne (Philadelphia: Sep. Winner & Son, 1003 Spring Garden Street, 1877).

Another edition, published in the same year, gives the composer and lyricist as Percy Guyer (LOC).

"Over My Heart," Alice Hawthorne (Philadelphia: Sep. Winner & Co., 933 Spring Garden Street, 1866), *To Miss Kate E. Healy.*

"Over the Stars is Rest," music by Franz Abt (from "Ueber den Sternen ist Ruh"), lyrics by Alice Hawthorne (Philadelphia: Sep. Winner & Son, 1003 Spring Garden Street, 1870).

"Parting Whispers," Alice Hawthorne (Philadelphia: Sep. Winner, 933 Spring Garden Street, 1863), *Miss Adele Roubaud.*

"Party at the Zoo, The," Apsley Street (Philadelphia: Sep. Winner & Son, 1736 Columbia Avenue, 1888).

"Pasaic Waltz," Septimus Winner (Philadelphia: Lee & Walker, unknown year), instrumental.

"Pass Us Not By," music by Alice Hawthorne, lyrics by George M. Vickers (Philadelphia?: W.F. Shaw, 1882).

"Passing Thoughts," Septimus Winner (Philadelphia: Sep. Winner & Co., 933 Spring Garden Street, 1865), *To Miss Adele Roubaud.*

Advertised as an "impromptu melody for the pianoforte" (KFR).

"Pavilion Model Polka," Septimus Winner (Philadelphia: Lee & Walker, 1875), instrumental.

Written in celebration of the national Centennial and notably the massive exhibits that took place as part of that celebration in Philadelphia. The very clever cover features cutouts from which one could construct a miniature version of the Centennial Pavilion.

"Peabody's Funeral March," Septimus Winner (New York: C.H. Ditson, unknown date), *In Memory Of "The World's Benefactor"*, instrumental.

"Penn-City March," Septimus Winner (unknown city: unknown publisher, unknown address, unknown date), instrumental.

"Pet of the Cradle, The," Alice Hawthorne (Philadelphia: Winner & Shuster, 1854), *To Miss S. Emily Davis.*

"Pray Tell Me the Wish of Thy Heart," Alice Hawthorne (Philadelphia: Lee & Walker, 1865), *To Misses Geneva and Ellen Bear.*

"Pretty Sally," music by M.S.C., lyrics by Septimus Winner (Philadelphia: Sep. Winner & Co., 933 Spring Garden Street, 1863).

"Pretty to Me," Alice Hawthorne (Philadelphia: Sep. Winner, 933 Spring Garden Street, 1864), *To and as Sung by J.A. Palmer, Esq.*

"Queer People There Be," Mark Mason (Philadelphia: Sep. Winner & Son, 1003 Spring Garden Street, 1870), *To Miss Emma P. Markley.*

"Race Horse Galop," Septimus Winner (Philadelphia: Lee & Walker, 1869), instrumental.

This instrumental quotes the Hawthorne ballad "Yes, I Would the War Were Over" (KFR).

"Rally for the Union," music by Septimus Winner, lyrics by C.M. Tremaine (unknown city: unknown publisher, unknown address, 1862).

"Rear Back Bob," Mark Mason (Philadelphia: Sep. Winner & Son, 1003 Spring Garden Street, 1869).

Listed by Myers as one of the few "Ethiopian" ballads written by Winner. The sheet music also makes note of its introduction by the singing duo of Duprez and Benedict.

"Rebecca at the Well," Alice Hawthorne (Philadelphia: Lee & Walker, 1854).

"Rebus Polka," Septimus Winner (Boston: Oliver Ditson, 1865), instrumental.

"Red Petticoat, The," Septimus Winner (Boston: Oliver Ditson, 1858).

"Resurgam," Septimus Winner (Philadelphia: Sep. Winner & Son, 1003 Spring Garden Street, 1871), *To A.R. Taylor, Esq.*

As noted earlier, this song seems to have been inspired by John Bunyan's *Pilgrim's Progress*. The title of this song is alternatively given as "I Will Rise Again" (PDM). (See "Mercy's Dream," "Shepherd Boy," "Vanity Fair" and "Wicket Gate").

"Reveille, The," Septimus Winner, (New York: S.T. Gordon, 1861), *To Mr. Herman Braungart,* instrumental.

"Robin's Roundelay, The," Septimus Winner (Philadelphia: Sep. Winner & Son, 1007 Spring Garden Street, 1882).
Advertised as a "concert song as sung by Miss Ritta Keller" (Myers).

"Rondo Polka," Septimus Winner (Philadelphia: Lee & Walker, 1862), *To Miss Mary A. Martin,* instrumental.

"Rosencrans Military Scottische," Septimus Winner (Philadelphia: Winner & Co., 933 Spring Garden Street, 1863), *Respectfully Dedicated to Maj. Genl. William S. Rosecrans,* instrumental.
The score of this song features several programmatic references including, "Introduction," "The Cross Fire," "Advance of the Cavalry." Winner clearly intended a programmatic reference in the minuet and trio structure.

"Rosine Waltzes," Septimus Winner (Philadelphia: Sep. Winner, 933 Spring Garden Street, 1865), *To Miss Rosine M. Roubaud,* instrumental.

"Royal March," Septimus Winner (Philadelphia: Wm. H. Keyser & Co., 1876), *To Miss May Royal, Germantown,* instrumental.

"Rubber Man, The," Septimus Winner (Philadelphia: Winner & Co., 933 Spring Garden Street, 1863).

"Ruby Scottische," Septimus Winner (Philadelphia: Wm. R. Smith, 1862), *To Miss Mary Delaney,* instrumental.

"San Francisco Scottische," Septimus Winner (Philadelphia: Sep. Winner, 148 North Eighth Street, 1858), *To Francis Dixey, Esq.,* instrumental.

"Scaley Polka," Septimus Winner, (Boston: Oliver Ditson, 1865), instrumental.
This song seems to have been a pedagogical study designed to introduce the performer to the various types of scales.

"Secretary Chase's March and Quickstep," Septimus Winner (Philadelphia: Lee & Walker, 1863), *To the Hon. Salmon P. Chase, Secretary of the Treasury,* instrumental.

"Shepherd Boy," Alice Hawthorne (unknown city: unknown publisher, unknown address, 1858).
Yet another song that refers to John Bunyan's *Pilgrim's Progress.* In an advertisement for the song it is described as a "Sabbath Ballad." (See "Mercy's Dream," "Resurgam," "Vanity Fair" and "Wicket Gate").

"Side by Side," Alice Hawthorne (Germantown, Pa.: Sep. Winner, 4742 Main Street, 1875), *To Miss Mary Jackson.*

"Silver Wedding March," Septimus Winner (unknown city: unknown publisher, unknown address, 1870), instrumental.

"Sister's Prayer, The," Mark Mason (Philadelphia?: W.F. Shaw, 1874). Listed as a temperance ballad (LOC).

"Snow-White Rose," Alice Hawthorne (Baltimore: Henry McCaffrey, 1861), *To Miss Rosine M. Rouband,* instrumental.

"Soldiers Are Passing, The," Septimus Winner (unknown city: unknown publisher, unknown address, 1882). Listed as being from the "melo-drama" *Heloise* (PDM).

"Some Happier Day," music by Alice Hawthorne, lyrics by Isaac Moffatt (Philadelphia: Louis Meyer, 1873), *To Mrs. I. Moffatt.*

"Song of Jokes, The," Septimus Winner (Philadelphia: Sep. Winner, 933 Spring Garden Street, 1864), *To Frank Moran, Esq.* A very clever arrangement that contains excerpts from more than twenty popular songs of the day combined into a coherent musical structure.

"Song of the Farmer," Alice Hawthorne (Philadelphia: Winner & Shuster, 110 North Eighth Street, 1854), *To Lawrence Shuster, Esq.*

"Song of the Winter Wind" (a.k.a., "Pity the Poor"), music by Alice Hawthorne, lyrics by William M. Clark (Philadelphia: Lee & Walker, 1869). Clark is listed as the editor of *Our Schoolday Visitor* (LOC).

"Sour Krout," Septimus Winner (New York: S.T. Gordon, 1873), *To Gus Williams, Sung by Fred Howard.*

"Spelling Bee, The," Septimus Winner (Philadelphia: Lee & Walker, 1875).

"Spring Carol (or Vocal Polka), A," music by Septimus Winner, lyrics by Alice Hawthorne (Philadelphia: Sep. Winner & Son, 545 North Eighth Street, 1892).

"Straight-Four Set," Septimus Winner (unknown city: unknown publisher, unknown address, unknown date), instrumental.

"Sue, My Darling Sue," Septimus Winner (Philadelphia: Sep. Winner & Son, 1736 Columbia Avenue, 1894), *To Miss Jessie E. Baker, Washington.*

"Summer of the Heart, The," Alice Hawthorne (New York: Firth Pond & Co., 1857), *To Malcom McCload Walker, Esq.*

"Sun Flower Polka," Septimus Winner (unknown city: unknown publisher, unknown address, unknown date), instrumental.

"Sunshine Scottische," Septimus Winner (Philadelphia: Sep. Winner, 933 Spring Garden Street, 1865), *To Miss Mattie Ward, "Sunshine,"* instrumental.

"Surprise Schottische," Eastburn (Septimus Winner?) (Philadelphia: S. Winner, 267 Callowhill Street, 1853).

Speculation that this was composed by a young Joseph Eastburn Winner makes authentication of this piece virtually impossible.

"Swallow-Tail Coat," music by Septimus Winner, lyrics by J.C. Williamson (Philadelphia: Hawthorne Publishing Company, 914 Spring Garden Street, 1875), *To Sam Rickey Esq., Comedian.*

"T'were Better That Words Were Unspoken," Alice Hawthorne (Philadelphia: Sep. Winner & Co., 933 Spring Garden Street, 1865), *To Miss Fannie Stevens.*

Advertised as being "sung with great success by Sophie Gimber Kuhn" (KFR).

"Take Me Mother in Thy Lap," music by Septimus Winner, lyrics by Alice Hawthorne (Cleveland: S. Brainard, 1871).

"Tapping at the Garden Gate," music by S.W. New, lyrics by J. Loker (Philadelphia: 1874).

Featured in *Peterson's Magazine.* While no independent verification exists to confirm that S.W. New and Septimus Winner are one and the same, the coincidence is too strong to dismiss.

"Ten Little Injuns," Septimus Winner (Boston: Oliver Ditson, 1868), *To Master Frank Dixey Winner.*

Two derivatives, "Ten Little Niggers" (Lee & Walker, 1869) and "Ten Undergraduates" (Lee & Walker, 1869) both credit Winner for the music but not the lyrics. Another version published under the name "Old John Brown" was also published by Oliver Ditson (year unknown) (NUC).

"That Little Church Around the Corner," Alice Hawthorne (Philadelphia: Lee & Walker, 1871), *To Joseph Jefferson, Esq.*

See the title of the same name by Winner's brother, Joseph Eastburn Winner (Appendix I).

"That's So," Mark Mason (unknown city: unknown publisher, unknown address, unknown date).

"There Is No One Like a Mother," Septimus Winner (Philadelphia: Sep. Winner, 531 North Eighth Street, 1862), *To Miss Matilda Lewis.*

"There Is Wealth for Honest Labor," Alice Hawthorne (unknown city: unknown publisher, unknown address, 1858).

"There's Not a Sorrow on My Heart," music by William Wither Jr., lyrics by Septimus Winner (unknown city: unknown publisher, unknown address, 1862).

"These Are Friends That We Never Forget," music by Septimus Winner, lyrics by Alice Hawthorne (Philadelphia: Sep. Winner & Son, 1003 Spring Garden Street, 1871).

The title is alternately given as "There Are Friends That We Never Forget" (Myers).

"This Land of Ours," Alice Hawthorne (Philadelphia: Lee & Walker, 1857), *To Tho's P. Heyl, Esq.*

"Thy Voice Hath a Charm," Alice Hawthorne (unknown city: unknown publisher, unknown address, unknown date).

"Tiny Bark, A," Alice Hawthorne (unknown city: unknown publisher, unknown address, unknown date).

"Tit-Tat-To Schottische," Marion Florence (Philadelphia: Winner & Shuster, 1855 (likely an error) and Philadelphia: Lee & Walker, 1860), *Respectfully Dedicated to Joseph Wood, Jr.,* instrumental.

"To Him That Giveth Let Us Sing," Alice Hawthorne (Philadelphia: Lee & Walker, 1856), *To Mrs. J.M. Evans.*

"Tobias and Biancos," Septimus Winner (Philadelphia: Lee & Walker, 1865).

"Tom Collins Is My Name," Septimus Winner (Philadelphia: W.H. Boner & Co., 1874), *To Mr. Frank A. Conly.*

This song may be the same as "I'm Here, I'm There, I'm Everywhere." Neither song has been obtainable.

"Trab-Trab Galop," Septimus Winner (Philadelphia: Sep. Winner, 531 North Eighth Street, 1862), *To Miss Emily H. Winner,* instrumental.

Like "General Halleck's Grand March," this song was also published with an opus number (927) (Myers).

"Under the Eaves," music by Septimus Winner, lyrics by Alice Hawthorne (unknown city: unknown publisher, unknown address, 1874).

"Vanity Fair," Alice Hawthorne (unknown city: unknown publisher, unknown address, unknown date).

Yet another song indicating the influence of John Bunyan's *Pilgrim's Progress* (Myers). (See "Mercy's Dream," "Resurgam," "Shepherd Boy" and "Wicket Gate").

"We Met No More," Alice Hawthorne (Philadelphia: Sep. Winner & Son, 1003 Spring Garden Street, 1871), *To Robert Boone, Jr.*

"We Will Walk in Thy Ways," Septimus Winner (unknown city: unknown publisher, unknown address, unknown date).

"Weeping Family, The," Mark Mason, (Germantown Pa.: Sep. Winner, 4742 Main Street, 1875).

One source also links this song with the name Frank Verdant, a name that comes up nowhere else in the Winner literature (PDM).

"What Care I?," Alice Hawthorne (Philadelphia: Sep. Winner & Co., 933 Spring Garden Street, 1866), *To Mrs. Mary A. Cox.*

The full title of this song is also given as "What Care I, Who Cares for Me?" (PDM).

"What Is Home without a Mother?," Alice Hawthorne (Philadelphia: Winner & Shuster, 110 North Eighth Street, 1854), *To Miss Ann Eliza P. Shuster.*

Already noted for the numerous parody songs it spawned (see page 47), one not mentioned includes the German parody "Vot Ish Life Mitout de Lager" (by John L. Zieber). Myers notes another, "What Is Hope Without a Father" as well as a London edition that advertised itself as being performed by the Christy Minstrels. If this were the case, it would have resulted in significant publicity for the song.

"What Shall I Offer Thee?," Alice Hawthorne (Boston: Oliver Ditson, 1860).

"When Mother Married Pap," Percy Guyer (unknown city: unknown publisher, unknown address, 1868).

One citation lists this song as being by Eastburn (Joseph Eastburn Winner) but the ascription is unlikely despite the fact the Joe Winner may have written a song with the same title with lyrics by Elmer Ruan Coates.

"When the Corn Is Gathered In," music by Alice Hawthorne, lyrics by A.G. Wolford (Philadelphia: Lee & Walker, 1870), *To Miss Adeline Sager.*

Listed as a companion song to "When the Corn is Waving" (Myers).

"Where Mother Is We Call it Home," Alice Hawthorne (Philadelphia: Lee & Walker, 1870), *To Mrs. Emma L. Gutekunst.*

"Wherefore," Septimus Winner (Germantown, Pa: Sep. Winner, 4742 Main Street, 1875), *To Miss Helen A. McCurdy.*

"Whirlwind Waltz," Septimus Winner (unknown city: unknown publisher, unknown address, unknown date), instrumental.

"Whispering Hope," Alice Hawthorne, (Philadelphia: Sep. Winner, 926 Spring Garden Street, 1868), *To Miss Dora Stiles, Stowe, Vt.*

Later published editions include ones by Oliver Ditson in 1881 and again in 1915, a testament to the song's popularity. The 1915 version publicized the song's popularity as a result of performances by Alma Gluck and Louise Homer. Hannah Winner would copyright the song again in 1910 to ensure continued royalties. This would result in at least three 1925 publications and another as late as 1949 following the song's popularity as a result of contemporary recordings.

"Who Will Kiss Those Ruby Lips?," Septimus Winner (unknown city: unknown publisher, unknown address, unknown date).

"Why Ask If I Remember Thee?," music by Gaetano Donizetti, lyrics by Alice Hawthorne (Philadelphia: Sep. Winner, 110 North Eighth Street, 1855).

Copy unavailable. Sources indicate that the melody was taken from Donizetti's *Lucia di Lammermoor* (Myers).

"Wicket Gate," Alice Hawthorne (unknown city: unknown publisher, unknown address, 1858).

Another in the series of songs inspired by John Bunyan's *Pilgrim's Progress.* (See "Mercy's Dream," "Resurgam," "Shepherd Boy" and "Vanity Fair").

"Widders Beware, Maidens Take Care," Septimus Winner (Boston: Oliver Ditson, 1857).

"Williamsport Schottische," Septimus Winner (Philadelphia: Sep. Winner, 716 Spring Garden Street, 1859), *To S.M. Grans Esq. (Burgess Of Williamsport),* instrumental.

"Winner's Banjo," Septimus Winner (Philadelphia: Lee & Walker, 1858), instrumental.

A solo piano work, it was advertised as "an imitation of this popular instrument." Myers notes that the music contains an excerpt from "Old Dan Tucker."

"Winstar Gavotte," Septimus Winner (Philadelphia: Sep. Winner & Son, 1736 Columbia Avenue, 1887?), instrumental.

"Winter Sweets," music by Septimus Winner, lyrics by Alice Hawthorne (Boston: Oliver Ditson, 1894), *To Miss Katherine Turner.*

"World Is Topsy Turvy, The," Septimus Winner (Philadelphia: Sep. Winner, 933 Spring Garden Street, 1864).

Another in the many songs that were introduced by E.F. Dixey.

"Wyoming Waltz," Septimus Winner (Philadelphia: Winner & Shuster, 110 North Eighth Street, 1854), *Respectfully Dedicated to Miss Maggie Swetland by her Friend S.W. Of Philadelphia,* instrumental.

Originally published under the name S.W. Winner would re-copyright the work in 1882, most likely for publication in *Peterson's Magazine*.

"Years Ago," Alice Hawthorne (Philadelphia: Beck & Lawton, 1856).

"Yes, I Would the War Were Over," Alice Hawthorne (Philadelphia: Winner & Co., 933 Spring Garden Street, 1863), *Respectfully Dedicated to Mrs. C. Henri.*

One advertisement described this song as follows: "The immense sale of this answer song to the popular song *When This Cruel War is Over* is enough to recommend it without further notice. It has been sung nightly at the Eureka Theatre in San Francisco by the popular vocalist Sig. Abecco amid unbounded applause. The sentiment is good and the melody beautiful" (Levy).

"You Can Never Win Us Back," A Lady of Kentucky (unknown city: unknown publisher, unknown address, unknown year).

Duke University Special Collections attributes this song to Winner but also indicates that it may be an arrangement. One source lists the author as Catherine Ann Warfield although this has not be independently verified.

"Yours Truly (Bessie Jane)," Alice Hawthorne (Philadelphia: Sep. Winner & Son, 1007 Spring Garden Street, 1880), *To My Friend A. Jackson, Esq.*

Notes

1. Claghorn, *Whispering Hope,* 6.

Appendix D
Pseudonymous Listing of Songs

This listing provides a chronological listing of songs published by Winner, sorted alphabetically by pseudonym. Songs written within a given year are organized alphabetically. Cross-reference with Appendix C for further information. Undated works are set apart.

The Hawthorne ballads chronology that Winner started at times, abandoned and then revived are noted in bold beside the appropriate titles. The reader can plainly see the haphazard nature of the system.

As *A Lady of Kentucky*

As stated several times, this pseudonym cannot be independently verified. It is included because it is listed in both Claghorn and Myers.

Undated
"You Can Never Win Us Back"

As *Eastburn*

Titles here are assumed to be by Septimus Winner publishing under the Eastburn name, due to their early composition date. If these songs, as most other Eastburn songs are, are by Septimus' brother, Joseph Eastburn Winner, they would have been written while he was still a teenager—an unlikely scenario.

"Night Spirit Polka," 1852
"Surprise Schottische," 1853

As *Marion Florence*

"Tit-Tat-To Schottische," 1860

As *Percy Guyer*

"When Mother Married Pap," 1868
"Meeting-House Gate, The," 1877
"I'll Plant a Rose beside Thy Grave," 1878
"Maid and Sparrow," 1878
"Don't Blame Your Wife," 1885
"Christmas Comes But Once a Year," 1887?

Undated
"Grandmother's Chair"
"Kettle and the Clock, The"

As *Alice Hawthorne*

"How Sweet Are the Roses?" 1853 (**Hawthorne Ballad #2**)
"My Cottage Home," 1853 (**Hawthorne Ballad #1**)

"Chimes of the Monastery, The," 1854
"Come, Gather 'round the Hearth," 1854
"I Set My Heart upon a Flower," 1854
"Mercy's Dream," 1854 (**Hawthorne Ballad #4**)
"Rebecca at the Well," 1854 (**Hawthorne Ballad #5**)
"Song of the Farmer," 1854 (**Hawthorne Ballad #6**)
"What Is Home without a Mother?" 1854

"Cast Thy Bread upon the Waters," 1855
"Days Gone By, The," 1855
"Dreams That Charmed Me When a Child," 1855
"Fond Moments of My Childhood," 1855
"Golden Moon, The," 1855
"Happiness of Home, The," 1855
"Let Us Live with a Hope," 1855
"Love of One Fond Heart, The," 1855
"My Early Fireside," 1855 (**Hawthorne Ballad #3**)
"Our Good Old Friends," 1855
"Pet of the Cradle, The," 1855
"Why Ask If I Remember Thee?" 1855

"Am I Not True to Thee?" 1856
"Hiawatha Polka," 1856
"Listen to the Mocking Bird," 1856
"To Him That Giveth Let Us Sing," 1856
"Years Ago," 1856

"As We Gathered in the Hay," 1857
"Flower Fadeth, The," 1857
"Heart's Mission, The," 1857 (**Hawthorne Ballad #34**)
"Home and Friends (When the Sun Goes Down)," 1857
"Summer of the Heart, The," 1857
"This Land of Ours," 1857

"Away From Home," 1858
"Gentle Maggie (I'm Coming Home from Sea)," 1858
"Good-Night But Not Good-Bye," 1858
"I Have Tidings," 1858 (**Hawthorne Ballad #39**)
"Motherless Kate," 1858
"Netty Moore," 1858
"Old Red Cent, The," 1858
"Shepherd Boy," 1858
"There Is Wealth for Honest Labor," 1858
"Wicket Gate," 1858

"Jenny, Darling Jenny," 1859 (**Hawthorne Ballad #41**)

"Look with Thy Fond Eyes upon Me," 1860 (**Hawthorne Ballad #63**)
"New Friends True Friends," 1860 (**Hawthorne Ballad #42**)
"What Shall I Offer Thee?" 1860 (**Hawthorne Ballad #43**)

"Cozy Nook, The," 1861 (**Hawthorne Ballad #49**)
"My Mother's Kiss," 1861
"Snow-White Rose," 1861 (**Hawthorne Ballad #47**)

"As Dear to Day as Ever," 1862 (**Hawthorne Ballad #45**)
"Friend of My Heart," 1862 (**Hawthorne Ballad #51**)
"Jovial Scottische," 1862?
"Le Solitaire Schottische," 1862

"Down upon the Rappahannock," 1863
"Lost Isabel (Isabel, Lost Isabel)," 1863
"Parting Whispers," 1863
"Yes, I Would the War Were Over," 1863

"Did You Think of Me to Day," 1864
"Pretty to Me," 1864

"I Am Dreaming of the Loved Ones," 1865
"Just as of Old," 1865
"Pray Tell Me the Wish of Thy Heart," 1865
"T'were Better That Words Were Unspoken," 1865

"Home Ever Dear," 1866
"I Was Thinking, Idly Thinking," 1866
"Link'd with Many Bitter Tears," 1866
"What Care I?" 1866
"Over My Heart," 1866

"Echoes from Afar," 1867

"Faded Leaves," 1868
"Friends We Love, The," 1868
"Lazaroni Maid, The," 1868
"Make Yourself at Home," 1868
"Our Own," 1868
"Whispering Hope," 1868

"Be Happy with Me," 1869 (**Hawthorne Ballad #85**)
"Cruel Words Unwisely Spoken," 1869
"Dance of the Sprites (Mazurka)," 1869
"Hearth and Home," 1869
"Love's Offering," 1869
"My Love to All at Home," 1869
"Song of the Winter Wind (Pity the Poor)," 1869

"Love Once Gone, Is Gone Forever," 1870
"No One to Weep When I Am Gone," 1870
"Over the Stars Is Rest," 1870
"When the Corn Is Gathered In," 1870
"Where Mother Is We Call it Home," 1870

"After Sundown," 1871
"Drifting from Home," 1871
"God Bless the Little Feet," 1871
"Take Me Mother in Thy Lap," 1871
"That Little Church around the Corner," 1871
"We Met No More," 1871

"Only Friends and Nothing More," 1872

"Bird and Mate," 1873
"Lord, Thou Knowest That I Love Thee," 1873
"Some Happier Day," 1873

"Bow in the Cloud, The," 1874
"Gates Are Ever Open, The," 1874
"Home By and By," 1874

"If My Wishes Could Come True," 1875
"Side by Side," 1875

"Out of Work," 1877

"Don't Forget to Say Your Prayers," 1879
"One Fond Heart," 1879

"Yours Truly (Bessie Jane)," 1880

"Pass Us Not By," 1882

"Good-Bye Dear Mother," 1888 (**Hawthorne Ballad "Aftermath Collection" #1**)

Undated
"Because Thou Art So Far Away"
"Bid Me Goodbye (The Soldier's Farewell)"
"Let Us Hope for the Best"
"Morn and Eventide"
"New Hearts and Faces"
"Only a Child"
"Only One"
"Thy Voice Hath a Charm"
"Tiny Bark, A"
"Vanity Fair"

As *M.A.I.*

"Hop De Dood'n Doo (Ethiopian ballad)," 1854
"Aunt Jemima's Plaster," 1855

As *Mark Mason*

"Lady All Skin and Bone, The," 1869
"Rear Back Bob," 1869
"Queer People There Be," 1870
"On the Board-Walk at Cape May," 1871
"And Yet I Am Not Happy," 1873
"Envy Not Your Neighbor," 1873
"I Don't Got Him Now?" 1873
"Sister's Prayer, The," 1874
"Weeping Family, The," 1875
"Ellen's Babies," 1877
"Johnny Get Your Hair Cut," 1887

"Let Her Go Gallagher! Don't Be a Clam," 1887
"Just Gone Out," 1888
"Lilliputian's Beer Song," 1892

Undated
"Boy and the Sparrow, The"
"That's So"

As *Paul Stenton*

"I Would Not Die Away from Home," 1878
"A Good Send Off to Thee," 1880

As *Apsley Street*

"Birdie's Ball, The," 1869
"Gone Where the Woodbine Twineth," 1870
"Party at the Zoo, The," 1888

As *Septimus Winner*

"Village Polka Quadrilles," 1850

"Let the Light of Days Depart," 1851

"Fireside Scottische, The," 1854
"Wyoming Waltz," 1854

"Kissing thro' the Bars," 1856

"Drama March," 1857
"Edwin Forrest Quickstep," 1857
"No One to Kiss!" 1857
"Nothing to Wear," 1857
"Nothing to Wear Polka," 1857
"Widders Beware, Maidens Take Care," 1857

"I'll Kiss You Quick and Stay," 1858
"Juana, Cuba's Fair Isle," 1858
"Red Petticoat, The," 1858
"San Francisco Scottische," 1858
"Winner's Banjo," 1858

"Williamsport Schottische," 1859

"Bully for You (Oh, I'm a Single Man)," 1861
"Colonel Ellsworth's Funeral March," 1861
"Contraband Scottische," 1861
"Reveille, The," 1861

"Away, Away the Morn is Brightly Breaking," 1862
"General Halleck's Grand March," 1862
"Give Us Back Our Old Commander, Little Mac, The People's Pride,"
    1862
"Rally for the Union," 1862
"Rondo Polka," 1862
"Ruby Scottische," 1862
"There Is No One Like a Mother," 1862
"There's Not a Sorrow On My Heart," 1862
"Trab-Trab Galop," 1862

"Comet Waltz," 1863
"Cruel War Quickstep," 1863
"Greenback Quickstep," 1863
"He's Gone to the Arms of Abraham," 1863
"Pretty Sally," 1863
"Rosencrans Military Scottische," 1863
"Rubber Man, The," 1863
"Secretary Chase's March and Quickstep," 1863

"Der Deutscher's Dog," 1864
"Drummer Boy's March," 1864
"Flash Scottische," 1864
"General Hancock's Grand March," 1864
"Kissing in Fun," 1864
"Love's Chiding's Waltz," 1864
"Our Flag o'er Georgia Floats Again," 1864
"Our Nation Calls for Peace Again," 1864
"Our Sweethearts at Home," 1864
"Song of Jokes, The," 1864
"World is Topsy Turvy, The," 1864

"Eyes Will Watch for Thee," 1865?
"Farewell Song of Enoch Garden (I'll Sail the Seas Over)," 1865
"Nation Mourns Her Martyr'd Son (An Honest Man's the Noblest
    Work of God), A," 1865
"Passing Thoughts," 1865
"Rebus Polka," 1865
"Rosine Waltzes," 1865
"Scaley Polka," 1865?
"Sunshine Scottische," 1865

"Tobias and Biancos," 1865?

"Mountain Rose Scottische," 1866

"Lady Art Thou Sleeping," 1868
"Ten Little Injuns," 1868

"Race Horse Galop," 1869

"Aberdeen Scottische," 1870
"Congress Scottische," 1870
"Silver Wedding March," 1870

"Blow the Horn for Supper, Kate," 1871 (**Winner's "Farm Ballads"**
     #1)
"Coolie Chinee, The," 1871
"Never a Care I Know," 1871?
"Resurgam," 1871
"These Are Friends That We Never Forget," 1871?

"Dolly Varden," 1872

"Bury Not Thy Neighbor," 1873
"Down the Quiet Valley," 1873?
"Good Words," 1873
"Old Boston Bay," 1873
 "Sour Krout," 1873

"Anna Polka," 1874
"Ball and Pin Galop," 1874
"Dear Mollie Magee," 1874
"Lover's Quarrel," 1874
"Tom Collins Is My Name," 1874
"Under the Eaves," 1874

"Archiduc Polka," 1875
"Pavilion Model Polka," 1875
"Spelling Bee, The," 1875
"Swallow-Tail Coat," 1875
"Wherefore," 1875

"French Polka," 1876
"Gay As a Lark (Canzonetta)," 1876
"Let Us Cross over the River," 1876
"Royal March," 1876

"Baby's Dance," 1880
"Creeds of the Bells," 1880
"Dado Waltz," 1880

"God Save Our President," 1881

"Fritz Lullaby," 1882
"Gypsy's Tent, The," 1882
"Little Fairy Polka," 1882
"Robin's Roundelay, The," 1882
"Soldiers Are Passing, The," 1882

"Winstar Gavotte," 1887?

"Spring Carol (or Vocal Polka), A," 1892

"Little Closer Please, A," 1893?

"Sue, My Darling Sue," 1894
"Winter Sweets," 1894

Undated
"Acceptance"
"Alice Vane"
"Arbor Day Waltz"
"Banner March"
"Bird Note Galop"
"Blue Note Galop"
"Bound Brook Polka"
"Bower Scottische, The"
"Chickey Polka"
"Come to Our Hearts and Abide"
"Commonwealth March"
"Companions of Old"
"Danish Dance, The"
"Dead Leaves Fall, The"
"Down Below"
"Easter Lilies Waltzes"
"Four-in-Hand Scottische"
"I'm Here, I'm There, I'm Everywhere"
"Kitty Tyrell"
"Maggie May Rondo"
"Old Maid"
"Pasaic Waltz"
"Peabody's Funeral March"
"Penn-City March"

"Straight-Four Set"
"Sun Flower Polka"
"We Will Walk in Thy Ways"
"Whirlwind Waltz"
"Who Will Kiss Those Ruby Lips?"

Appendix E
Arrangements

Because Winner published arrangements under his own name, titles are listed here alphabetically. In many cases, publication records are unknown as many of these pieces are only referred to obliquely in biographical sketches or on advertisements in other publications. Attempts to uncover these arrangements from contemporary sources have proved largely unsuccessful. In addition, given the number of pseudonyms Winner did use, it is very likely that there are other arrangements that may never be uncovered.

"Annie Laurie Scottische" (Philadelphia: Lee & Walker, 1857), *Respectfully Dedicated To Miss Mary L. Dennison.* According to Spaeth (p. 81), the inspiration for this song was very likely the song "Annie Laurie" by Lady John Douglas Scott (born Alicia Ann Spottiswood; 1810-1900) which was highly popular among the British troops fighting in the Crimean War.

"Aria Alla Schozzese" (N.d./n.p., 1870). Arranged for violin and piano from *The Budget of Music.*

"Ballad Set Cotillions" (Philadelphia: Winner & Shuster, 1855). From Winner's *Plain Cotillions* series.

"Be My Mother Til I Die" (N.d./n.p., 1863). Melody by Elmer Ruan Coates, lyrics and arrangement by Winner.

"Black Diamond Cotillions" (Philadelphia: Sep. Winner & Son, 1872). From the *Fashionable Round and Square Dance* series.

"Black Swan Set" (Philadelphia: Winner & Shuster, 1855). From the *Plain Cotillions* series.

"Bonanza Polka Quadrilles" (N.p.d.).

"Captain Jinks of the Horse Marines" (Philadelphia: Lee & Walker, 1868). After T. Maclagan.

"Child's Own Set Cotillions" (Philadelphia: Winner & Shuster, 1855). From the *Plain Cotillions* series.

"Chimes of Normandy Waltz" (Philadelphia: Sep. Winner & Son, 1878). After Planquette.

"Cruel War Quickstep" (Philadelphia: Lee & Walker, 722 Chestnut Street, 1863), instrumental. Although this piece has not been examined, it is a dance arrangement of the song Hawthorne's "Yes, I Would the War Were Over."

"District Quickstep" (Philadelphia: Sep. Winner, 1852).

"Dolly Varden Cotillions" (Philadelphia: Sep. Winner & Son, 1872. From the *Fashionable Round and Square Dances* series.

"Eagle Quadrilles" (Philadelphia: G. Andre & Company, 1876).

"Ellie Rhee" (a.k.a. "Carry Me Back to Tennessee") (Boston: Oliver Ditson, 1865, republished in 1893). Claimed by Winner as of 1865 but traced back to "Ella Ree" by C.E. Stuart and James W. Potter from 1853. Claghorn notes that it is Winner's version that popularized the song and went on to fame in the Reconstruction era.

"Erminie and Nanon Gavotte" (Philadelphia: J. Gibson Winner, 1887). Advertised as "Containing popular melodies from these operas. Excellent for dancing."

"Fancy Cotillions" (Philadelphia: Lee & Walker, 1857). Number twelve of *Twenty Duets for Violin and Piano*.

"Flower Song" (Boston: Oliver Ditson, n.d.). After Lange.

"Flying Trapeze, The" (Philadelphia: Lee & Walker, 1868). Arrangement for voice and guitar.

"French Polka" (Philadelphia: Sep. Winner, 1865). A four-hand version was published by Oliver Ditson in 1876 and by F.A. North in 1904.

"Gasperone (Merry Go Round) Waltz" (Philadelphia: Sep. Winner & Son, 1873).

"Gentlemen's Bloomer Waltz" (Philadelphia: Sep. Winner, 257 Callowhill Street, 1851), instrumental.

"Glory Hallelujah" (Boston: Oliver Ditson, 1862).

"Grafulla's Favorite Waltz" (Philadelphia: S. Winner, 267 Callowhill Street, 1851), *To W.G. Stevenson, Esq.*

"Heaven's a Great Way Off" (Philadelphia: J.E. Winner, n.d.).

"Hoist up The Flag" (Philadelphia: Winner & Co., 1864). Claghorn lists this song as having words by Billy Holmes and music by Winner. Conversely, PDMusic.org lists it as having music by Billy Holmes and words/arrangement by Winner. An advertisement for the song found at the Library of Congress gives Holmes credit for both the lyrics and music and credits Winner with only the arrangement.

"Madame Angot Waltz" (Germantown, Pa.: Sep. Winner, 1875).

"Maggie May Rondo" (N.p.d.), instrumental.

"Maryland, My Maryland" (Philadelphia: Sep. Winner, 1862). This song is an adaptation of popular words to the tune of "O Tannenbaum." The National Union Catalog credits Charles W. Ellerbrock as composer and Winner as only an arranger. The poet, James R. Randall, was a Maryland-born Confederate sympathizer who lived in Louisiana where he was professor of English at Poydras College. Randall wrote the poem (first published in April 26, 1861, and reprinted extensively throughout the South) hoping that Maryland would join the Confederacy. Winner's version is not so much an adaptation but an answer song featuring new words encouraging Marylanders to be careful of Confederate influences: "The rebel horde is on thy shore, Maryland my Maryland, arise and drive him from thy door, Maryland my Maryland."

"Medley Set Cotillions" (Cincinnati: W.C. Peters & Sons, 1857). From the *Plain and Fancy Cotillions* series.

"Mocking Bird Cotillions" (Philadelphia: Winner & Shuster, 1856). Issued later in the *Mocking Bird Echoes*.

"National Set Cotillions" (Philadelphia: Winner & Shuster, 1855). From the *Plain Cotillions* series.

"Never A Care I Know" (Philadelphia: Sep. Winner & Son, 1003 Spring Garden Street, 1870), *To Frank A. Conly, Esq., the American Mimic and Vocalist.* Myers notes that this song was introduced in the popular play *Rainbow*. It is likely that this song was an arrangement as it is listed as such when it was published in *Peterson's Magazine*.

"O Ye Tears!" (Philadelphia: W.A. Trumpler, 1866). An arrangement for voice and guitar possibly by Franz Abt (ascription uncertain).

"Pasaic Waltz" (Boston: Oliver Ditson, 1865). Republished in 1893.

"Patchwork (Medley Song)" (N.p.d., 1873).

"Picnic Set Cotillions" (Cincinnati: W.C. Peters & Sons, 1857). From the *Plain and Fancy Cotillions* series.

"Pins & Needles Galop" (Philadelphia: J.E. Ditson, 1877).

"Rally for the Union" (Philadelphia: Lee & Walker, 1862). Advertised "as sung by [The Tremaine Brothers] nightly with unbounded applause at Dr. Colton's Exhibitions."

"Rosalie Schottische" (Boston: Russell & Richardson, 1857). Arranged from the song "Rosalie, The Prairie Flower" by George F. Root.

"Saileur [*sic*] Boys Set Cotillions" (Boston: Oliver Ditson, 1858), *Dedicated to the Crew of the Leviathan.* Original source of arrangement unknown.

"Shepherd Boy, The" (Boston: Oliver Ditson, 1877). Listed as being by G.D. Wilson, Myers conjectures that this may be another pen-name as there is a tune by Winner of the same name (see Appendix C).

Solos from the Opera (Philadelphia: E.M. Kerk, date unknown), *Dedicated to E.M. Kerk.* Myers lists as "arrangements for violin and flute with piano. A collection of more than fifty pieces originally issued separately. One of Winner's most elaborate works." The collection was published variously and much of it separately by Sep. Winner, Lee & Walker and Oliver Ditson between 1856 and 1867. Pieces include arrangements from *Il Trovatore, La Somnambula, Norma, Martha, Lucia di Lammermoor, La Fille du Regiment, La Traviata, Les Vespres Siciliennes, Don Pasquale, Lucrezia Borgia, The Barber of Seville, The Bohemian Girl, Zampa, I Puritani, Beatrice di Tenda, Ernani, Don Juan, Der Freischutz, Muette de Portici, I Montecchi e Capuletti, Guillaume Tell, Rigoletto, Die Zauberflote, A Night in Granada, Figaro, Faust, Le Postillon de Lonjumeau, Fra Diavolo, La Dame Blanche, L'Elisir D'Amour, Oberon, Fidelio, L'Africaine, La Grande Duchesse, Le Belle Helene, Barbe-Bleue, Orphee aux Enfers, Maritana, Genevieve, La Fille de Madame Angot, Mignon, Aida* and *La Vie Parisienne.*

"Star-Spangled Banner, The" (Philadelphia: Sep. Winner, 1898). Arranged as a solo for mandolin, violin, banjo or guitar with piano accompaniment or, alternately, accompanied by a second banjo or second guitar.

"That Lady in the Cars" (Philadelphia: Sep. Winner, 926 Spring Garden Street, 1868), *To Mr. Sam'l Kelly.*

"Tip Top Set" (Cincinnati: W.C. Peters & Sons, 1857). From Winner's *Plain and Fancy Cotillions* series.

"Topsey Set Cotillions" (Cincinnati: W.C. Peters & Sons, 1857). From Winner's *Plain and Fancy Cotillions* series.

"Village Polka Quadrilles" (Philadelphia: S. Winner, 257 Callowhill Street, 1850), *Respectfully Dedicated to John W. Gaul, Leader of the Original Philadelphia Brass Band.*

"Wedding Set Quadrilles" (Philadelphia: Sep. Winner & Son, 1003 Spring Garden Street, 1872). From the *Fashionable Round and Square Dances* series.

"Willie Schottische (Willie We Have Missed You)" (New York: Firth Pond & Co., 1857), *To Miss Emily Hawthorne Winner.*

Winner's Dance Folio (Philadelphia: Sep. Winner & Son, 1007 Spring Garden Street, 1882). Piano arrangement containing marches for weddings, promenades, round and square dances, plain quadrilles, fancy quadrilles, lancer quadrilles, schottisches, gavottes, hornpipes, Danish dances, five step waltzes, cotillions waltzes, polka-waltzes, mazurkas, redowas, and reels (Myers).

Winner's Octavo Music (Philadelphia, Sep. Winner & Son, 1736 Columbia Avenue, date unknown). Apparently, this was a series of songs issued under this title featuring both arrangements and original songs.

"Yankee Doodle and The Fisher's Hornpipe" (Philadelphia: Sep. Winner & Co., 1867). Published in the *Musical Journal.*

"Yankee Set Cotillions" (Cincinnati: W.C. Peters & Sons, 1857). FromWinner's *Plain and Fancy Cotillions* series.

Other arrangements for violin and piano include: *The Banner Folio*; *Choice Gems*; *Winner's Collection of Music for Violin* (Sep Winner, 1851; Lee & Walker, 1853; Davis, 1853); *Winner's Collection for Violin* (Ditson, 1892); *Septimus Winner's Dime Book of Tunes for Violin*; *Winner's Excelsior Collection*; *Folio of Violin and Piano Duets*; *Musical Garland of First Class Duets* (Ditson, 1874); *Musical Pastime Collection* (Lee & Walker, 1872; Ditson, 1900); *Winner's New American Collection* (White-Smith, 1884); *Septimus Winner's New Idea for Violin*; *New Set of First-Class Duets*; *Operatic Selections* (M.D. Swisher, 1895); *Social Pastime* (Ditson, 1881 and 1884); *Winner's Tunes of the World* (Lee & Walker, 1863, and containing music popular among the Army and Navy); *Twenty Duets* (Winner & Kerk, 1857); *Union Collection* (Ditson, 1862); *Violin Amusements Collection* and *Winner's Violin Folio* (Goetting, 1891).

Other miscellaneous arrangements: *Winner's Dance Music*; *Music and Steps for Round and Square Dances* (Ditson, 1870); *Winner's Band of Four*; *Choice Melodies* (for Mandolin, Ditson, 1893); *Evening Hour Collection* (for mandolin or guitar with piano, Ditson, 1893); *Fifty Parlor Duets*; *Grand Opera Melodies* (for mandolin); *Grand Opera*

Melodies (for guitar); *Light Opera Melodies* (for mandolin); *Light Opera Melodies* (for guitar); *Musical Present Collection*; *Operatic Selections for Cornet*; *Pages from the Opera for Beginners* (Sep. Winner, 1856); *Sep Winner's Penny Music*; *Winner's Select Duets for Cornet and Piano*; *The 'Starbeams' Collection for Piano or Reed Organ* (J.M. Stoddart, 1877) and *Winner's Tunes of the World* (featuring separate editions for clarinet, accordion, fife, and flageolet).

Appendix F
Pedagogical Materials

This appendix is listed by instrument.[1] Within each instrument, publications are listed chronologically. Where known, the publisher and year are provided.

Accordion

Winner's Improved Accordeon Method (Philadelphia: Winner & Shuster, 1854).

Winner's Accordion Songster (Philadelphia: Wm. Shuster, 1856; Philadelphia: Lee & Walker, 1857).

Winner's Accordion and Flutina Primer (New York: Firth Pond & Co., 1857).

Winner's Perfect Guide for Accordeon (Boston: Oliver Ditson, 1861).

Winner's Excelsior Method for the Accordeon (Boston: Oliver Ditson, 1864).

Winner's New Primer for Accordeon (New York: Firth Pond & Co., 1864).

Winner's Easy System for Accordeon (Philadelphia: Sep. Winner & Co., 1866).

Winner's Easy System for German Accordeon (Philadelphia: Lee & Walker, 1869).

Winner's New School for Accordeon (Boston: Oliver Ditson, 1869).

Winner's New School for the German Accordeon (Boston: Oliver Ditson?: 1870).

Winner's Primary School for the German Accordeon (Cleveland: S. Brainard, 1872).

Winner's American Instructor for German Accordion (Boston: White-Smith, 1883).

Winner's Practical School for Accordion (N.p.: Banes, 1886).

Winner's Self-Instructor for Accordeon (Philadelphia: M.D. Swisher, 1887).

Winner's Champion School for German Accordeon (N.p.: Robert C. Kretschmar, 1889)

Winner's Eureka Method for Accordion (Boston: Oliver Ditson, 1892, 1920).

Banjo

Winner's New Primer for Banjo (New York: Firth Pond & Co., 1864).

Winner's Easy System for the Banjo (Philadelphia: N.p., 1870).

Winner's New School for Banjo (Boston: Oliver Ditson, 1872, 1900).

Winner's Primary School for Banjo (Cleveland: S. Brainard, 1875).

Ideal Method for Banjo (Boston: Oliver Ditson, 1882).

Winner's American Banjoist (Philadelphia?: W.F. Shaw, 1882).

Winner's New American School for Banjo (Boston: White-Smith, 1883).

Winner's Practical School for Banjo (Philadelphia?: Banes, 1884).

Winner's Self-Instructor for Banjo (Philadelphia: M.D. Swisher, 1887).

Winner's Champion School for Banjo (N.p.: Robert C. Kretschmar, 1890).

Winner's Eureka Method for Banjo (Boston: Oliver Ditson, 1892).

Winner's Easy System for Banjo (Boston: Oliver Ditson, 1897).

Winner's Imperial School for Banjo (Indianapolis: Wulschner & Son, 1899).

Eureka Method for Banjo in C (Boston: Oliver Ditson, 1920).

Eureka Method for Tenor Banjo (Boston: Oliver Ditson, 1924).

Clarinet

Winner's Perfect Guide for Clarionet (Boston: Oliver Ditson, 1861, 1889).

Winner's New Primer for Clarionet (New York: Firth Pond & Co., 1864, republished in 1892).

Winner's New School for Clarionet (Boston: Oliver Ditson, 1870)

Winner's Primary School for Clarionet (Cleveland: S. Brainard, 1872).

Winner's Clarionet Gamut (Philadelphia: Sep. Winner & Son, 1877).

Winner's American Clarionettist (Philadelphia?: W.F. Shaw, 1881).

Ideal Method for Clarinet (Boston: Oliver Ditson, 1882).

Winner's New American School for Clarinet (Boston: White-Smith, 1886).

Winner's Self-Instructor for Clarinet (Philadelphia: M.D. Swisher, 1887).

Winner's Eureka Method for Clarinet (Boston: Oliver Ditson, 1891).

Concertina

Winner's Easy System for German Concertina (Philadelphia: Lee & Walker, 1869).

Winner's Perfect Guide for Concertina (Boston: Oliver Ditson, 1869).

Winner's Primary School for Concertina (Cleveland: S. Brainard, 1872).

Winner's New American School for Concertina (Boston: White-Smith, 1883).

Winner's New Primer for German Concertina (New York: Firth Pond & Co., 1897).

Cornet

New School for the Cornet (Boston: Oliver Ditson, 1870).

Winner's Primary School for the Cornet (Cleveland: S. Brainard's Sons: 1872).

Winner's Cornet Gamut (Philadelphia: Sep. Winner & Son, 1877).

Ideal Method for Cornet (Boston: Oliver Ditson, 1882).

Winner's New American School for Cornet (Boston: White-Smith, 1883).

Hurst's Model Cornet School (N.p.: Hurst, 1884).

Self-Instructor on Cornet in B-flat (N.p.: Pepper, 1886).

Self-Instructor on Cornet in E-flat (N.p.: Pepper, 1886).

Winner's American Cornetist (Philadelphia?: W.F. Shaw, 1889).

Winner's Eureka Method for Cornet (Boston: Oliver Ditson, 1891).

Double Bass

Winner's Eureka Method for Double Bass (Boston: Oliver Ditson, 1894)

Drum

Winner's Drum Book (Philadelphia: Lee & Walker, 1861; Boston: Oliver Ditson, 1861).

Winner's Eureka Method for Small Drum and Glockenspiel (Boston: Oliver Ditson, 1905).

Fife

Winner's Perfect Guide for Fife (Boston: Oliver Ditson, 1861, 1889).
Winner's New School for Fife (Boston: Oliver Ditson, 1870).
Winner's Primary School for Fife (Cleveland: S. Brainard, 1872).
Winner's Fife Gamut (Philadelphia: Sep. Winner & Son, 1877).
Winner's American Fifer (Philadelphia?: W.F. Shaw, 1881; Bath, ME: Thos. P.O. Magoun, 1881).
Ideal Method for Fife (Boston: Oliver Ditson, 1882).
Winner's Self-Instructor for Fife (Philadelphia: M.D. Swisher, 1887).
Winner's Eureka Method for Fife (Boston: Oliver Ditson, 1891).

Flageolet

Winner's Perfect Guide for Flageolet (Boston: Oliver Ditson, 1861).
Winner's New School for Flageolet (Boston: Oliver Ditson, 1870).
Winner's Primary School for the Flageolet (Cleveland: S. Brainard's Sons, 1872).
Winner's New American School for Flageolet (Boston: White-Smith, 1885).
Winner's Eureka Method for Flageolet (Boston: Oliver Ditson, 1892).

Flute

Winner's Flute Primer (New York: Firth Pond & Co., 1857, 1864).
Winner's Perfect Guide for Flute (Boston: Oliver Ditson, 1861).
Winner's Easy System for Flute (Philadelphia: Sep. Winner & Co., 1866).
Winner's New School for Flute (Boston: Oliver Ditson, 1870, 1898).
Winner's Primary School for the Flute (Cleveland: S. Brainard's Sons, 1872, 1900).
Winner's Flute Gamut (Philadelphia: S. Winner, 1877).
Winner's Excelsior Method for the Flute (Boston: Oliver Ditson, 187?).
Winner's American Flutist (Philadelphia?: W.F. Shaw, 1880).
Winner's New American School for Flute (Boston: White-Smith, 1883).
Winner's Practical School for Flute (Unknown City: Banes, 1884).
Winner's Self-Instructor for Flute (Philadelphia: M.D. Swisher, 1887).
Improved Method for Flute (Toledo OH: W.W. Whitney & Co., 1891).
Winner's Eureka Method for Flute (Boston: Oliver Ditson, 1891).

Guitar

Winner's Guitar Primer (New York: Firth Pond & Co., 1858).

Winner's Perfect Guide for Guitar (Boston: Oliver Ditson, 1861, 1889).

Winner's New Primer for Guitar (New York: Firth Pond & Co., 1864).

Guitar Gems: Exercises and Melodies (Philadelphia: Sep. Winner, 1866).

Winner's Easy System for Guitar (Philadelphia: Sep. Winner, 1866).

Winner's New School for the Guitar (Boston: Oliver Ditson, 1870).

Winner's Primary School for Guitar (Cleveland: S. Brainard, 1873).

Ideal Method for Guitar (Boston: Oliver Ditson, 1882).

Winner's New American School for Guitar (Boston: White-Smith, 1883).

Winner's National Guitarist (Philadelphia: W.F. Shaw, 1885).

Winner's Self-Instructor for Guitar (Philadelphia: M.D. Swisher, 1887).

Guitar Without a Master (Boston: Oliver Ditson, 1890).

Winner's Eureka Method for Guitar (Boston: Oliver Ditson, 1891, 1919, 1924).

Winner's Imperial School for Guitar (Indianapolis: Wulschner & Son, 1899).

Mandolin

Complete Method for Spanish Mandoline (Boston: Oliver Ditson, 1884).

Winner's New American School for Mandolin (Boston: White-Smith, 1890).

Winner's Eureka Method for Mandolin (Boston: Oliver Ditson, 1891, 1919, 1925).

Winner's American Mandolinist (Boston: Oliver Ditson, 1897).

Winner's Imperial School for Mandolin (Indianapolis: Wulschner & Son, 1899).

Melodeon

Winner's Melodeon Primer (New York: Firth Pond & Co., 1860).

Winner's Perfect Guide for Melodeon (Boston: Oliver Ditson, 1861).

Easy System for the Melodeon (Philadelphia: Lee & Walker, n.d.).

Organ

Winner's Easy System for Organ (Boston: Oliver Ditson, 1865).

Winner's New School for Cabinet Organ (Boston: Oliver Ditson, 1870, republished in 1898).

Winner's New Method for Reed Organ (Cleveland: S. Brainard, 1872).
Winner's American Organist (Philadelphia?: W.F. Shaw, 1880).
Ideal Method for Cabinet Organ (Boston: Oliver Ditson, 1882).
Marshall's National Method for Reed Organ (Philadelphia: M.D. Swisher, 1888).
Excelsior Practical and Progressive School for Reed Organ (N.p.: Banes, 1889).
Winner's Perfect Guide for Cabinet Organ (Boston: Oliver Ditson, 1889).
Shorter Parlor Organ Method (Atlanta: Phillips & Crew, 1890).
Winner's Eureka Method for Organ (Boston: Oliver Ditson, 1892).

Piano

Winner's Pianoforte Primer (New York: Firth Pond & Co., 1857; Boston: Oliver Ditson, 187?).
Winner's Perfect Guide for Piano (Boston: Oliver Ditson, 1861).
Winner's New Primer for Piano (New York: Firth Pond & Co., 1864).
Winner's Easy System for the Pianoforte (Boston: Oliver Ditson, 1865).
Winner's Easy System for Pianoforte or Melodeon (Philadelphia: Sep. Winner, 1865).
Winner's New School for the Piano (Boston: Oliver Ditson, 1870; Chicago: Lyon & Healy, 1898).
Winner's American Pianist (Philadelphia?: W.F. Shaw, 1880).
Winner's New American School for Piano (Boston: White-Smith, 1883).
Winner's Practical School for Piano (N.p.: Banes, 1884).
Marshall's National Method for Pianoforte (Philadelphia: M.D. Swisher, 1888).
Winner's Eureka Method for Piano (Boston: Oliver Ditson, 1892, 1918).
Winner's Piano Tutor (Boston: Oliver Ditson, 1896).
Winner's New School for Piano (Boston: Oliver Ditson, 1898).

Piccolo

Winner's New School for the Piccolo and Boehm Flute (Boston: Oliver Ditson, 1870; New York: C.H. Ditson, 1870).
Eureka Method for the Piccolo (Boston: Oliver Ditson, 1919).

Trombone[2]

Winner's Eureka Method for Trombone (Boston: Oliver Ditson, 1905).
Eureka Method for the Slide Trombone (Boston: Oliver Ditson, n.d.).

Ukulele[3]

Eureka Method for Ukulele, Ukulele Banjo & Tiple (Boston: Oliver Ditson, 1924).

Violin

Winner's Improved Method for Violin (Philadelphia: Winner & Shuster: 1854).
Winner's Violin Primer (New York: Firth Pond & Co., 1858).
Winner's Perfect Guide for Violin (Boston: Oliver Ditson, 1861).
Winner's New Primer for Violin (New York: Firth Pond & Co., 1864).
Winner's Easy System for Violin (Philadelphia: Sep. Winner, 1866).
Winner's New School for Violin (Boston: Oliver Ditson, 1869).
Winner's Pocket Preceptor for Violin (Philadelphia: Sep. Winner & Son, 1870)
Winner's Violin Study (Philadelphia: Septimus Winner, 1873).
Winner's Violin Gamut (Philadelphia: Sep. Winner & Son, 1877).
Ideal Method for Violin (Boston: Oliver Ditson, 1882).
Hurst's Model Violin Method (N.p.: Hurst, 1884).
Winner's National Violinist (Philadelphia?: W.F. Shaw, 1884).
Winner's Practical School for Violin (N.p.: Banes, 1884).
Winner's Violin Tutor (Philadelphia: Lee & Walker, 1884).
Self-Instructor for Violin (N.p.: Pepper, 1886).
Winner's Self-Instructor for Violin (Philadelphia: M.D. Swisher, 1887).
Grand Method for Violin (Book I) (Philadelphia: Sep. Winner & Son, 1889).
Winner's Champion School for Violin (Philadelphia: Robert C. Kretschmar, 1889).
Winner's Violin Practice (Philadelphia?: W.F. Shaw, 1889).
Improved Method for Violin (Toledo: W.W. Whitney & Co., 1890).
Winner's Boston Method for Violin (Boston: White-Smith, 1890).
Winner's Eureka Method for Violin (Boston: Oliver Ditson, 1891).
Winner's Imperial School for Violin (Indianapolis: Wulschner & Son, 1899).

Violoncello

Winner's Easy System for Violoncello (Philadelphia: Lee & Walker, 1872)

Winner's Primary School for Violoncello (Cleveland: S. Brainard, 1875).

Winner's New American School for Violoncello (Boston: White-Smith, 1890).

Winner's Eureka Method for Violoncello (Boston: Oliver Ditson, 1894).

Voice

Winner's Singing Method (Philadelphia: Lee & Walker, 1860).

Winner's School of Vocal Music (Philadelphia: Sep. Winner & Co., 1867). Published in 12 installments in the *Musical Journal*, edited by Alice Hawthorne.

Winner's Primary School of Vocal Music (Cleveland: S. Brainard, 1872).

Zither

A Complete Method for Zither (Boston: Oliver Ditson, 1884).

Winner's New American School for Zither (Boston: White-Smith, 1890).

Winner's Eureka Method for Zither (Boston: Oliver Ditson, 1894, 1922).

Notes

1. While Myers provides an excellent listing of pedagogical materials by Winner (included here), this listing has been augmented by publication records from the National Union Catalog (Pre-1856 Imprints).

2. While earlier publications must exist, any record of their publication is currently unavailable.

3. Earlier editions for ukulele must also exist but cannot be found in publication records currently available.

Appendix G
Books and Articles

Hawthorne, Alice. *The Book of Adventures*. Philadelphia: C.H. Davis, 1854 and New York: James Miller, 1869 and New York: Allen Brothers, 1869.

An 1854 advertisement listed this book as "comprising stirring incidents and adventures of hunters, sailors and travelers in different parts of the world. Written in a beautiful and easy style for children."

Hawthorne, Alice. *The Book of Curiosities*. Philadelphia: C.H. Davis, 1854 and New York: James Miller, 1854.

An advertisement for this set of one- to two-page descriptions of marvels from around the world describes it as "containing a description of many remarkable things in nature and art, among which are Eddystone lighthouse, cave of the elephants, Peter Botte mountain, the Giant's Causeway, &c. &c." As with many other of these Hawthorne-penned children's books, they capitalize on the public's ever-increasing desire to learn more about the world in which they lived.

Hawthorne, Alice. *Hawthorn [sic] Leaves*. Louisville, Ky.: Gazette Press, 1886.

This collection of poetry, published later in Winner's life, is a series of lyrics not used for any of his popular songs. None of the poetry is reused for the later volume *Cogitations of a Crank at Three Score and Ten* (possibly because these poems were intended to appear under the Hawthorne name only).

Hawthorne, Alice. *Our Jenny: A Story for Young People*. Philadelphia: C.H. Davis, 1854 and New York: James Miller, 1854.

Advertised as "a very pretty story of the adventures of a little girl, written in a pleasing and easy style and embellished with numerous engravings."

Hawthorne, Alice. *Stories of Africa*. Philadelphia: C.H. Davis, 1854.

Advertised as "a beautiful book of instruction and entertainment, containing many pretty stories about the people and customs of Africa, written in a manner to please and interest young readers."

Hawthorne, Alice. *Stories of Asia*. Philadelphia: C.H. Davis, 1854.

Advertised as "combining instruction and entertainment in a pleasing manner for the young, containing interesting stories of the countries, people and customs of Asia."

Hawthorne, Alice. *Stories of Remarkable Birds for the Amusement of My Young Friends*. Philadelphia: C.H. Davis, 1854 and 1855.

Advertised as "containing many pretty anecdotes of cage birds and the little wild warblers of the woods, beautifully illustrated with numerous engravings of the principal birds of all countries."

Hawthorne, Alice. *Stories of Wild Animals*. Philadelphia: C.H. Davis, 1854.

Advertised as "a beautiful volume for the amusement and instruction of children, with numerous anecdotes of the sagacity; haunts and habits of the principal animals of the earth. Full of illustrations."

Hawthorne, Alice and Septimus Winner. *The Musical Journal*. Philadelphia: Sep. Winner & Company, 1867.

A musical magazine published by Winner and edited by Hawthorne that lasted twelve issues only. Each magazine included approximately four or five songs (many of them original Hawthorne and Winner works), poetry, commentary on musical matters, humor and an ongoing section on vocal pedagogy.

Winner, Septimus. *Cogitations of a Crank at Three Score and Ten*. Philadelphia: Drexel Biddle, 1903.

An extensive collection of poetry that we might assume was written following the issuance of the *Hawthorn Leaves* collection (1886). The poems are divided into nine categories, each one, presumably, reflecting a different side of Winner's creative artistry or according to his belief as to the significant uses of poetry. The categories include emotional, pastoral, lyrical, cynical, satirical, incidental, occasional, ironical and sentimental.

Appendix H
Published Poetry

While there are numerous examples of poetry by Winner that he wrote in his journals or in letters to his wife (especially during their court-ship), many cannot be accurately dated nor were they ultimately in-tended for publication.[1] This appendix only features poetry Winner wrote, under his own name and as Hawthorne, that was intended for publication over the course of his lifetime. Poems are listed alphabeti-cally by publication. For bibliographic details on each publication, please refer to the listings in Appendix G.

From *Graham's Magazine* (1846) as Septimus Winner
"Song"

From the *Musical Journal* (1867). In many cases, Winner provided a byline for the author. This listing includes only those poems that were not credited in the publication and are, therefore, assumed to be original works. One might speculate on Winner's intentions as far as their authorship as Hawthorne was technically the editor.
"Cogitation"
"Men of Mention"[2]
"My Nosegay"
"Old Music"
"Sea Music"
"Sweet Misery"
"The Musical Wife"
"What Care I"

From *Hawthorn* [*sic*] *Leaves* (1886) as Alice Hawthorn(e)[3]
"A Dream of Home [Song]"
"A Heavy Rainfall"
"April"
"Beautiful Lamp"
"Beauty Land"

"Bessie's Christmas Wreath"
"Bloom of the Heart, The"
"Brave McWhirter, The"
"Broken Heart"
"Cave Hill - The Silent City"
"Celestine"
"Christmas Tide"
"Dew Drops"
"Drummer Notes"
"Edith (or Beauty in the Arms of Death)"
"Hawthorn Flower, The"
"Hill-Side Tryst, The"
"Hopeful Heart"
"In The Park at Grayson"
"Kiss Me Mother Dear"
"Let the Christmas Lights Be Burning"
"Let the Sunshine In"
"Little Foot-Prints"
"Little Tot's Dress, The"
"Marble Heart [Marco and Raphael]"
"Merciless River, The [The flood of 1884]"
"Month of Roses, The"
"My Heart is Aching For Thee"
"My Love For You"
"Only a Rose-Bud"
"Our Confederate Dead"
"Sewing Machinist, The"
"Skeptic's Soliloquy, The"
"Southern Woman, The"
"To Will"
"Under the Willow"
"Woman's Brightest Jewel"

From *Cogitations of a Crank at Three Score and Ten* **(1903)** as Septimus Winner. As cited earlier, this volume was one of Winner's last
projects and ultimately, was published posthumously by his grandson.
In the introduction, Winner's grandson wrote:

> This little volume is presented to you, not as a literary produc-
> tion of great merit, but as indicative of the thought and tem-
> perament of a man who has done much to impress his indi-
> viduality on a past generation. It has been said of the author
> "that while his verses are frequently crude, yet time and time
> again, in their simple earnestness, they appeal to the affections
> and emotions of a multitude of his countrymen."[4]

None of the poems have titles and are, therefore, listed by first lines. Winner divided the poems into nine sections, presumably reflecting the different sides of his personality or the different uses that poetry might serve. That division is preserved in the listing below.

Emotional
"A Little Anchor Holds a Mighty Ship . . . "
"Beneath the Stars There is No Rest . . . "
"God is the architect of this vast world . . . "
"God is the Master of the Universe . . . "
"Oh Earth! Thy Scenes are Glorious to My Soul . . . "
"When Life is Sweet and All is Well . . . "

Pastoral
"Dead Leaves Fall, And One By One, The"
"Early Sunlight Greets the Dewy Earth, The"
"Go Rest Awhile Within the Quiet Wood . . . "
"Go, Tiny Ant, I Would Not Crush Thee, No! "
"Grand Trees! Companions in My Solitude . . . "
"I Wandered Along Through the Meadows in Springtime . . . "
"Though Man May Culture, With a Certain Pride . . . "

Lyrical
"Ah! What in This Life is as Dear . . . "
"In Years Agone—But All is Over . . . "
"Something Seems Telling Me Ever . . . "
"Southern Roses Brightly Bloom . . . "
"Than Thine No Fairer Face I See . . . "
"When the Sun of Life is Shining . . . "
"Which is Life's Most Happy Season . . . "

Cynical
"Alas That Man Should Feign to Worship God . . . "
"A Vaunt Ye Teachers of the Olden Time . . . "
"But Three-Score Years and Ten! How Brief the Span . . . "
"Man Who Buildeth For Himself a Vane, The"
"One in Love With One's Own Selfish State, The"
"Religion is a Grace Befitting All . . . "
"Show Sympathy for Weaker Minds, Possessed . . . "
"Spring Grows Garden's O'er the Sunny Earth, The"
"Stars that Shine Above Us in the Day, The"
"That Truth is 'Mighty and it Must Prevail' . . . "
"We Never Know Until the Day is Done . . . "
"We Sin As Easily in Manner Much . . . "

Satirical
"A Critic is the One Who "Kens it All" . . . "
"A Vale of Tears, Indeed, How Many Say . . . "
"A Wise Man Sayeth That He Knoweth What . . . "
"Alas! The Fact to All is Surely Plain . . . "
"E'en in a Land Where Royalty is Scorned . . . "
"Fidelity, Thou Hollow, Empty Word . . . "
"King Solomon Was Wise When He Declared . . . "
"Love is a Fever That No Drug Can Break . . . "
"Man is a Riddle Woman Cannot Guess . . . "
"Traits of Humankind are Much the Same, The"

Incidental
"A Mortal Man of Forty Years or More . . . "
"A Nation Hungers After Lands Galore . . . "
"A Pinhole May Disclose to Eyes Far More . . . "
"He Was a Noble Beast, and From His Eye . . . "
"I Look From My Window and What Do I See? "
"Rags! Rags! Rags! From the Street Comes a Cry . . . "
"That Talent Never Can Be Bought for Cash . . . "

Occasional
"Fame Builds Her Structure on the Acts of Life . . . "
"Fruit That Drops Untimely to the Ground, The"
"Heaven Makes Not Matters Unto Man's Desire . . . "
"If Talent Could Bequeath its Store of Brains . . . "
"Of All the Evil's Underneath the Sun . . . "
"Scented Grass that Beautiful the Sod, The"
"There's Nothing on the Earth Brought Forth in Vain . . . "
"We Know Too Well that We Can Never Take . . . "

Ironical
"Full Many Maxims of Our Former Years . . . "
"I Close My Eyes to All the World . . . "
"Sore-Footed and Weary the Multitude Went . . . "
"They Brought Him Forth in His Garment of Blood . . . "
"Time is Flying, Our Hopes Denying . . . "
"Toil, Toil, Till the Daylight is Set . . . "

Sentimental
"Another Heart May Love Thee Well . . . "
"Another Noble Head Lies Low . . . "
"Cheerful Bird May Take its Flight, The"
"Oh Dreary Was the World to Me! "
"Sweet Moments of My Childhood . . . "
"When O'er the Scenes of Happier Days I Ponder . . . "

Notes

1.   Several examples of Winner's poetry to his wife can be found in this volume.

2.   This poem was something of an epic undertaking for Winner. Organized in cantos, it was published over the course of several issues and ultimately numbered more than thirty stanzas. Interestingly, Winner appears to have either forgotten the poem or chose to abandon it, as the poem was never completed. The last published cantos bear the notation "to be continued" but it never is in any of the remaining issues.

3.   The origin of the misspelling of Hawthorne's name is unknown. It is possible it was a publisher error. Winner never used this alternate spelling in any musical publication.

4.   Claghorn, William C., Introduction to *Cogitations of a Crank at Three Score and Ten* by Septimus Winner, 5.

Appendix I
Joseph Eastburn Winner

Joseph Eastburn Winner may not have had as successful a career as his brother, but he did publish a variety of songs, at least one of which is fondly remembered today. He published exclusively under the nom de plume Eastburn and this alphabetical listing uses that pseudonym.

"Alice Vane" (a.k.a. "Down by the Field"), music by Eastburn, lyrics by Eastburn (Philadelphia: J.E. Gould, 1863).

"All in a Hundred Years," music by Eastburn, lyrics by "Arline" (N.p.: T.A. Bacher, 1876).

"Angel Friends," music by Eastburn, lyrics by Eastburn (Philadelphia: Sep. Winner, 1862), *Dedicated to Charles N. Mann, Esq.*

"Died in the Streets," music by Eastburn, lyrics by Claude DeHaven (Philadelphia: J.E. Winner, 1869).

"Friendless and Sad," music by Eastburn, lyrics by Elmer Ruan Coates (Boston: White-Smith, 1874), *Dedicated to J.E. Winner.*

"Friends of Our Early Days," music by Eastburn, lyrics by George Cooper (Philadelphia, J.E. Winner, 1868).

"Gates Are Forever Open, The," music by Eastburn, lyrics by Eastburn (Cleveland: S. Brainard's Sons, 1873).

"Grecian Bend, The," music by Eastburn, lyrics by Elmer Ruan Coates (Philadelphia: J.E. Winner, 1868).

"Growing Old Together Love," music by Eastburn, lyrics by "Arline" (Philadelphia?: W.F. Shaw, 1877).

"Happy as a Birdie in Its Nest," music by Eastburn, lyrics by Eastburn (Philadelphia: J.E. Winner, n.d.).

"He Never Says a Word," music by Eastburn, lyrics by Eastburn (New York: Jno. L. Peters, 1869).

"He's Just Like All the Men," music by Eastburn, lyrics by Eastburn (Philadelphia: J.E. Winner, 1895).

"Hearty Welcome Home," music by Eastburn, lyrics by Eastburn (Philadelphia: Wm. R. Smith, n.d.).

"Home Is Not Home without Thee" (a.k.a. "Return to Me"), music by Eastburn, lyrics by Eastburn (Philadelphia: Wm. R. Smith, 1865).

"How Are You Maximilian?" (a.k.a. "Off for Mexico"), music by Eastburn, lyrics by Eastburn (Philadelphia: Wm. R. Smith, 1865).

"How the Gates Came Ajar," music by Eastburn, lyrics by Eastburn (Cleveland: S. Brainard, 1871?).

"I Hear the Soft Wind Sighing," music by Eastburn, lyrics by Carolla H. Criswell (Philadelphia: Wm. R. Smith, n.d.).

"I'm Dying for Someone to Love Me," music by Eastburn, lyrics by Eastburn (Philadelphia: W.F. Shaw, 1877), *Dedicated to Miss Mamie B. Winner.*

"Kettle and the Clock, The," music by Eastburn, lyrics by Elmer Ruan Coates (Philadelphia: J.E. Winner, n.d.).

"Little Brown Jug," music by Eastburn, lyrics by Eastburn (Philadelphia: J.E. Winner, 1869). Advertised as being "put into shape and filled up by Eastburn." Later editions used the pseudonym Betta on the cover. Other names associated with the song include Wellman Jr. and J.L. Miller. A highly successful edition was published after Winner's death (New York: Vogel Music Company, 1938).

"Little Crib beside the Bed, A," music by Eastburn, lyrics by "Miriam" (Philadelphia: C. Sivori Winner, 1871).

"Little Homeless One, The" (a.k.a. "No One to Kiss Me Good-Night"), music by Eastburn, lyrics by Elmer Ruan Coates (Boston: Oliver Ditson, 1867).

"Little Lone Mary," music by Eastburn, lyrics by Eastburn (Philadelphia: Lee & Walker, 1874).

"Lone Heart, The," music by Eastburn, lyrics by Eastburn (Philadelphia: Wm. R. Smith, 1865).

"Maid of Athens," music by Eastburn, lyrics by "Lobd [*sic*] Byron" (Boston: Oliver Ditson, 1866).

"Matchless Schottische," music by Eastburn (Philadelphia: J.E. Winner, 1871). Instrumental.

"Meet Me with a Kiss," music by Eastburn, lyrics by Elmer Ruan Coates (Philadelphia: J.E. Winner, 1867).

"My Darling Is Waiting for Me," music by Eastburn, lyrics by Eastburn (Cleveland: S. Brainard's Sons, 1877).

"Never Censure," music by Eastburn, lyrics by Eastburn (Philadelphia: J.E. Winner, 1868).

"Oil on the Brain," music by Eastburn, lyrics by Eastburn (Philadelphia: J. Marsh, 1865).

"Old Log Hut, The," music by Eastburn, lyrics by Eastburn (Philadelphia: Wm. R. Smith, 1865).

"One Good Term Deserves Another," music by Eastburn, lyrics by Grace Carleton (Cleveland: S. Brainard's Sons, 1872).

"Only This I Ask of Thee," music by Eastburn, lyrics by B.W. Lacy (Philadelphia: J.E. Winner, 1867).

"Peerless Polka," music by Eastburn (N.p.d.). Instrumental.

"Planchette," music by Eastburn, lyrics by Elmer Ruan Coates, (Philadelphia: J.E. Winner, 1868). Dedicated to Lewis E. Meginley.

"Prisoner's Release, The" (a.k.a. "The Dear Old Flag Has Come"), music by Eastburn, lyrics by Eastburn (Philadelphia: Wm. R. Smith, 1865), *Dedicated to George F. Root, Esq., "author of the beautiful ballad, The Prisoner's Hope."*

"Safe within Thy Little Bed," music by Eastburn, lyrics by Eastburn (Cleveland: S. Brainard's Sons, 1870).

"Sallie of the Dell," music by Eastburn, lyrics by H.C. Duffield (Philadelphia: J.E. Winner, 1868).

"Sandman, The," music by Eastburn, lyrics by Eastburn (Philadelphia: Roberts & Hall, 1884). Patter song.

"Send For Mother, Birdie's Dying," music by Eastburn, lyrics by Eastburn (Boston: White-Smith, n.d.).

"Shadows," music by Eastburn, lyrics by Eastburn (Philadelphia: J.E. Winner, 1871).

"Sing to Me Softly Dear Sister," music by Eastburn, lyrics by Mrs. L.S. Nichols (Cleveland: S. Brainard's Sons, 1867), *Dedicated to Mrs. Sophie E. Wray.*

"Some One to Weep When I Am Gone," music by Eastburn, lyrics by George Cooper (Philadelphia: J.E. Winner, 1871), *Dedicated to Miss Allie A. Francis.*

"Song of Conundrums," music by Eastburn, lyrics by Eastburn (New York: Wm. A. Pond Co., 1893).

"Sweet Little Girl That I Love, The," music by Eastburn, lyrics by B.W. Lacy (Philadelphia: Wm. R. Smith, 1867).

"That Little Church around the Corner," music by Eastburn, lyrics by Grace Carleton (Cleveland: S. Brainard, 1871). See same title by Septimus Winner.

"That's Where the Laugh Comes In," music by Eastburn, lyrics by Eastburn (New York: Wm. A. Pond Co., 1865), *Dedicated to Louis P. Bourquin, Esq.*

"They Say," music by Eastburn, lyrics by Eastburn (Cleveland: S. Brainard's Sons, 1875).

"'Tis But a Rosebud Faded," music by Eastburn, lyrics by A. Marshall Ross (Philadelphia: Wm. R. Smith, 1866).

"Traitor and the Laws," music by Eastburn, lyrics by Daniel McAleer (Philadelphia: J. Marsh, 1864), *Dedicated to Major General George B. McClellan.*

"Triumph of the Old Flag" (a.k.a. "Our Flag o'er Richmond Waves Again"), music by Eastburn, lyrics by Eastburn (Philadelphia: Wm. R. Smith, 1864?).

"Tune the Old Cow Died On, The," music by Eastburn, lyrics by George Russell Jackson (Boston: John F. Perry & Co., n.d.). Advertised as "the funniest song ever written."

"Vanished Dreams," music by Eastburn, lyrics by Eastburn (Philadelphia: J.E. Winner, 1869), *Dedicated to Mrs. Joel J. Bailey.*

"We Have Met, Loved and Parted," music by Eastburn, lyrics by Eastburn (Boston; Oliver Ditson, 1869, 1896).

"When Mother Married Pap," music by Eastburn, lyrics by Elmer Ruan Coates (Philadelphia: J.E. Winner, 1868), *Dedicated to L. Simmons, Esq.* Advertised as being "sung with immense success by Frank A. Oliver."

"When the Shadows of the Evening Have Fallen," music by Eastburn, lyrics by H.G. Duffield (Boston: Oliver Ditson, 1868, 1896).

"Will You Come and Wander with Me?" music by Eastburn, lyrics by Hattie I. Brainard (Philadelphia: Wm. R. Smith, 1866).

Bibliography

Austin, William W. *Susanna, Jeanie and the Old Folks at Home: The Songs of Stephen Foster*. New York: MacMillan, 1975.

Bewley, John. Keffer Collection of Sheet Music, ca. 1790-1895 of the University of Pennsylvania. http://www.library.upenn.edu/special/keffer, [accessed October 17, 2001].

Birdseye, George. "American's Song Composers, No. VI: Septimus Winner," *Potters American Monthly*, June 1879.

Booth, Mark W. *American Popular Music: A Reference Guide*. Westport, Conn.: Greenwood Press, n.d.

Bowers, Jane. "Feminist Scholarship and the Field of Musicology I," *College Music Symposium*, vol. 20, no. 1, 1989.

Bowers, Jane and Judith Tick. *Women Making Music: The Western Art Tradition, 1150-1950*. Urbana Ill.: University of Illinois Press, 1987.

Bronson, William White. *The Inscriptions in St. Peter's Churchyard, Philadelphia*. Camden N.J.: Sinnickson Chew, 1879.

Citron, Marcia J. *Gender and the Musical Canon*. Cambridge: Cambridge University Press, 1993.

Claghorn, Charles Eugene. *The Mocking Bird: The Life and Diary of Its Author, Sep. Winner*. Philadelphia: Magee Press, 1937.

Claghorn, Charles Eugene. *Whispering Hope: The Life of Composer Septimus Winner*. Unpublished manuscript, 1977.

Dichter, Harry and Elliott Shapiro. *Early American Sheet Music*. New York: R.R. Bowker, 1941.

Divine, Robert A., et al. *America Past and Present*. Volume 2 From 1865. New York: HarperCollins, 1995.

Douglas, Ann. *The Feminization of American Culture*. New York: Alfred A. Knopf, 1977.

Duke University Rare Book, Manuscript and Special Collections Library. http://www.scriptorum.lib.duke.edu, [accessed September 22, 2001].

Emerson, Ken. Doo-Dah! Stephen Foster and the Rise of American Popular Culture. New York: DaCapo Press, 1998.

Ewen, David. Songs of America. Chicago: Ziff-Davis Publishers, 1947.

Ewen, David. Popular American Composers from Revolutionary Times to the Present: A Biographical and Critical Guide. New York: H.W. Wilson Company, 1962.

Fisher, William Arms. One Hundred Years of Music Publishing in the United States. Boston: Oliver Ditson Co., 1933.

Gammond, Peter. The Oxford Companion to Popular Music. Oxford: Oxford University Press, 1991.

Garraty, John A. 1001 Things Everyone Should Know about American History. New York: Doubleday, 1989.

Gerson, Robert A. Music in Philadelphia. Philadelphia: Theodore Presser, 1940.

Gormley, Beatrice. First Ladies: Women Who Called the White House Home. New York: Scholastic, 1997.

Hamm, Charles. Music in the New World. New York: W.W. Norton and Company, 1983.

Hamm, Charles. Yesterdays: Popular Song in America. New York: W.W. Norton, 1979.

Hawthorne, Alice. The Book of Adventures. Philadelphia: Charles H. Davis, 1854 and New York: James Miller, 1869 and New York: Allen Brothers, 1869.

Hawthorne, Alice. The Book of Curiosities. Philadelphia: Charles H. Davis, 1854 and New York: James Miller, 1854.

Hawthorne, Alice. Hawthorn [sic] Leaves. Louisville, Ky.: Gazette Press, 1886.

Hawthorne, Alice. Our Jenny: A Story for Young People. Philadelphia: C.H. Davis, 1854 and New York: James Miller, 1854.

Hawthorne, Alice. Stories of Africa. Philadelphia: Charles H. Davis, 1854.

Hawthorne, Alice. Stories of Asia. Philadelphia: Charles H. Davis, 1854.

Hawthorne, Alice. Stories of Remarkable Birds for the Amusement of My Young Friends. Philadelphia: Charles H. Davis, 1854 and 1855 and New York: James Miller, 1869

Hawthorne, Alice. *Stories of Wild Animals*. Philadelphia: Charles H. Davis, 1854.

Hawthorne, Alice and Septimus Winner. *The Musical Journal*. Philadelphia: Sep. Winner & Company, 1867.

Hournstra, Jean and Heath, Trudy. *American Periodicals 1741-1900*. Ann Arbor, Mich.: University Microfilms, 1979.

Korn, Jerry (ed.). *This Fabulous Century: 1870-1900*. New York: Time-Life Books, 1970.

LaRue, Jan. *Guidelines for Style Analysis*. New York: W.W. Norton, 1970.

Lester S. Levy Sheet Music Collection at the Milton S. Eisenhower Library of the Johns Hopkins University. http://levysheetmusic. mse.jhu.edu/index.html, [accessed October 15, 2001].

Levy, Lester S. *Picture the Songs: Lithographs from the Sheet Music of the Nineteenth-Century*. Baltimore: Johns Hopkins University Press, 1976.

Loesser, Arthur. *Men, Women and Pianos: A Social History*. New York: Simon and Schuster, 1954.

McClary, Susan. *Feminine Endings: Music, Gender and Sexuality*. Minneapolis: University of Minnesota Press, 1991.

Music for the Nation: American Sheet Music, 1870-1885. American Memory Collection. Library of Congress. http://memory.loc.gov/ ammem/smhtml, [accessed October 17, 2001].

Musical Fund Society of Philadelphia: A Brief History (Philadelphia: University of Pennsylvania Libraries, n.d.). No credited author, provided to the author by the librarians of the Keffer Collection of Sheet Music.

Myers, Howard Leo. *The Music of Septimus Winner*. Master's thesis, University of North Carolina at Chapel hill, 1951.

The National Union Catalogue, Index of Subjects in Two Volumes. Washington DC: United States Government Printing Office, 1869.

Silber, Irwin and Jerry Silverman. *Songs of the Civil War*. New York: Dover, 1995.

Solie, Ruth A. (ed.). *Musicology and Difference: Gender and Sexuality in Music Scholarship*. Berkeley, Calif.: University of California Press, 1993.

Spaeth, Sigmund. *A History of Popular Music in America*. New York: Random House, 1948.

Spillane, Daniel. *The History of the American Pianoforte: Its Technical Development and the Trade*. New York: D. Spillane, 1890.

Stephens, Autumn. *Wild Women: Crusaders, Curmudgeons and Completely Corsetless Ladies in the Otherwise Virtuous Victorian Era.* Berkeley, Calif.: Conari Press, 1992.

Tawa, Nicholas E. *The Way to Tin Pan Alley: American Popular Song, 1866-1910.* New York: Schirmer Books, 1990.

Tick, Judith. *American Women Composers before 1870.* Rochester, N.Y.: University of Rochester Press, 1979.

Tubb, Benjamin Robert. *Public Domain Music.* http://www.pdmusic. org, [accessed October 14, 2001].

Winner, Septimus. *Cogitations of a Crank at Three Score and Ten.* Philadelphia: Drexel Biddle, 1903.

Winner, Septimus. Collection, 1845-1902. Pennsylvania Historical Society. Diaries, letters, and music notebooks of Septimus Winner, American composer. Original manuscript of "Listen to the Mocking Bird;" catalog of music for piano and organ, 1874; music for violin; Hannah Winner's illustrated volume of songs with music by Winner under the pseudonym of Alice Hawthorne. Gift of Charles Eugene and Donald Claghorn, 1946.

Index

Note that all numbers in **bold** represent citations for figures, photographs and musical examples.

About the Author

Michael Remson is a composer, librettist and musicologist. He received his doctorate in composition and libretto writing/playwriting from the University of Houston where he studied with Grammy Award winner Carlisle Floyd, Pulitzer Prize-winning playwright Edward Albee and Robert Nelson. Dr. Remson earned two master's degrees from the University of Houston (musicology) and Carnegie Mellon University (composition). He is an alumnus of New York University (B.A.), and also attended Columbia University.

Dr. Remson has written both the music and libretto for operas featured by such organizations as Houston Grand Opera's "Opera To Go!," the Society for the Performing Arts (Houston) and the New York City Opera "Showcasing American Composers" series. His vocal and choral works have been performed and recorded throughout the United States and in Europe. He was composer-in-residence with the Ulster Orchestra (Northern Ireland) through a prestigious award from the Americans for the Arts foundation and was also a fellow at both the Virginia Center for the Creative Arts and the Ragdale Colony.

Currently Dr. Remson is managing director of the American Festival for the Arts summer music conservatory where he has also served as director of the department of composition, music theory and history. He serves on the board of Dragon's Gate, a Houston-based non-profit working to bring the arts to disenfranchised communities. He is currently an adjunct faculty member at his alma mater, the University of Houston, and has written several articles and presented at national conferences. *Septimus Winner: Two Lives in Music* is his first book. More information on Septimus Winner can be found on his website: www.michaelremson.com.